DEACCESSIONED

A Workable Government?

THE AMERICAN ASSEMBLY was established by Dwight D. Eisenhower at Columbia University in 1950. Each year it holds at least two nonpartisan meetings which give rise to authoritative books that illuminate issues of United States policy.

An affiliate of Columbia, with offices at Barnard College, the Assembly is a national, educational institution incorporated in the state of New York.

The Assembly seeks to provide information, stimulate discussion, and evoke independent conclusions on matters of vital public interest.

CONTRIBUTORS

SHIRLEY S. ABRAHAMSON, Wisconsin Supreme Court, & DIANE S. GUTMANN

STEPHEN L. CARTER, Yale Law School

LLOYD N. CUTLER, Wilmer, Cutler & Pickering

FRANK H. EASTERBROOK, U.S. Court of Appeals

NICHOLAS DEB. KATZENBACH, Riker, Danzig, Scherer, Hyland & Perretti

BURKE MARSHALL, Yale Law School

H. JEFFERSON POWELL, University of Iowa

MARK V. TUSHNET, Georgetown University Law Center

ALAN F. WESTIN, Columbia University

THE AMERICAN ASSEMBLY
Columbia University

A Workable Government?

The Constitution After 200 Years

BURKE MARSHALL

Editor

W·W·NORTON & COMPANY
New York   *London*

Copyright © 1987 by the American Assembly
The Influence of Judicial Review on Constitutional Theory © 1987
by Frank H. Easterbrook
All rights reserved.

Published simultaneously in Canada by Penguin Books Canada Ltd.,
2801 John Street, Markham, Ontario L3R 1B4.
Printed in the United States of America.

The text of this book is composed in Baskerville.
Composition and manufacturing by The Haddon Craftsmen, Inc.

First Edition

ISBN 0-393-02480-6

ISBN 0-393-30431-0 PPK

W. W. Norton & Company, Inc., 500 Fifth Avenue,
New York, N. Y. 10110

W. W. Norton & Company Ltd., 37 Great Russell Street,
London WC1B 3NU

1 2 3 4 5 6 7 8 9 0

Contents

Preface

In this bicentennial year of the Constitutional Convention it is particularly appropriate that the Seventy-third American Assembly, cosponsored by the Commission on Public Understanding About the Law of the American Bar Association, should have focused on the adequacy of our present constitutional structure in the light of rapid change over the last two centuries and of persistent and increasingly complex domestic and foreign problems. For the last twenty-five years, doubts about the present political structure and various proposals to change it have been raised. Some would alter the terms of the president and members of the Senate and House of Representatives, or make changes in the roles of Congress and the executive branch on foreign policy matters. Others have proposed a more radical move toward something approximating parliamentary government.

The American Assembly discussions focused on such issues and on the present relationship between the central government and the states. On April 23, 1987, the Assembly brought together at Arden House distinguished participants from various sectors of our society. They discussed an agenda prepared by Professor Burke Marshall of Yale University and developed from background papers prepared for the participants by several constitutional scholars, judges, and former public officials. The background papers have been compiled into the present book.

As is customary, The American Assembly participants issued a report on their findings and views on these important issues. The report is included as an appendix to this book.

In addition to the support of the cosponsors, the Wallace Funds, The Coca-Cola Foundation, the Charles A. Dana Foundation, and The New York Times Company Foundation provided funding for this project. We are grateful for their assistance. The opinions in this volume are those of the individual authors and not necessarily those of the financial supporters or of The American Assembly and the Commission on Public Understanding About the Law, which do not take stands on issues they present for public discussion.

Mark I. Harrison
Chairman
Commission on Public Understanding
  About the Law
American Bar Association

Stephen Stamas
President
The American Assembly

A Workable
Government?

Introduction

BURKE MARSHALL

In April 1952 President Harry Truman declared that an impending steel strike "would immediately jeopardize and impair our national defense and the defense of those who joined us in resisting aggression" in Korea and "would add to the continuing danger of our soldiers, sailors, and airmen employed in combat in the field." Therefore, he said, it was necessary to authorize the secretary of commerce "to take possession of all or such of the plants, facilities, and other property of the steel companies" as he may deem necessary in the interest of national defense.

The *Steel Seizure* case which followed culminated in an injunction prohibiting the secretary from obeying the president's order. Six justices each explained their reasons, separately, for deciding the order was unconstitutional. The best

BURKE MARSHALL is Nicholas deB. Katzenbach Professor of Law at the Yale Law School, where he has taught since 1970. In the past he has been a partner in the Washington, D.C. law firm of Covington & Burling, assistant attorney general of the United States in charge of the Civil Rights Division, and general counsel and senior vice-president of IBM Corporation.

known of these opinions, and the one that has most clearly withstood thirty-five years of scrutiny, is that of Justice Robert H. Jackson, an eloquent yet crystal-clear legal writer who in the *Steel Seizure* case reminded his brethren (especially, I believe, Justice Hugo Black, who delivered the official opinion of the Court) of the obvious: that the framers of the Constitution were indeed brilliant and learned men skilled in the exposition of political theory, but that they came together as practical men who wanted to put together a system of government that would work, as the one they were operating under plainly did not. Justice Jackson wrote:

> The actual art of governing under our Constitution does not and cannot conform to judicial definitions of the power of any of its branches based on isolated clauses or even single Articles torn from context. While the Constitution diffuses power the better to secure liberty, it also contemplates that practice will integrate the dispersed powers into a workable government.

There are, of course, many other currents of government flowing from the Constitution. Among them are its concern, expressed in most instances through the amendments (including those enacted many years after its ratification), with principles of the individual dignity and rights of the people, government fairness in dealing with the people, and of the great urge toward equality. But Justice Jackson was dealing with an exercise of power, with the issue whether it could properly start from the executive instead of the legislative branch, and hence with the structure of government. Surely matters of structure and government institutions were also a principal, if not the primary, concern of the framers in 1787, and should be such for the people of the United States today. The question still is whether the Constitution integrates the "dispersed powers" it disposes, not just within the federal government, but also among the nation and the states, into "a workable government" for the end of the twentieth century, and on into the twenty-first.

Putting the question this way in no sense implies that the problems and changes created for the United States by revolutionary improvements of technology, indivisible national and international economies, and a politically interdependent world change the Constitution, or justify exercises of government power which are forbidden by the specific constraints in the Bill of Rights and elsewhere. It is still rather the other way around, and it is still a prime function of the Article III judicial system, as well as of state court judges acting both under Article VI and their own state constitutions, to protect the people from unconstitutional behavior by officials acting under color of law. This is the subject, at least in part, of the chapters by Justice Abrahamson, Judge Easterbrook, and Professor Tushnet, and is the focal point for most writing about the Constitution. The bulk of this book is concerned at core, however, with whether the government established in the document of 1787 continues to be workable.

Jefferson Powell's chapter, like much of his other works, establishes a historical backdrop. The framers started almost immediately arguing with each other, and with the people, about exactly what they had in mind when they agreed on the structure presented in the proposed Constitution. Was it primarily political theory, or the need for a unitary government effectively displacing the economic and political anarchy of the states under the Articles of Confederation, or simply a drive toward a codification of the process of government? Clearly the answer to issues such as that raised by the *Steel Seizure* case might depend on which of these three roads was the one that led to the original plan. Yet it is just as plain from Professor Powell's powerful presentation of the evidence from the writings and speeches of the framers in the years after 1787 that there is no single road, no shared master plan or strategy, no original intent. Structural decisions about such specifics as what powers should be given Congress under Article I, Section 8, the relationship between the Congress and the president, and the status and function of the federal judiciary were the result of the meeting of minds starting from quite different premises as to ultimate goals and principles. Political forces at work in the first years of the nation brought these differences to light, and made them available to the people even during the period when the archives of the 1787 convention were shut away. Thus it is impossible accurately now to say that such and such is so because Madison, or Jefferson, or Hamilton, or Gouverneur Morris, or even Washington said it was so, unless the speaker chosen can be assumed to have written and ratified the Constitution all by himself.

Does this leave modern government officials, such as Article III judges, completely at sea and left to their own devices in deciding structural questions arising under the Constitution? That is clearly not the lesson Professor Powell wants drawn from his writings. All he wants is freedom from a historical myth that this is a discoverable original intent that must control. It remains the fact that all the delegates in 1787 who signed on to the proposed Constitution, and undoubtedly the dominant majority of the public figures, such as John Marshall, who participated in its ratification, wanted to put together a government that would work indefinitely. That is a postulate, an operating hypothesis, against which the text and interrelationships of the Constitution can be measured. The *Steel Seizure* case did not say, for example, that the government could not do what was necessary then, but only that the participation of Congress was possible, and therefore constitutionally necessary.

Lloyd Cutler would put emphasis on the reality of the word "possible" in response to this proposition about the *Steel Seizure* case. Of course, the participation of Congress in resolving the labor dispute in the steel industry at the time was constitutionally possible, and therefore possibly constitutionally necessary, as is the participation of Congress in dealing with the budgetary and trade deficits of the 1980s. The question to Mr. Cutler, who worked closely with one president and has known several others, is whether congressional action is politically possible so that a president in the position that Truman was, for example, can reasonably be expected to behave, can in fact effectively behave, in the way the Constitution contemplates. That in turn depends, in Mr. Cutler's view, on an institution that the Constitution nowhere mentions or takes account of, and that the framers either did not imagine, or perhaps deplored. The institution is that of the major political parties. Mr. Cutler's chapter posits a decline in "the cohesion of the political parties," and attributes to that decline an apparent paralysis in the political system set up by the Constitution, which in this view requires party accountability in Congress, preferably to the president. There are many who might argue, of course, with all parts of this premise—the historical facts and the political assumptions. Mr. Cutler, however, has been working on the matter for some years as a matter of personal conviction and as a leader of the Committee on the Constitutional System, which he helped to form. If the premise is accepted, then there are institutional changes which come to mind that should strengthen the party system. Some of them are specifically constitutional, as in the case of those changes dealing with the terms of members of the House and Senate. Others are clearly or possibly susceptible of legislation. Many believe, for example, that the Constitution does not prohibit reforms in campaign financing and spending, which is part of the agenda, despite the decisions of the Supreme Court looking the other way. Mr. Cutler lucidly outlines these problems and proposals in a way that will contribute to an important forthcoming debate.

The other major current concern of those concerned with effective but democratic government is the allocation of power with respect to foreign affairs, and especially decisions and actions relating to war. Is foreign policy being conducted in the manner contemplated by the Constitution? The United States has, since World War II, twice participated in wars undeclared by Congress. The Supreme Court apparently treated the Korean conflict as something different from a constitutional "war" in the *Steel Seizure* case, and took note on several occasions of the absence of a congressional declaration of war in Vietnam. Has the United States been acting unconstitutionally in these critically important matters? What about the invasion of Grenada? Finally, there is an ongoing dispute between Congress and the president—clearly not dependent on

who controls Congress, or who is president—about the fact
and degree of congressional participation in foreign policy
decisions. Examples now are the questions of continued adherence to the 1972 SALT agreement, the position of the
United States on the ABM treaty, nuclear testing, and potential arms control arrangements. What is the appropriate congressional role with respect to intelligence functions and covert activities?

Nicholas Katzenbach surveys this changing scene in his
chapter on the Constitution and foreign policy, but he is too
wise to attempt crisp answers. Even where the Constitution
appears specific, as in the grant of power "to declare War," the
allocation of powers is in fact vague. What is to be made of the
absence of a declaration, for example, when there is continuing congressional support for a war-in-fact, through exercise
of its power "to raise and support Armies," and to "provide
and maintain a Navy," or when there is an open-ended approval of unspecified future presidential action, as in the case
of the Gulf of Tonkin Resolution? Further, the president is,
after all, the constitutional "Commander in Chief of the Army
and Navy of the United States, and of the Militia of the several
States, when called into the actual service of the United
States." Again, the president has the power to "make" treaties, but needs the advice and consent of the Senate in doing
so, and the concurrence of two-thirds of the senators present
at a vote on ratification. The constitutional text is unclear,
perhaps deliberately so, with so many skillful draftsmen,
whether the advice and consent is a required process separate
from final concurrence. The Senate says yes, and the president
says no. It is tempting perhaps to try some revisions to clear
up such matters. Mr. Katzenbach, however, would leave them
to be worked out in the political process from time to time, and
I think he is right.

A corresponding set of constitutional ambiguities in domestic affairs lies in the fit, or rather lack of fit, between the apparent structural neatness of the constitutional structure and the
modern administrative state. In recent years, as Stephen
Carter points out, the Supreme Court has appeared to move

toward an unraveling of policy making by administrators, and executive action by legislators, in its decisions with respect to the legislative veto and the intended role of the comptroller general in the scheme of deficit control enacted in Gramm-Rudman-Hollings. Those decisions seemed to many to take a mechanistic view of who can do what: legislative-type policy can only be made in the legislative manner set forth in Article I, with bicameralism and presentment to the president for signature, while executive action can be taken only by clearly executive branch officials, appointed and removable by the president. The myriad administrative agencies created since the Interstate Commerce Commission in 1888 seemed unclear under such a rigid view of the classification and separation of powers in Articles I and II. There was for a while a consequent semipanic among the many observers of the administrative scene, who were used to a relaxed view by the Supreme Court of the confusion of the policy-making and executive roles of the agencies. Professor Carter's incisive and clear comment on these matters is therefore soothing. In his view, and as a growing number of constitutional scholars have been noting, the Court's decisions in an area such as this are in some sense part of a conversation that the Court is having with the other separate, but equal, branches of the federal government. The Congress and the president can now respond, as they see fit, but the machinery of government in general will continue to run as it has come to during the past century.

The separation of powers is, of course, only one-half of the complex structure of government created, or left intact, by the Constitution. The other half is the system of federalism. There are tens of direct or implied references to the states in the body of the Constitution and its amendments, although they in the main assume rather than define the states' role in the constitutional scheme. One consequence is the extraordinarily difficult network of court systems, and the interrelationships among state systems and between state systems and the federal system. The state systems are as bound under Article VI to implement supervening federal law, and the constitutional commands, as are the Article III courts, but the need for uniformity as well as compliance with federal law requires direct Supreme Court, and in rare cases lower federal court, supervision of the state courts. Thus the state courts must act as federal courts in cases arising under the Constitution, laws, and treaties of the United States, but the federal courts must pretend they are state courts, except on matters of procedure, in diversity cases between citizens of different states.

Justice Shirley Abrahamson and Diane Gutmann address a specific part of this maze—the role of the state courts in protecting individual rights. It is a role almost completely overlooked by the civil liberties and civil rights bar until recently, although there is strong evidence that the framers looked to the state rather than the federal courts for such matters in the first instance. In other areas, especially that of economic regulation, there is no question but that the nationalization of the economy, the revolution in information technology, the increasing mobility of the population, and many other factors have subdued areas of traditional state policy making. Those trends have been the subject of laments by some members of the Supreme Court (a minority, at the end) in the recent series of cases which first struck down, but later legitimated, federal regulation of state employees. Undoubtedly some federal spending programs have had similar effects. It is clear, however, that the state judicial systems are alive and well, and that in this critical corner of federalism at least, the federal structure has thus far survived the historical forces working against it.

Federalism is of course dependent for its vitality on the proper functioning of the political systems of the several states, and here there have been two major flaws that were not self-correcting. The first, notorious for many decades despite the command of the Fifteenth Amendment, was the blatant deprivation of black people of access to the franchise in several states. The second was endemic and gross malapportionment of state legislatures such that the city populations had no proportionate say in the political decisions of the states. Mark Tushnet analyzes the resulting federal, mainly judicial except for the Voting Rights Act of 1965, corrective measures taken in the name of the Constitution. At the time the measures were taken, many viewed them as destructive of the federal system, because of direct federal interference with state political structures. Certainly they were so characterized again and again in the long struggle for voting rights. Yet the result is truly protective of the constitutional scheme, for the federal measures made it work again, and were in that sense a triumph of constitutionalism.

Of the three branches of the national government, the federal courts under the Supreme Court have played the critical role in policing the federal system, as they also do, of course, in confining the Congress and the president to constitutionally permissible exercises of power. It has long ceased to seem strange, in a democratic society, that such authority can be exerted over politically responsive government by an institution accountable to no one, and composed of people appointed for life and not removable except by the constitutional process of conviction on articles of impeachment. Yet the legitimacy of the power of judicial review must be justified over and over again to each generation of law students, lawyers, and judges even when it has become for the people of the United States an accepted part of the political process. Judge Frank Easterbrook takes a fresh look at this process of regeneration, and finds judicial review vibrant and legitimate as a constitutional function, but undercut by what he sees as the dominant strains of modern substantive constitutional theory, that is to say theory concerned with the sources and content of constitutional law rather than the process issue of who decides. His analysis moves the issue accordingly back to where it should be, to the debate over how federal judges decide constitutional questions about the power of the other branches, or the states, to pass certain laws, or do certain things, not whether the judges have authority to decide such questions at all.

In sum, the authors of these chapters come with different backgrounds, different experiences, different political beliefs, and different priorities. Their common commitment and shared experience was to measure the government created by

the Constitution 200 years ago against a standard of useful-
ness and effectiveness today and for the foreseeable future.
The changes in two centuries are, of course, extraordinary.
Alan Westin recounts an aspect of them in his chapter on the
effects of explosion of information technology. Yet it is clear,
at least to me, in the end, that all is still vital, though obviously
not perfect, in the core instruments of constitutional government examined in this book. The failures of government are
due to the intractability of problems, forces of history far beyond the control of any nation, and other currents not caused
or diverted by the constitutional structure.

1

How Does the Constitution Structure Government?

The Founders' Views

H. JEFFERSON POWELL

No one reading the text of the 1787 Constitution can doubt the founders' intense concern with the structure of government. Americans in the late twentieth century, to be sure, usually think of rights against government when they think of matters constitutional: the rights of religious freedom, free speech and press, security of person and property, protection from arbitrary or discriminatory oppression by government. Eighteenth-century Americans, on the other hand, seem more usually to have thought of the powers and organization of government: who is to govern, how they are to be chosen, how public power and responsibility are to be distributed. For them, in other words, a "constitution" is primarily *constitutive,* a declaration or description of how a government is to be structured.

H. JEFFERSON POWELL teaches law at the University of Iowa and in 1986–87 was a visiting associate professor at the Yale Law School. He has served as a law clerk to the Honorable Sam J. Ervin, III, of the U.S. Court of Appeals for the Fourth Circuit. Since earning his J.D. from Yale in 1982, Mr. Powell has published several articles on constitutional history.

It is worth pondering for a moment why the ordinary conno-
tation of "constitutional" has shifted over the last two centuries from "having to do with structure" to "having to do with
rights." The founders, after all, had a lively concern with what
the Declaration of Independence called "unalienable Rights,"
and we in our turn frequently debate the authority and relationship of Congress, president, federal courts, and state governments. One reason for the shift, I suspect, is the very success of the founders in constituting a workable government.
Every other year since the Constitution went into effect,
Americans have voted to retain or replace our federal representatives and one-third of the U.S. Senate; every fourth
year, in crisis and calm, peace and war, a president has been
chosen. Only once over all that time, in all those elections, has
a defeated party ultimately refused to accept the result of the
political process the founders created. And even on that occasion, the dissidents did not deny Abraham Lincoln the presidency, but instead attempted to withdraw themselves altogether from the founders' handiwork. Despite two centuries of
social, economic, and political change, the constitutive me-
chanics of government devised by the founders (and in a few
respects modified by subsequent amendment)—their answers
to the questions of "who" and "how chosen"—have persisted
and functioned with remarkable success and consistency. A
great deal, then, of what the founders debated when they
discussed "constitutional" issues has become unproblematic
for us due to their very success. No wonder that for us the
highest level of political discussion that English speakers call
"constitutional" focuses on other questions.

It obviously would be wrong, however, to assume that all
issues of governmental structure were settled in 1787, or that
the radically different world of almost the year 2000 does not
present new problems in constituting and organizing power.
Identifying and discussing in detail those problems is the concern of other chapters, but we should note a few here. Is
Congress, as presently elected and organized, capable of rational discussion and legislation in the public interest? Has the
presidency grown dangerously imperial, or (perhaps, most

frightening, "and") is it an institution on the brink of failure? Have federal judges, and above all the justices of the Supreme Court, escaped the limits of their commission to interpret and apply the law? What role ought the vast federal bureaucracy, so often free of effective executive or legislative control, play in our constitutional system? Is there some residuum of governmental authority and responsibility that belongs to the states exclusive of federal control? The list could be continued almost indefinitely, but the issues outlined above suffice to show that we, like the founders, must address important and controversial questions about how to constitute power.

In addressing those questions, it is natural, inevitable, and appropriate that we should look to the founders for enlightenment. The founding era was a period of sustained debate— carried out at a remarkably high level of sophistication—over the theory and practice of structuring government. And the people who carried on that great debate were, despite two centuries of change, our direct cultural and political ancestors. Perhaps most fundamentally, we listen to the founders because they *were* the founders: they created our Republic, and the written Constitution, which is the framework and touchstone of our own constitutional discussions.

There are several ways in which we can interrogate the founders on issues of governmental structure. The most familiar is through investigation of the history of the Constitution's framing and ratification. Study of the records of the Philadelphia convention that wrote the text, and of the state assemblies that adopted it, reveals a rich and complicated debate over what that text ought to say, and how it would be interpreted. When the public debates are supplemented by individual commentary in the newspapers (the preeminent example, of course, is *The Federalist*) and in private correspondence, we have a great deal of information about what individual founders said and thought between 1787 and 1789. Modern lawyers frequently undertake such investigations, and a vast literature has grown up around the search for the "original intent" of the founders.

A second approach to the founders' opinions is through the

methods of intellectual history: the search for the sources of
their ideas, the influences on their viewpoints, and the intellectual and cultural context within which we must understand the
positions they took. In the last few decades, studies of this sort
have opened up entire new perspectives on the founders and
their achievements. Machiavelli, Hume, and a host of lesser-
known English thinkers of the seventeenth and early eighteenth centuries have joined John Locke and the Baron de
Montesquieu as philosophical forebears of the U.S. Constitution.

In this chapter, we shall try a different approach to the
founders' thinking. Rather than asking what the founders and
their mentors put *into* the Constitution of 1787, we shall ask
what the founders drew *out of* that instrument after its ratification. We shall ask how the founders, after they had created the
Constitution, understood what they had accomplished. It is
clearly a fact, although one easy to forget, that in important
respects the founders in 1789 or 1799 or 1810 faced the same
basic question we must answer today: how ought we to interpret and apply the Constitution that stands apart from and
before us as the fundamental law of the nation? For them, no
less than for us, the Constitution was something unto itself.
Their superior knowledge of its creation did not render its
meaning and import wholly clear to them; indeed, at times
they suggested that knowledge of the Constitution's origins
was a hindrance, a source of bias rather than of enlightenment.
It is tempting for us to assume that the Constitution, for the
founders, was like a personal letter: the letter writer cannot be
mistaken about his or her meaning (leaving aside the possibility of forgetfulness) even though he or she may have put that
meaning into written words imperfectly. In similar fashion, we
sometimes think that the founders must have known what they
meant, even if they were not always successful in communicat-
ing that meaning to us.

This assumption, however attractive, is simply false for at
least three reasons. In the first place, it is a matter of historical
fact that the founders began debating the Constitution's
meaning immediately upon its adoption. Their debates at

times were over matters of detail, but often the disagreement centered on basic, constitutive issues of power and governmental structure. In 1801 an exasperated newspaper correspondent writing as "An Impartial Citizen" complained of the Philadelphia framers that "neither two of them can agree to understand the instrument in the same sense." "An Impartial Citizen" was exaggerating, it is true, but his hyperbole was understandable: the single most striking characteristic of the founders' constitutional discussions between 1789 and around 1805 is controversy—fundamental, principled, and sustained. Whatever consensus may or may not have existed while the founders were creating the Constitution, their implementation of it revealed deep-rooted disagreement.

The Constitution's partial lack of clarity to the founders themselves was not solely a product of the political squabbles of the 1790s. Indeed, it dated back to the very writing of the Constitution. The founders argued over what they had done, but they agreed that whatever they had accomplished, it was the product of compromise. In 1803 Uriah Tracy of Connecticut informed the Senate that "the members of the Convention who formed the instrument have, in private information and public communications, united in the declaration that the Constitution was the result of concession and compromise." Tracy particularly had in mind the compromise between large and small states, which afforded the latter equal representation in the Senate and disproportionate weight in the electoral college in return for representation according to population in the House, but his remark was generally applicable. On a series of central issues—state equality, the extent of congressional power, national control of state legislation, the mode of electing the president, the method of taking slave populations into account for the purposes of representation and taxation—the Philadelphia framers compromised, agreeing to satisfy wholly neither of two deeply held positions. The product of such compromises was inherently ambiguous. The Constitution, for example, secured to each state two senators, but was this equality of representation a symbol and guarantor of continuing state sovereignty, or a grudging concession to localism

carved out of an essentially nationalist Constitution? Nothing
in the 1787 text unambiguously answered that or other, parallel questions, and individual founders were free to argue sin-
cerely for either interpretation or neither.

There is at least one other reason why we cannot expect that
even the founders would find the Constitution invariably clear
and unambiguous in meaning: they themselves did not expect
to be able to resolve all "constitutional" issues, all questions
about the structuring of government, with the stroke of a pen
in 1787. Two remarks of Gouverneur Morris, who was the
principal stylist for the original text, illustrate the point. Soon
after the Philadelphia convention adjourned, a friend compli-
mented Morris on the fine Constitution the framers had written. Morris rejected the compliment with the remark, "That
depends on how it is construed." At about the same time,
Morris wrote George Washington, whose presence at
Philadelphia was, for many Americans, the best argument for
ratifying Philadelphia's handiwork. "Custom," actual experience of an institution's working, is "the great commentator of
human Establishments," Morris stated. "No Constitution is
the same on Paper and in Life."

In this chapter, then, we shall explore what the founders
learned about the Constitution they set down "on Paper"
when they turned to administer it "in Life." I will address the
fundamental question—how does the Constitution structure
our government?—by asking what sorts of answers the founders themselves gave it during roughly the first decade and a
half of the new system, from the institution of the government
in 1789 through the beginning of Thomas Jefferson's second
administration.

Three basic tendencies or approaches to understanding our
constitutional structure of government emerged during those
years, I suggest. I shall label them the Theoretical, the Nationalist, and the Textualist. The Theoretical approach viewed the
Constitution through the lens provided by one or the other of
the political theories current in eighteenth-century thought.
The Nationalist approach took as its starting point certain
assumptions about the Constitution's ends, and interpreted

the specifics of text and theory as subordinate to the accomplishment of those ends. The Textualist approach, in contrast, found the key to America's structure of government precisely in the specifications of the constitutional document.

This threefold division of the founders' thought on how the Constitution structures government is not equivalent to other, more familiar classification schemes. The three approaches did not directly translate into specific political parties; there were adherents to all three among both Hamiltonian Federalists and Jeffersonian Republicans. Adherence to differing approaches did not prevent political alliance or even close political friendship. Thomas Jefferson's constitutional thought revolved primarily within the Theoretical sphere, James Madison's in the Textualist; yet the two men shared common political goals throughout the period. Different people adhered with different degrees of consistency to a particular approach: Madison was a more thoroughgoing Textualist than Jefferson a Theoretician, and John Adams was radically eclectic in his thinking on structural issues. Finally, adherence to an approach did not necessarily limit the adherent's choice of specific argumentative technique. Nationalist Alexander Hamilton and Theoretician Jefferson sometimes made use of argument over the proper construction of constitutional provisions, while Textualist Madison occasionally invoked well-known political theories even though they were not, in the end, of fundamental significance in his constitutional thought.

The value and power of differentiating the Theoretical, Nationalist, and Textualist approaches are not so much to enable us to draw lists of adherents as to illuminate the range of thought present in the founders' discussions of the constitutional structure of government. It is all too easy, as observed above, to see in the founders an unhistorical consensus of viewpoint about the Constitution. It is, perhaps, equally possible to see nothing but ad hoc argument grounded in political expediency. By identifying these three approaches, I believe that we can recapture the variety and complexity of the founders' thought while retaining an appropriate, historical sense of the principled nature of their disagreements. In understanding their debates, I believe it is not too much to hope that we will learn something about our own.

The Theoretical Approach

The political science and philosophy of the eighteenth century offered an astounding variety of theoretical discussion about governmental structure. Americans familiar with the literature—and it is remarkable how many of the founders displayed a surprising breadth of knowledge on these subjects—were thereby acquainted with the intellectual legacy of the ancient Mediterranean world: the philosophical theories of Plato and Aristotle, the philosophically informed historical works of Polybius, Livy, Tacitus, and Plutarch, as well as "modern" classical scholarship. Invocations of Greek and Roman thought and example are almost ubiquitous in the founders' discussions.

Another source of theoretical enlightenment lay in what some contemporary scholars call the Atlantic republican tradition. Despite an important debt to the image of the ancient Greek polis, this tradition has its real origins in Renaissance humanism and in the city-states of northern Italy. The historical and political writing of Machiavelli and a number of idealized portraits of the Venetian Republic influenced the founders, both directly and through the works of seventeenth-century English political writers like James Harrington. More insular in origin was the great British tradition of political philosophy that stretched from Thomas Hobbes, through John Locke and Scottish thinkers like Thomas Hutcheson, to David Hume and Adam Smith. Foreign only in his person was the influential and admiring philosophical account of the British Constitution by the Baron de Montesquieu.

Still another theoretical influence on the founders came from the legal tradition. The standard international law treatises of the day—Grotius, Vattel, Burlamaqui, Rutherford—were replete with discussion of the nature and governmental structure of unitary states and confederations, while the English common law tradition necessarily had produced a body of learning about the distribution and limitation of royal and parliamentary power.

With such a rich theoretical background, it would have been quite amazing if the founders had not made explicit use of it in construing the constitutional structure they had erected. The influence of contemporaneous political theory can be traced throughout the founding era, both in terms of broad conceptions of proper governmental structure and in terms of specific interpretations of the Constitution. An example of the latter concerns the Senate's relationship to the president. A structural device strongly recommended by many of the theorists with whom the founders were familiar was the executive council, a body of advisers to the chief executive magistrate whose advice he ought to be constitutionally mandated to seek and (at least usually) to follow. The underlying concern was to constrain the executive both from improvident action and from tyrannical designs, and in the first flush of overthrowing what they saw as an overweening executive (George III), the Revolutionary patriots embodied the concept in a number of state constitutions. The 1787 Constitution, however, failed explicitly to create such a mechanism. The executive department heads to whom the Constitution does refer were clearly not an "executive council" in the contemporaneous political science sense: instead of being *obligated* to consult them, the president was *empowered* to require their "opinion in writing . . . upon any subject relating to the Duties of their respective Offices" at his discretion.

Some Americans, however, did not regard the text's silence as dispositive of whether the Constitution in fact created an executive council. Noting the Senate's explicit role in appointments and treaties, these founders perceived in that body the superficially missing, but Theoretically necessary, council. Indeed, George Washington himself seems to have toyed with this Theoretical interpretation of the relation between Senate and president. Washington personally presented the first treaty his administration negotiated to the senators, formally requesting their "Advice and Consent." The senators not unreasonably construed this as an invitation to debate the merits of the treaty's details rather than simply to approve or disapprove the executive's actions, and the resulting legislative discussion so angered Washington that he never repeated the procedure. Henceforth, indeed up to the present day, presidents would regard the Senate's role as exclusively one of giving or withholding consent rather than of proffering substantive advice. Despite the grumblings of some early senators, and the persistent arguments of a few writers like St. George Tucker, the Theoretical claim that the Senate should act "in quality of an executive council" (reported by Massachusetts politician Fisher Ames in a mid–1789 letter) has been rejected in practice.

The idea of an executive council is a specific structural mechanism, although it rests on a broader Theoretical basis. Founders of a Theoretical bent were likely, however, to perceive the entire Constitution through some broader concept. Three such concepts were widely shared in the founding era, and indeed remain of importance in modern American constitutional discussion: the ideas of checks and balances, separation of powers, and federalism. Each of these concepts had a quite specific meaning in eighteenth-century political science, each was frequently used to interpret the U.S. Constitution, all were as frequently denounced as "general borrowed misapplied phrases" (Senator William Branch Giles of Virginia, speaking in the Senate in 1808).

Checks and Balances

For eighteenth-century political scientists, checks and balances were the governmental mechanism that properly corresponded to a particular form of government, which they usually called "mixed." The notion of mixed government ultimately derived from ancient and Renaissance reflection on the merits and faults of the Greek city-states and the Roman Republic. The Romanophile Greek historian Polybius had portrayed Rome's military and political successes as the product of the mixture of the Republic's two great social classes in its government. The largely patrician upper class wielded its

influence through the Senate and through its de facto monopoly on the consular office, while the common people exerted
authority through the popular assemblies. In this way, the
wisdom of the aristocrats and the energy of the commons were
balanced, while the inherent social antagonism of the classes,
acting through the opposing governmental structures of Senate, consuls, and assemblies, checked the tendency of both
classes to seize power.

Machiavelli's widely read commentary on the Roman historian Livy, whose work in turn relied heavily on Polybius, presented a still more complex example of a heterogeneous society with a mixed government, classical Sparta. According to
Machiavelli, the primeval Spartan legislator Lycurgus de-
served "the highest praise," because he "combined under the
same constitution a prince, a nobility, and the power of the
people" so that "these three powers" could "watch and keep
each other reciprocally in check." It was unsurprising, Machiavelli thought, that such a government should endure "for
over eight hundred years in the most perfect tranquility,"
since it embodied in its constitutional structure the social realities of its people, and thereby balanced the virtues and
checked the evil propensities of those realities.

Machiavelli's argument, transmitted through the English
radical politicians of the tumultuous seventeenth century, was
enormously influential since it seemed so closely to parallel
the traditional English Constitution. Since the High Middle
Ages, English lawyers from time to time had conceptualized
England's political structure as a balance between the three
estates of Parliament: the nobility (Lords Temporal), the
higher clergy (Lords Spiritual), and the commons. The post-
Reformation decline in status of the Lords Spiritual and the
imperial pretensions of Tudor and Stuart monarchs rendered
a reformulation of the medieval account along Machiavelli's
lines attractive. The "ancient Constitution" of England, according to many seventeenth- and eighteenth-century writers,
was a mixture of monarchy, aristocracy, and democracy (a
political trinity dating back to Aristotle): king, lords, and commons mutually balanced and checked one another in a Parlia-

ment that therefore combined all three elements of English society.

Many founders were deeply influenced by the equation of free government with mixed government. As Congressman Albert Gallatin of Pennsylvania told the House of Representatives in 1798, the mechanism of checks and balances was, and ought to be, utilized in independent America just as it was "fully established by the theory and practice of the Government of that country from which we derive our political institutions." The Constitution was the reduction to paper of this theory, according to Gallatin. "We have always been taught to believe that, in all mixed Governments and especially in our own, the different departments mutually operated as checks one upon the other." The Constitution, according to Theoreticians like Gallatin, recognized in its structuring of government a fundamental political principle: the tendency of any social class to destroy freedom when, in John Adam's words (in a 1790 letter to his cousin Samuel Adams), "possessed of the *summa imperii* in one body, without a check." Unless checked and balanced through governmental structure, all social classes historically display the desire to dominate, to bring about tyranny: not just nobles, John warned Samuel, but so have all classes behaved, "so have the plebians; so have the people; so have kings; so has human nature, in every shape and combination, and so it ever will."

In the founding era, the Theoretical claim that the U.S. Constitution structures government in accordance with the theory of mixed government and by the mechanism of checks and balances was powerful and, to many, persuasive. There are also more recent supporters of that claim. In 1926 Justice Louis Brandeis wrote that both checks and balances and the separation of powers were adopted "not to avoid friction, but, by means of the inevitable friction . . . to save the people from autocracy."

Despite its attractiveness and its prominent adherents, the theory of mixed, checked, and balanced government did not command the allegiance of most founders. To begin with, its critics argued, the whole idea rested on fallacious assumptions about America. Britain might be a country divided by a social class structure of royalty, nobility, and commons, but the United States knew no such divisions. The very defining characteristic of American society—fluidity of status and equality of political and legal rights—undercut the Theoretical justification for a governmental structure of checks and balances. Even while the Philadelphia framers were deliberating, John Adams's use of the concept of mixed government was under attack: Reverend James Madison wrote his cousin James (the framer and future president) that "nothing is more illusory on most Occasions than the Use of metaphorical Language. I question whether, this Balance, which Adams talks so much about, has not served somewhat to mislead him."

Attacks on the Theoretical invocation of checks and balances accelerated after the Constitution's ratification. Numerous founders reiterated Reverend Madison's argument that America fortunately lacked the antagonistic social structure that the theory of mixed government presupposed. In a congressional speech in 1796, Fisher Ames, one of the least egalitarian if most brilliant politicians of the founding era, denounced the notion that America had European-style social classes: "Our countrymen, almost universally, possess some property and some pretensions of learning"—the two primary characteristics differentiating an English or continental aristocracy from the common folk. America's lack of social class heterogeneity, Congressman William Vans Murray asserted about the same time, undercut any Theoretical claim that the various federal constitutional organs should attempt to check the actions of other organs. Vans Murray told his colleagues:

[The House of Representatives] is elected by the people, not to struggle with [the Senate), but to give action to the Constitution; and no right can be assumed by any one branch that gives a power of making the Constitution incentive or inefficient to its great ends. To overturn this Constitution is not merely to oppose it by violence. To refuse to act, to withhold an active discharge of the duties it enjoins upon the different branches, would as effectually prostrate it as open violence could do.

The "imported doctrine of checks," Delaware Representative James Bayard asserted two years later, therefore results in "absurdities": "consequences which tend to paralyze the powers of the Constitution, and effectually to stop the wheels of Government." Balancing and checking the powers of the branches of government may be sensible when the governed constitute separate estates; when they do not, the majority of the founders agreed, to do so is a constitutional solecism and an intellectual error.

Separation of Powers

The Theoretical concept of separation of powers is often equated today with that of checks and balances (as in the opinion of Justice Brandeis quoted above), and indeed on occasion Americans in the founding era also combined or confused them. In origins, in eighteenth-century political science, and in the minds of most founders, however, the two ideas are quite distinct. The theory of mixed government sought to avoid the tyrannical domination of any one social class or "estate" by providing every estate a governmental check on the others. The theory of separation of powers, on the other hand, rested on the premise that tyranny was the consequence of placing all governmental power in a single individual or group of allied individuals. Mixed government Theorists were unconcerned about concentrating power as long as the interests of the different estates were in balance; separation of power Theorists did not object to the domination of government by a single social class as long as different persons wielded the functionally distinct governmental powers.

Separation of powers also differed from checks and balances in that the former was essentially a creation of English and English-influenced writers. In the seventeenth century, political and constitutional crisis stimulated the development in Britain of a functional approach to what constitutes free government. Already in 1648, Clement Walker, a member of the Long Parliament, wrote that for any one man, or any Assembly, Court or Corporation of men (be it the two Houses of Parliament) to usurpe these three powers: 1. The Governing power. 2. the Legislative power. 3. And the Judicutive power, into themselves, is to make themselves the highest Tyrants, and the people the basest slaves in the world.

Early discussions of separation of powers, to be sure, vacillated in the number and character of distinct government functions that ought to be separated. Many writers identified only two functions (the legislative and executive, with the courts regarded as a special subset of the executive function), while others thought the most useful analysis would distinguish a third, "federative" power, that of negotiating and entering into treaties and compacts. By the late eighteenth century, however, Walker's quite modern-sounding test for separation had become standard, especially through the influence of Montesquieu's *The Spirit of Laws*. (Montesquieu's actual discussion was subtly nuanced: he accepted the theoretical location of the judicial power within the executive sphere but nonetheless believed that the function of making legal judgments ought not to be exercised by those who carry them out. The founders tended to read Montesquieu as simply adhering to a straightforward legislative/executive/judicial scheme.)

For many founders, it seemed self-evident that the U.S. Constitution was the practical implementation of the separation of powers theory. "Our Government," Edward Livingston of New York told the House of Representatives in 1798, "is founded on the establishment of the principles which constitute the difference between a free Constitution and a despotic power; a distribution of the legislative, Executive, and Judiciary powers into several hands . . . strongly marked, decisively pronounced." In 1789, in one of the first congressional debates involving a constitutional issue (whether the president alone could remove officers appointed with the advice and consent of the Senate), Virginian Richard Bland Lee reminded his fellow legislators that several states had explicitly incorporated the principle into their constitutions: the 1776 Virginia Constitution, for example, declared that "the legislative, executive, and judiciary departments shall be separate and distinct, so that neither exercise the Powers properly belonging to the other." (Indeed, the Virginia framers regarded the principle as so important that they incorporated it into their Declaration of Rights as well as into the body of the state constitution proper.) Nor could Lee believe that the Philadelphia framers, who "came from among the people, who venerated this general principle," could have failed to incorporate it into the federal Constitution. That instrument's lack of an explicit separation of powers provision was therefore no problem: "the general spirit of the Constitution" in its entirety embodied the Theoretical concern that the three powers not be "blended in or exercised by one body."

In a superficial way, no one could deny that separation of powers theory had influenced the Constitution. The document's functional breakdown of federal authority into legislative, executive, and judicial powers, and perhaps even the form of its first three articles, obviously were devised by men who had read Montesquieu. The problem with using the theory to interpret the Constitution, as James Jackson of Georgia replied to Lee in 1789, is that the framers had so thoroughly *rejected* the object of the threefold functional analysis—to keep in separate hands the different powers. "Are the Legislative, Executive, and Judicial powers kept separate and distinct? No, Mr. Chairman, they are blended . . . in all the possible forms they are capable of receiving." The actual Constitution—as opposed to the imaginary one Theoreticians like Lee had conjured up out of their own ideas—was one long repudiation of the separation of powers theory. The document commanded the Senate to exercise powers properly executive (in appointments and treaties) and judicial (in trying impeachments), the House to exercise in certain circumstances the executive function of prosecution (impeachment), and the president to wield legislative power (the veto). Nor was the Constitution's disregard of the separation of powers confined to its explicit blending of powers; in practice too, Hamilton observed in a 1796 letter, the constitutional system often required a branch of the government to function outside its theoretical sphere.

The Constitution's "injunctions & restrictions on congressional power," for example, could serve to convert Congress's legislative power of deliberation and decision to the mere execution of the constitutional command. Hamilton gave as an instance of this the Constitution's requirement that the compensation of federal judges "not be diminished during their Continuance in office." With regard to the salaries of judges presently sitting, Congress's only legitimate function was to execute that command.

Some of the Theoreticians who endorsed the idea of separation of powers recognized the force of the anti-Theoretical critique. In late 1801 Edmund Pendleton, president of the Virginia Court of Appeals and one of that commonwealth's most famous Revolutionary patriots, wrote a newspaper essay entitled "The Danger Not Over." Pendleton's theme was that Americans ought to take advantage of Jefferson's electoral success by ensuring constitutionally that Federalist abuses would not recur, and one of his primary concerns was to eliminate the 1787 Constitution's deviations from the separation of powers. In order to do so, Pendleton proposed a series of constitutional amendments that would have confined Senate and president to their Theoretically proper roles.

Federalism

The third great Theoretical concept used by some founders to interpret the Constitution was the idea of federalism. Eighteenth-century legal and political theorists distinguished between consolidated and confederate states. A consolidated, "perfect" or "entire" state was one in which there was a single government possessed of all legitimate political authority—in St. George Tucker's words in 1803, "all the essential parts of civil power." A confederacy (confederation, federation, and confederate state all were synonymous) was, in contrast, "a kind of assemblage of societies" created by "a convention by which several petty states agree to become members of a larger one" (Montesquieu). Only a consolidated state properly could be termed "sovereign," or a "nation," or its instrumen-

talities "national." (One of the more bemusing aspects of
American political discourse in the 1790s is the amount of heat
generated by references to the U.S. government as the "national" government. Madison, who tended to use that expression, once denounced with asperity those who thereby attributed to him a desire to convert the federal union into a
consolidated state. But Madison's critics were not simply being
sticklers for linguistic punctilio; the terms "nation" and "national" were freighted in the eighteenth century with highly
significant political connotations. If Madison was in fact inno-
cent of the desire for "consolidation" that the critics alleged,
on this matter he was unreflective about his choice of words
to an extent remarkable in one so habitually concerned with
the niceties of language.)

It is well known that the primary, and most damaging,
charge against the Constitution during the ratification struggle
was the allegation that it would effect a consolidation of what
had been, until 1787, a (con)federation. The old Massachusetts Revolutionary Samuel Adams wrote a fellow opponent of
ratification in December 1787 that "I confess, as I enter the
Building I stumble at the Threshold. I meet with a National
Government, instead of a Federal Union of Sovereign States."
Adams went on to complain that "if the several States in the
Union are to become one entire Nation, under one Legislature, the Powers of which shall extend to every subject of
Legislation, and its Laws be supreme & control the whole, the
Idea of Sovereignty in these states must be lost." Supporters
of the Constitution varied in their responses: some claimed,
disingenuously, that if contemporaneous political science
were taken seriously, the Constitution did not disturb the federal character of the union. A few others came close to accepting the indictment and endorsing it as good—most promi-
nently James Wilson (who later became a U.S. Supreme Court
justice) in the Pennsylvania state convention. Wilson flatly
rejected the applicability of notions of compact and federalism
to the proposed Constitution. The most common response of
the proratification founders, however, was best put by Madison in *Federalist Paper No. 39:* the Constitution is "neither

wholly *national,* nor wholly *federal";* at times one or the other, at other times neither. The Constitution for Madison, and probably for most of his allies in 1787–1789, simply could not be accurately described through the categories of contemporaneous political science.

The Theoreticians who were proponents of a truly federal constitution for the United States lost their battle to defeat the product of the 1787 Philadelphia convention, but they did not thereby concede the political war. Almost as soon as the Constitution was put into effect, Theoretical "federalists" began challenging the claims of those who denied the confederate nature of the instrument (but who had usurped the label "Federalist"). Secretary of State Jefferson's cabinet opinion denying the constitutionality of a national bank was the most important of these early Theoretical interpretations of the Constitution as an instrument of federalism. Jefferson described "the foundation of the Constitution as laid on this ground: That 'all powers not delegated to the United States, by the Constitution, nor prohibited by it to the states, are reserved to the states or to the people' " (quoting the Tenth Amendment). Jefferson's argument rested on the "maxim of political law" that a "sovereign state" never delegates or surrenders any powers by implication (St. George Tucker's formulation), and assumed that the Constitution was a compact among sovereign, "perfect" states. Seven years later, Jefferson penned the canonical statement of the Theoretical interpretation of the Constitution as a "federal" document in the Kentucky Resolutions of 1798. "The several states composing the United States of America . . . by compact . . . constituted a general government for specific purposes . . . reserving, each state to itself, the residuary mass of right to their own self-government." Others were equally emphatic; in 1803 anti-Jeffersonian Congressman Roger Griswold of Connecticut described the U.S. government as "strictly federal," and as a "Confederacy," and claimed that "the federative principle . . . remains the great and leading feature of the Constitution." At about the same time, Tucker, professor of law at William & Mary College, wrote the first academic discussion of the

Constitution. For the Theoretician Tucker, the Constitution merely created a "general federal council" without disturbing the states' "civil state." "Each is still a perfect state, still sovereign, still independent," each enjoying the same powers as "any other state, or nation." The Constitution, for these founders, did not fundamentally affect the states' sovereign political status; it merely put "constraints," by way of contractual agreement, "upon the exercise of that sovereignty."

The "federal" Theoreticians faced an uphill struggle in the period following ratification, since their essential argument was that the Constitution was not what most of its proponents, and all of its foes, claimed it was. Throughout the first fifteen years of the Constitution's effective existence, anti-Theoretical Americans repeatedly ridiculed the claim that the Constitution after 1789 was what its opponents wanted it to be during the previous ratification campaign. Tennessee Representative George Campbell's 1803 speech was typical: "I am, sir, of opinion that our Government was formed by the people of the United States in their capacity as such, by their immediate representatives in the General Convention, and not by the several states convened in their State capacities." The Constitution emphatically was not, in Campbell's words, "a Confederation of States," but instead a national government which, in a very few of its features, "partakes of a compromise of powers and rights between the small and large states."

The most striking repudiation of Theoretical "federalism" in the founding era is to be found in the Virginia Report of 1800, drafted by Madison to explain and justify the apparently anti-Nationalist resolutions of 1798. Despite his sincere political alliance with Jefferson, whose Theoretical Kentucky Resolutions of 1798 presented an unequivocal "federal" (confederate) interpretation of the Constitution, Madison's report carefully avoided a Theoretical perspective. The Virginia Resolutions described the "powers of the federal government as resulting from the compact to which the states are parties"; the report explained that by "states" the resolutions had meant "the people composing those political societies, in their highest sovereign capacity." The Constitution, in other words, was *not* a "convention," an "assemblage of societies" already organized into separate and "perfect" polities, but the creation of the people acting in their most fundamental constitutive role. Many years later, in the nullification crisis of 1828–33, Madison made plain his rejection of Theoretical "federalism" in a variety of settings, most clearly in a letter to Senator Daniel Webster of Massachusetts. Madison there denied that his 1800 state compact account of the Constitution differed in anything other than historical assertion from Webster's claim that the Constitution was the creation of the American people en masse. For Madison, as for most of his contemporaries, the Constitution undercut, did not embody but instead repudiated, "federalism."

The Rejection of Theory

As we have seen above, Theoretical descriptions of the Constitution were hotly contested during the early founding era. Adherents of the mixed government, separation of powers, and federalism concepts usually did not—indeed with consistency could not—accept one another's Theoretical interpretations, while many, probably most, founders rejected the Theoretical approach in principle. These latter founders agreed with Pennsylvania Chief Justice Thomas M'Kean, who stated in a 1798 judicial opinion that "our system of government seems to me to differ, in form and spirit, from all other governments that have heretofore existed in the world." "Our own reason and our constitution are the best guides" to fundamental questions of governmental structure, Madison wrote in 1793, for the political writers on whom American Theoreticians rely "wrote before a critical subject was paid to those objects, and with their eyes too much on monarchical governments," or were "evidently warped by a regard to the particular government of England." As a result, study of the Theoreticians' sources was "a field of research which is more likely to perplex than to decide." The attitude of the anti-Theoretical majority of the founders was well put by Senator John Pope in 1811: "We are misled very much, I believe, by theories and terms more applicable to other Governments than our own."

The Nationalist Approach

The second general approach to interpreting the Constitution that can be identified in the founders' discussions is perhaps best labeled "Nationalist," for its central premise was that the Constitution created a national government empowered to pursue whatever goals the people, through their representatives, perceived to be necessary or proper for national resolution. Nationalists disdained the Theoretical concepts of checks and balances, separation of powers, and federalism, for each of those modes of interpreting the Constitution impeded rather than facilitated the national government's accomplishment of its purposes. In similar fashion, Nationalists tended to reject the Textualist concern with precise construction of the textually enunciated compromises of 1787. The Nationalists saw Textualism as an overnice concern with verbal manipulation that trivialized constitutional discourse, converting it from the high-minded discussion of how best to carry out whatever goals enjoyed "the strongest wishes of the country" (Fisher Ames, in a 1792 speech) into a species of literary criticism.

Nationalists, like those Theoreticians who endorsed the notion of separation of powers, were able to draw on pre–1787 ideas in their post–1789 arguments, for from the beginning there had been Americans who rejected the (con)federation interpretation of the United States. When, on the eve of the Philadelphia convention, Dr. Benjamin Rush published an address describing Congress as "the only *sovereign* power in the United States" and asserting that Congress ought to be "the only sovereign, supreme and absolute authority over, in and throughout every part of the United States," he was only giving forthright expression to the constitutional views of many others. James Wilson declared in 1785 what Nationalists believed: the Continental Congress possessed "general rights, general powers, and general obligations, not derived from any

particular states, nor from all the particular states, taken separately; but resulting from the union of the whole." From its
origins, Justice William Paterson wrote in 1795, the Congress
was "the general, supreme and controlling council of the nation, the centre of union, the centre of force, and the sum of
the political system." Like the British Parliament, Congress's
powers were coextensive with the nation's needs. "To determine what their powers were," Paterson wrote, "we must in-
quire what powers they exercised."

Postratification Nationalists often accused their opponents
of willfully refusing to acknowledge plain facts. "It seems
strange indeed," Judge Alexander Addison wrote in 1800, that
anyone would apply hypertechnical readings of the Constitution's text to limit national power, since the main goal of the
instrument was to give to Congress "all legislative power, for
the execution of their duties," duties which even under the
Articles of Confederation extended to the "common defense
and general welfare." The Constitution's purpose was to make
"the government of the United States a complete government
with all powers within itself for general purposes." (Addison
was explicitly making use of the usual political science definition of a "compleat" or "perfect" state, which was central to
the views of the Theoretical "federalists," to make a Nationalist point: to the extent that theoretical notions of sovereignty
have any validity, it is the United States and the federal government, rather than the individual states and their governments,
that possess sovereignty.)

The Nationalists' understanding of how the Constitution
structured American government was founded on a remarkably expansive view of the national government's proper responsibilities. Richard Bland Lee, whose constitutional
thought combined a Theoretical analysis of intrafederal issues
with a generally Nationalist understanding of the Constitution
as a whole, described in 1794 the "evils" the Constitution was
created to address. They included not only the international,
commercial, and political weaknesses of the Confederation,
but internal and social disorder as well: "The ties of confidence between man and man, and consequently, the ties of

morality were broken asunder." Using biblical imagery for the
good society, Lee asserted that "the intention of the Constitution" was to ensure that "every man is safe under his own vine
and his own fig tree, and there is none to make him afraid."
In more prosaic language, Hamilton spelled out the Nationalist premise in his 1791 Report on Manufactures. The Constitution "of necessity left to the discretion of the National Legislature, to pronounce, upon the objects, which concern the
general Welfare." He went on to write that "there seems no
room for a doubt that whatever concerns the general interests
of *Learning* of *Agriculture* of *Manufactures* and of *Commerce* are
within the sphere of the national Councils." Hamilton, to be
sure, linked Nationalism in a lawyerly fashion to an interpretation of Article One's grant of power "to pay the Debts and
provide for the common Defense and general Welfare," and
thereby conceded that Congress's plenary "general welfare"
power, unlike its enumerated powers of regulation, extended
only to "an application of money." Other Nationalists—and
Hamilton's critics—could see no difference between Hamilton's position and an overt recognition that Congress was
constitutionally empowered to address all issues of national
importance and interest. To think otherwise, Addison wrote,
was to suggest that Congress's "authority extends only to *some*
cases of the general welfare. The Constitution is not so absurd.
It gives to Congress power over the means, and imposes the
duty of providing for the general welfare in all cases whatever,
to which in its discretion the means ought to be applied."
Many Nationalists were rather impatient with what they saw as
the trivialization of constitutional questions through their reduction to lawyers' word games. In a 1791 speech, Fisher
Ames criticized Madison's tendency to labor over the fine
points of textual interpretation. Any construction, Ames said,
"may be maintained to be a safe one which promotes the good
of society." A year later, Ames told his colleagues in the House
of Representatives that when a governmental project or action
enjoyed popular support, "it is our duty to provide means for
[its] accomplishment."
Nationalist thinking on governmental structure was not,

then, dominated by the belief that the Constitution embodied some preexisting political theory, nor was it overly concerned with parsing the constitutional text. Instead, Nationalists addressed issues of structure in the light of their premise that the Constitution was meant to address—or to create a national government capable of addressing—society's problems generally. Their constant concern was to insist on the energy, efficiency, and competence of the new government to achieve that goal, and their specific constitutional arguments concentrated on saying what the national authorities *could* do, rather than on what they *could not*. Our actual governmental structure, in the words of a 1789 letter by Dr. Benjamin Rush, must correspond to the "vigorous, ballanced, and triple-powered Constitution" that created it. (Rush's reference to "ballance" is probably not a Theoretical allusion to the idea of checks and balances, but instead an invocation of the mechanical imagery sometimes invoked by the founders in discussing government. The purpose of balance in a machine to eighteenth-century thinkers was to enable it to operate effectively and efficiently, not to impede or constrain its activity, as the idea of balance functioned in mixed government theory.)

The fundamental problem with the Nationalists' position according to their critics was that, intentionally or not, their views amounted to a repudiation of the root notion of "constitution." Soon after the outbreak of the Revolution, an anonymous writer published a discussion of the questions at issue between Great Britain and the American colonies, and in the course of it he asserted that "a Constitution, and a form of government, are frequently confounded together, and spoken of as synonimous things, whereas they are not only different, but are established for different purposes." The "particular business of a Constitution," he went on, was "to mark out *how much*" power the people had granted their government. This same understanding of the central purpose of a constitution informed much of the criticism of the 1787 document during the ratification campaign by those who feared that the text would be construed as the Nationalists of the 1790s said it ought to be read. An opponent of ratification published a newspaper essay in early 1788 declaring that the "only true point of distinction between arbitrary and free governments seems to be, that in the former the governors are invested with powers of acting according to their own wills, without any other limits than what they themselves may understand to be necessary for the general good"—an almost prophetic description of how Nationalists would be describing the constitutional structure of government little over a year later! Unsurprisingly, critics of Nationalist thought made similar arguments in the 1790s. In a 1792 speech, Madison warned that if the Nationalist arguments were accepted as constitutional orthodoxy, "everything from the highest object of state legislation down to the most minute object of police, would be thrown under the power of Congress." The Nationalist position, Jefferson warned in his 1791 cabinet opinion opposing a national bank, amounted to a federal attempt to lay claim to powers "no longer susceptible of any definition." The Nationalists, their opponents claimed, answered questions of how the Constitution structured government by denying that it really did so and by simply authorizing the national authorities to act however they believed appropriate.

The Nationalist response to this critique was implicitly to accept its premise—that the Nationalist account of governmental structure was in the end the simple picture of a body of magistrates entitled to take whatever action they thought was for the common good through the most expedient means available—but to deny that this interpretation converted the Constitution into a grant of unlimited power. The federal government, Nationalists conceded, was not entitled to infringe or disregard express restrictions on its power, although, as the 1798 debate over Congress's power to punish seditious libel revealed, the Nationalists generally were willing to construe such restrictions narrowly. Sometimes Nationalists added that actions "repugnant to the natural rights of man" (Fisher Ames in a 1791 speech) were also beyond the government's legitimate reach. Most fundamentally, however, the Nationalists insisted that the primary limit on federal power was the republican one of the people's exercise of the fran-

chise. To the theme of energy, Nationalist thought on governmental structure added the concept of responsibility. The
Constitution's second great improvement on the Articles of
Confederation, next to the empowerment of Congress to carry
out what even the Articles gave it the duty to consider, was the
creation of strong and direct lines of responsibility between
the people and the federal government. Directly by the right
to elect the House of Representatives, more obliquely through
state legislative choice of senators, the electoral college's selection of the president, and the Congress's ability to impeach
and remove federal judges, the Constitution had insured that
the people could control the national authorities. This being
the case, it was simply absurd to worry about the extent of
those authorities' powers. To fear that a Congress so responsible would extend its competence to "all cases whatever" was
a "supposition so extravagant, that I cannot persuade myself,
it will ever be honestly and seriously urged," Addison wrote.
But in a burst of candor on this issue not always characteristic
of Nationalist spokesmen, Addison denied that such a remote
possibility was to be feared, if it should come to pass: "Is it a
greater evil, that the general welfare of the United States
should be provided for by one body of representatives of the
people, instead of several; or should be left altogether unpro-
vided for?" For Addison, as for Nationalists generally, the
latter possibility—that there were matters of the common
good which no governmental body rightfully could address—
was quite unthinkable, and Addison's admitted preference for
the efficiency and energy of a single, omnicompetent legislature was the logical conclusion of the Nationalist vision.

The Textualist Approach

In 1805 Maryland Congressman Roger Nelson addressed
the House of Representatives in opposition to a bill (to re-
trocede the District of Columbia to Maryland and Virginia) the
constitutionality of which he thought doubtful. In the speech,
Nelson addressed the question of what a constitution is, and
provided an answer significantly different from the functional

definitions offered by Nationalists and their critics (discussed above). "Before the American Revolution," Nelson said, "no power on earth had a Constitution"; indeed "the word itself was never fully understood." England's boast of a free constitution was the product of deluded imaginations. "Fine words truly; but where is the thing itself to be found? Is it reduced to writing? No. Who has seen it? No man. Is it known to any man?" But in America, the word was understood and the concept a reality. "How different, how honorably different, is the American Constitution. With us it is reduced to writing. It is in every man's hand; it is known to the whole world." For the Textualist, the fundamental characteristic of the Constitution, and hence the key to how it structured government, was its written, specific, particular nature. Theoretical accounts of the Constitution were objectionable because they repudiated this basic reality in favor of lapsing back into the uncertainties of European political thought. The Nationalist approach was equally in error: in their lack of concern for correct interpretation of the text's specific language, the Nationalists, Madison warned in 1792, were "trying to convert the Government from one limited" by that language into "an indefinite Government . . . without any limits at all." To do so, he went on, would be to "subvert the very foundation and transmute the very nature" of the Constitution and the government "established by the people of America."

The great charter of Textualism was Madison's famous speech in February 1791 opposing the national bank bill. The bulk of Madison's opening remarks did not directly concern banks at all, but was instead a small treatise on how to interpret a written constitution, with the bank bill serving as one of several examples. Madison made it plain that, for him, constitutional discussion *was* discussion about the meaning of a particular document rather than about good political theory or efficient national government. The great questions of federal authority and governmental structure were to be answered by construing the text and not by the extratextual concerns of the Theoreticians and Nationalists. Where the text's "meaning is clear," Madison asserted, "the consequences, whatever they are, are to be admitted." If the text failed to embody a Theoretical mechanism that would benefit the country, or failed to empower the government to pursue an important, even essential, Nationalist goal, that fact only showed the Constitution's imperfection. Rejecting the Nationalist premise that all powers "necessary and proper for the Government or Union" must of necessity be vested somewhere, Madison said that the argument ignored "the peculiar nature of the Government; no power, therefore, not enumerated, could be inferred from the general nature of Government." To "take a single step" beyond the text, Jefferson told President Washington in 1791, would be "to take possession of a boundless field of power" and thereby to convert the federal government into an unlimited despotism. The answer to this danger, in Madison's words, was to "keep close to our chartered authorities."

The Textualists' insistence on linking great issues of political power to debate over how to read a document often seemed to critics the worst sort of lawyers' wrangling, but Textualists themselves viewed it as nothing other than obedience to the declared will of the people. What we are contending for, the Textualist editor of the *Philadelphia National Gazette* wrote in 1792, is "a regular observance of the Constitution, equally when it limits as when it grants power." If constitutional questions were not to be settled by Textualist interpretation, then the document was "a useless and dead letter; and it would be to no purpose, that the States, in Convention assembled, had framed that instrument to guide the steps of Congress" (unidentified speaker in the House of Representatives, 1792). The object of Textualism, Madison wrote in 1800, was "to maintain what the Constitution has ordained."

Obedience to the Constitution as once written down was a necessary consequence for some Textualists not only of its written nature, but also of its origin in debate and agreement. "Is it not, in its essence, a compact, a bargain, a perfect compromise?" asked Benjamin Huger of South Carolina in 1803. As individuals and states, Americans were bound only by the textual provisions upon which they had agreed, "by the articles and conditions in the written contract—the Constitution—which has been acceded to by them all."

Sophisticated Textualists were, of course, aware that the Constitution's language was not wholly free of ambiguity. Soon after the Philadelphia convention sent the instrument to Congress, Madison conceded in a letter to Jefferson that it had proven impossible to write a text so clear "as to be free from different constructions by different interests, or even from ambiguity on the judgment of the impartial," and Madison's fellow Virginian John Page even suggested that some of the Philadelphia framers had conspired to create textual ambiguity "ingeniously contrived . . . to suit two events—a Republican or a Monarchical issue." (Page thought that whatever some cryptomonarchists at Philadelphia might have wished, the people plainly had adopted the Constitution in its republican sense.) In cases of ambiguity, Madison asserted in his bank bill speech, that interpretation was superior that hewed as closely to what was textually clear as possible; on the other hand, an "interpretation that destroys the very characteristic of the Government"—its textually prescribed and limited nature— "cannot be just."

Most of the contemporaneous objections to the Textualists have already been noted. Textualism was an unworkable approach to understanding the American structure of government, Fisher Ames stated in the 1791 bank bill debate, and from the beginning Congress had rejected it: "We have scarcely made a law in which we have not exercised our discretion with regard to the true intent of the Constitution." Furthermore, Ames continued, the Textualists' claims that their approach was necessary in order to avoid uncertainty about federal power were bogus. Textualism, in fact, was no solution to the danger of congressional overreaching: "Do they mark out the limits of the power which they will leave to us with more certainty than is done by the advocates of the bank? Their rules of interpretation . . . will be found as obscure, and of course as formidable as that which they condemn; they only set up one construction against another." Textualism was a subtle method of attacking the governmental structure the people had erected: in a letter written in 1801, U.S. diplomat Charles Cotesworth Pinckney described Textualist arguments as "attempts . . . to construe away the Energy of our Constitution, to unnerve our Government, and to overthrow that System by which we have risen to our present prosperity." Textualism was intellectually dishonest, some critics added, in that it assumed rather than proved that Textualism followed from the existence of a written Constitution; Addison attacked Madison's famous report of 1800 on these grounds. "The Virginia Report argues not fairly," Addison wrote, because it started with a Textualist "presumption" and then swiftly proceeded to a Textualist conclusion. Indeed, Fisher Ames wrote in 1805, the very notion that governmental structure could be created or administered in obedience to discussions about documentary construction amounted to "the insane belief that an engrossing clerk can make a constitution. Mere words, though on parchment, though sworn to, are wind, and worse than wind."

Reflections

How does the Constitution structure government? The first Americans to ask that question of the Constitution as an operating instrument of governance—the founders in the decade or two following 1789—proposed a rich, indeed at times almost bewildering, variety of answers. Some claimed that the written Constitution was the embodiment of some preexisting political theory and its correlative governmental mechanisms; questions of governmental structure for these founders were to be answered by going behind the 1787 document to whatever theory they saw reflected in it. Others saw in the Constitution not a preexisting theory but a novel injunction to pursue and accomplish those political goals identified through the national political process. The details of governmental structure and the niceties of textual interpretation were subordinate for these founders to the overriding imperative that the nation's government have the competence to address the nation's concerns. Still others insisted that neither theory nor felt necessity was

the proper key to understanding the Constitution's structuring
of government; constitutional questions for these founders
were questions about the meaning of a particular text, and they
rejected calls to go beyond or behind the text's provisions in
the interest of political theory or expediency. And, as we have
observed, some founders varied in the approach they endorsed, or simply held inconsistent positions.

These three fundamental approaches to our question—the
Theoretical, the Nationalist, and the Textualist—informed
and shaped the founders' discussions over specific structural
questions: the extent of congressional power, the nature of
state autonomy, the relationship between Congress and president, and between the House of Representatives and the other
two elected federal organs, and the status and role of the
federal judiciary. While other factors entered into those specific debates, the influence of the three approaches identified
here is everywhere evident, and often decisive, in determining
what position a given founder took.

Invocations of the founders' debates over particular questions of governmental structure are a common feature of contemporary constitutional debate, particularly among lawyers
and in the opinions of the justices of the Supreme Court.
Those attempts often illuminate our constitutional problems
through the brilliance and passion of the founders' thought,
but they are also prone at times to confuse or obfuscate, as
advocates strive to force the founders' varied and conflicting
views into the straightjacket of a unitary "original intent," or
when our twentieth-century problems simply do not correspond to their eighteenth-century answers. It may be useful,
therefore, to look for the founders' contribution not just in the
particularities of their specific constitutional debates but also
in the broader forms their discussions took. The Theoretical,
Nationalist, and Textualist approaches are such forms, and in
conclusion, I would like briefly to go beyond my historical
purpose and to suggest a few ways in which these approaches
may provide some modest help to us as we seek to understand
how the Constitution structures, and ought to structure, government today.

My first observation is that, at least in the short term, the Textualist won the general debate. One consequence of the Jeffersonian electoral "revolution of 1800" was the permanent expulsion of the generally Nationalist party of Adams and Hamilton from control of the presidency and Congress. Even John Marshall's Supreme Court, in many respects the heir of Adams and Hamilton, was, at least stylistically, as Textualist as it was Nationalist, and increasingly so as time went on. And when, in the middle and late 1810s, the political heirs of Jefferson wished to adopt broadly Nationalist governmental policies, they felt it necessary to justify doing so through Textualist arguments. Justice Joseph Story's classic opinion upholding Supreme Court review of state decisions (*Martin v. Hunter's Lessee*, 1816) and the arguments of Henry Clay and John C. Calhoun on behalf of a federal internal improvements program (1816–1818) proposed conclusions the old Nationalists would have endorsed in terms distinctively Textualist. From 1800 onward American constitutional discourse has remained, in a fundamental sense, discussion about how to read a text.

It might be replied that the Textualist victory was largely illusory, that contemporary constitutional debate is more likely to revolve around the meaning of judicial opinions than around words penned in 1787, and that the actual structure of government of the late twentieth-century United States is vastly different from anything the original Textualists expected. But these observations, although largely true, do not invalidate or reverse the Textualists' early victory: our present governmental structure, however much novelty and expediency have marked its development, has evolved through a process of deliberation that has given primacy of honor—and sometimes of decision—to construing the text. Constitutional positions that are difficult to reconcile with the document's language—supporting the legitimacy of a legislative veto, for example, or endorsing an innovative budget-control scheme—face an uphill struggle for acceptance or survival because of our Textualist legacy.

Our allegiance to Textualism ought to make us particularly interested in the founding-era critique of that approach. At least two elements of that critique seem of permanent importance. The first is the charge that Textualism is a trivializing and unworkable account of how the Constitution could structure government. Anti-Textualist founders forcefully argued that fundamental questions of high politics could not and should not be wholly reduced to discussion over the meaning of the words on the page, and their contention deserves consideration. Contemporary constitutional discussion would not fully serve our needs as a national community if it were nothing more than a lawyers' debate over the construction of a document.

The second contribution of the anti-Textualist critique is its reminder that Textualism necessarily involves the admission that the Constitution may be defective, that we may encounter national needs or desires which are constitutionally, in Madison's 1792 language, "an omitted case." This is so not only in the obvious and explicit sense—we might *need* the legislative veto and yet decide the text would not permit it—but in a subtler way as well. By providing a specific and therefore limited vocabulary in which to discuss questions of governmental structure, the Textualist Constitution channels and constrains the ways in which we can speak and even think about those questions. A common idiom of discussion has obvious benefits; it may also carry with it less apparent blindnesses and limitations.

The Theoreticians' contribution to modern constitutional thought on governmental structure is somewhat less pervasive. Their most fundamental gift to us, perhaps, is the critique they stimulated of Theoretical approaches to the Constitution. No American constitutionalist in over half a century has seriously endorsed one of three great Theoretical concepts—checks and balances, separation of powers, or federalism—in anything remotely approaching its eighteenth-century meaning. Justice (later Chief Justice) William Rehnquist's defense of federalism is perhaps the most apparent counterexample, but Rehnquist's federalism is so limited a revival, so pale a reflection of the eighteenth-century theory, that from the viewpoint of any of the great Theoretical "federalists," Jefferson, say, or St. George Tucker, Rehnquist's constitutional views would have seemed essentially Nationalist. The anti-Theoretical critics have been proven correct, at least as prophets of the course of constitutional thought: few Americans since the founding era have viewed the Constitution from a genuinely Theoretical perspective. This fact of our history raises a serious question about the tendency of the Supreme Court, on scattered but important occasions, to invoke one of the three main Theoretical concepts as the justification for overturning contemporary practice as unconstitutional. Should we, or the justices, continue to employ ideas that history has confused (think of the modern difficulty in distinguishing checks and balances from separation of powers) or repudiated and that none of us is willing to accept with their original range and significance?

On the positive side, while little of the Theoreticians' particular ideas can be translated easily into meaningful contemporary terms, their shared insistence that governmental structure must correspond to social and political realities is, I believe, of continuing value. Contemporary American constitutional debate faces the constant temptation to deny theoretical, moral, or philosophical commitments. The Theoretical founders' message is that such a denial can be at most a self-delusion. The positions we take with respect to the constituting of government's structure inevitably will be fraught with theoretical implication and moral decision; we would be wise to imitate the original Theoreticians in admitting and openly discussing that reality.

The Nationalists' continuing significance for us is perhaps less obvious. Their central object—to insure that the Constitution would be recognized as creating a national government fully competent to address the nation's needs—has been substantially achieved. Furthermore, this object was of such overriding concern to them that they had relatively little to say about the type of intrafederal issues that concern us in an era of national omnicompetence. We have the energetic federal government they desired, and we have created lines of responsibility between the president and Congress, and the people, that (formally at least) far exceed the degree of popular control the early Nationalists thought necessary to render such a government politically safe. More than either the Textualist or Theoretical approaches, I believe the Nationalist offers questions rather than answers: beyond the safeguards necessary to maintain electoral responsibility and equal representation, ought there to be limits on what the elected, national representatives of the people can do in a republic? And conversely, as anti-Nationalist founders asked two centuries ago, can a free people dare to entrust its central government with plenary power and responsibility over objects as broad as the common defense and the general welfare?

2

Political Parties
and a Workable Government

LLOYD N. CUTLER

Many Americans are deeply concerned about the government's seeming inability to tackle critical problems, such as the need to make the decisions necessary to correct our continuing budget and trade deficits. That inability does not derive from a lack of consensus about the gravity of these problems. Indeed, there is virtual unanimity among our elected leaders that the twin deficits are spreading cancers that may soon become irreversible. Every one of them has a cure

---

LLOYD N. CUTLER is a member of the Washington law firm Wilmer, Cutler & Pickering. He has a long history of public service, including several advisory positions for various U.S. presidents. He was a senior consultant for the President's Commission on Strategic Forces during 1983–1984. From 1979 to 1980 he was counsel to the president and special counsel to the president on ratification of the SALT II Treaty. He was the president's special representative for Maritime Resource and Boundary Negotiations with Canada from 1977 to 1979. Mr. Cutler is a member of several civic and educational boards, and he has published widely on issues of domestic and international law. Along with Senator Nancy Kassebaum and Douglas Dillon, he is a cochair of the Committee on the Constitutional System.

to propose, but they are unable to agree on what cure to adopt. Meanwhile, the cancers continue to grow.

Although we are now celebrating the 200th anniversary of the Constitution, few of us associate these massive failures of the political system with faults in our political structure. Most of us blame the individuals we elect to office. Like horseplayers disappointed in our choices for the last race, we turn immediately to the entries in the next. But by and large, the 537 incumbents we elect today—435 members of Congress, 100 senators, the president, and the vice-president—are as able and decent as the incumbents of 1937 or 1887. If the national government has greater difficulties in meeting its responsibilities today than at earlier times, the reasons must lie elsewhere.

One glaring reason is the recent decline in the cohesion of the political parties. It is true, of course, that the Constitution makes no mention of political parties, and that James Madison warned against the "rise of faction" in *Federalist Paper No. 10.* But to the political theorists of the eighteenth century, there were three kinds of faction, based on allegiance to a person or family, on a desire for personal political power, or on a shared view of the national interest. There is strong circumstantial evidence that the framers were more concerned about the first two rather than the third. When the new government was formed, Madison and Thomas Jefferson, along with Alexander Hamilton and John Adams, quickly took the lead in establishing two broadly based political parties rooted in their differing views of the national interest. During their presidencies, Adams, Jefferson, Madison, and James Monroe were the de facto leaders of their parties' delegations in Congress. And until President Andrew Jackson, at odds with the congressional wing of his party, invented the national political convention to achieve his renomination, the congressional caucus of each party played the dominant role in nominating the party's presidential candidate.

While the constitutional separation of the executive and legislative branches did exert its intended centrifugal effect, presidents and legislators of the same party worked remarkably well together to govern the young nation. John Adams and Jefferson never had to cast a single veto, Madison did so only seven times, and Monroe only once. During the seven consecutive terms of these four presidents, divided government (one party holding the White House and the other party a majority of one or both houses) never occurred. In fact, only three nineteenth-century presidents (Millard Fillmore, Rutherford B. Hayes, and Grover Cleveland in his first term) were elected without carrying majorities for their parties in both houses. In the twentieth century, this did not happen until 1956, when President Dwight D. Eisenhower, even while winning his own reelection by a huge margin, failed to carry a majority for his party in both houses. This phenomenon of divided government resulted in five of the eight presidential elections from 1956 to 1984—more often in these three decades than in the first 170 years of the Republic. In the presidential elections from 1968 to 1984, it occurred four times out of five.

Woodrow Wilson campaigned against divided government when he ran for president in 1912, a time when the Republicans held the presidency and a majority of the Senate, and the Democrats held a majority of the House. Wilson said:

[Under divided government] you have an arrested government. You have a government that is not responding to the wishes of the people. You have a government that is not functioning, a government whose very energies are stayed and postponed. If you want to release the force of the American people, you have got to get possession of the Senate and the presidency as well as the House.

Wilson won the presidency and a solid majority for the Democrats in both houses. His first term carried out the party program by laying the legislative foundation of the New Freedom, generally regarded as the most productive period of American government between the abolition of slavery and the New Deal.

This recent trend toward divided government parallels the growing weakness of the political parties. That weakness has several causes.

First, voters have lost their earlier sense of party consciousness. In 1900, 4 percent of the nation's congressional districts cast a majority vote for one party's presidential candidate and for the other party's candidate for the House of Representatives. Ticket splitting increased to the point where this happened in 45 percent of all districts in 1984. Polls taken in 1987 showed that nearly one-third of all voters did not think of themselves as adhering to a party.

Second, party cohesion in Congress, and between the legislators and president of the same party, has been greatly weakened by twentieth-century reforms such as the civil service system, the primary elections, and the "democratization" of Congress, as well as by technological innovations such as radio and television. National, state, and local party leaders no longer select or provide most of the financing to the party's candidates for federal office; the candidates get themselves nominated and financed with little or no help from party leaders. Well-heeled single-interest groups have accelerated this process. They have learned they can exert greater influence on the single issues they care about by contributing directly to the candidate and by making additional "independent expenditures" on his or her behalf than by contributing indirectly through the party. For the past two decades, congressional candidates have become less and less dependent on the parties' leaders to get themselves elected and reelected, and they have little incentive to support these leaders while in office.

Two features of the Constitution itself have accelerated the weakening of political parties. One is the ban, which the Supreme Court has read into the First Amendment, on laws limiting campaign expenditures. Congress may set such limits only as a condition imposed on those candidates who accept public financing, which is currently available only to presidential nominees. This ban enhances the divisive power of single-interest blocs willing to spend any amount to achieve their goals. The other constitutional feature that has weakened political parties is the staggering of electoral terms and the brief two-year term of the House of Representatives—the shortest of any major democratic nation. Presidents are elected for a four-year term, but all representatives and one-third of the senators always face an election within two years. With the carefully balanced sharing of legislative and executive power that is designed into the Constitution, the shorter time horizon of most legislators becomes dominant and creates deadlock between the branches and between the president and the legislators of the president's party. It is a political truism that nothing can be done to reduce deficits in an election year, which now means nothing can be done every other year.

The results are apparent. The percentage of congressional votes in which a majority of one party is on one side and a majority of the other party is on the other side has fallen below 50 percent. Most controversial legislation is passed by cross-party coalitions whose makeup shifts from one issue to the next. With so little cohesion on either side of the aisle, the party holding the White House has great difficulty in legislating the program on which its candidates ran for office. This is especially true at times of divided government, when the administration's success rate on major bills is only about 66 percent (except in 1981, President Ronald Reagan did no better). Even at times when the administration party has majorities in both houses, its success rate is only 80 percent. These rates considerably overstate the actual degree of success, because they include many bills in which the administration has accepted major modifications it dislikes in order to get at least half of what it wants.

The sum of all these decisions is often inconsistent and self-defeating. Moreover, neither party nor any individual we elect can fairly be held accountable for the hodgepodge of unwanted outcomes such as the huge budget and trade deficits. Indeed, they mostly succeed in escaping accountability. About 90 percent of the incumbent legislators of *both* parties who run for reelection are reelected, even when their party loses the White House. And Presidents Eisenhower, Richard Nixon, and Reagan, who ran for reelection at times of divided government, were reelected by landslide margins.

Benjamin Franklin's 1776 maxim, "We must all hang together, or most assuredly we shall all hang separately," is a dead letter for either party's incumbents today. They adhere more closely to the motto of the Damon Runyon character who said, "It's every man for theirself."

The values of a strong national party system are threefold. First, a broadly based party, able to select and finance its own candidates and maintain cohesion among them in office, can serve as a moderating force between the financial and voting pressures of single-interest groups and the individual candidates we elect to conduct the government. Second, it can blend these conflicting pressures and a broader view of the national interest into a coherent program for governing. Third, if it wins the presidency and a working majority of both houses, it can legislate and execute that program, and stand clearly accountable at the next election for its good, bad, or indifferent results.

Nevertheless, some believe that weak parties and divided government are better than their opposites. They fear that stronger political parties and a greater degree of party government would lead to wild swings of the pendulum between extreme policies, such as the shifts between nationalization and privatization in Britain. But wild extremes did not happen under the stronger parties that took turns governing this nation for most of the first 150 years of our history. They have not happened in the Federal Republic of Germany or in our own state governments, many of which still function under strong and cohesive state party systems. The centrifugal forces in our constitutional structure and in our ocean-to-ocean continent of a nation are far too strong for such extreme swings to occur.

Some also believe that the primary reason for deadlock and incoherence is a lack of public consensus on major controversial issues, and that it is the duty of elected officials to reflect this lack until a true public consensus forms. But the framers never intended the national government to be run as a town meeting of the entire citizenry. The framers created *representative* government, and expected these elected representatives to govern by making decisions in the national interest as they saw it. They did not intend these representatives to vote in perfect reflection of the weekly public opinion polls.

Is it too late to strengthen the political parties to the point where they can resume their natural functions of intermediation and accountability? Some of us believe it is not too late. For the past several years, the Committee on the Constitutional System, composed of several hundred present and former senators and representatives, cabinet officials, White House staffers, academics, and grass-roots political, business, and labor leaders, has been studying this question. It has just published its analysis and recommendations.

The committee recognizes the many virtues in our 200-year-old constitutional structure and in the reforms of the political party system that have been made during this century. It sees no reason to reverse any of these reforms or to alter the basic constitutional framework, and accepts that in any event it is not feasible to do so. But a broad consensus of the committee agrees that a few modest improvements in our electoral arrangements would greatly improve the chances of strengthening the parties and enabling them to resume the role they filled so well until the 1950s. Some of these suggestions would require changes in party rules, some would require legislation, and some would require very moderate changes in the Constitution itself. The following are among the most important improvements.

Change Party Rules for Presidential Nominating Conventions. Give the party's nominees for the House and Senate races plus the holdover senators 535 additional seats as uncommitted voting delegates. This would give them a major voice in close races for the presidential nomination, make them politically accountable for the convention's choice, and enhance the possibilities of party cohesion with the president after the election.

Provide Funding for Congressional Election Campaigns. Enact a statute to provide public funding for congressional election campaigns, as we now do for presidential elections. Nominees who accept public funding would be barred from raising or spending any other funds, as the presidential nominees are now barred, and as the Supreme Court approved in *Buckley v. Valeo* (1976). Half or more of the funds would be allocated to the nominees directly under a population-based formula. The balance would go to each party's congressional campaign committees, usually made up of party leaders in each house, to be allocated among the close races as the committees decide in order to maximize the party's chances of winning majority control. This would reduce the pressure of well-heeled single-interest groups on nominees and incumbents, and improve their cohesion with the party's legislative leaders after election.

Limit Campaign Expenditures. Amend the Constitution to permit Congress to set reasonable limits on all campaign expenditures in primaries and general elections, something the Supreme Court has held the Constitution presently forbids. In 1986 midterm election candidates raised and spent $350 million, most of which was contributed directly or spent on behalf of individual candidates by wealthy single-interest pressure groups. This was considerably above the amount spent four years earlier, and the trend is moving steadily up. These pressure groups weaken party cohesion and are largely responsible for the hodgepodge of inconsistent government actions we see today.

Change Terms of Office. Amend the Constitution to establish a four-year term for the House of Representatives, running simultaneously with the presidential term, and an eight-year term for the Senate, with two classes of senators rather than the present three. Every four years we would vote at the same time for president, vice-president, all members of the House, and one senator from each state. This would create a common political time horizon of at least four years for all elected officials. It would lengthen the "honeymoon" period in which major but controversial legislation can be enacted, such as deficit-reduction measures that may create unpopular pains within two years, but produce popular benefits within four. It would also cut the cost of campaigning in half and assure a much larger voter turnout for congressional elections than the 35 percent of eligible voters who turned out for the 1986 midterm election. It would enhance the party consciousness of voters and, since they all would be running in the same election and reelection, it would enhance cohesion among each party's elected officials while in office.

Change Vote Required for Treaties. Amend the Constitution to change the vote required for advice and consent to treaties from two-thirds of the Senate to a majority of both houses. If the Senate balks at sharing this prerogative with the House, the required Senate vote should be reduced at least to 60 percent. The two-thirds rule dates from a time when the young nation, separated by an ocean from other menacing powers, could be governed in isolation, and when entangling alliances were justly to be feared. That day, of course, has long since passed. The U.S. government today cannot meet its economic, political, and security responsibilities except by making numerous agreements with other nations. We need a process that facilitates such agreements instead of obstructing them, as a minority of senators obstructed the Treaty of Versailles despite Senate majorities (below two-thirds) in its favor.

All of these are modest proposals. None would shake the pillars of our political structure. But separately or in combination, they should help to improve the effectiveness and accountability of our elected government and its chances of coping with the daunting responsibilities it will face in its third century, when it must act jointly with other nations to manage the volatile, interdependent global economy, to defend the democratic tradition, and to prevent nuclear war.

Some will say that since "it ain't broke, don't fix it." There were many Americans of this view in 1787, but the framers were not among them. They were more discerning in their analysis and more daring in their design of remedies. As Thomas Jefferson wrote:

I am certainly not an advocate for frequent and untried changes in laws and constitutions . . . But I know that laws and institutions must go hand in hand with progress of the human mind. As that becomes more developed, more enlightened, as new discoveries are made, new truths disclosed, and manners and opinions change with the change of circumstances, institutions must advance also and keep pace with the times.

To conduct a critical analysis of our political structure on its 200th anniversary does not show any lack of respect or admiration for the framers. It pays homage by emulating and building upon their enduring work. Let us hope that our generation will carry on this task as wisely and courageously as the framers did in theirs.

3

The Constitution and Foreign Policy

NICHOLAS deB. KATZENBACH

Introduction

Any discussion of how the Constitution allocates the conduct of foreign policy among the branches of the federal government starts from the premise that the United States is one sovereign nation and that the federal government speaks and acts for that nation. While that premise is beyond dispute, it is curious that it cannot be found anywhere in the words of the Constitution itself. What can be found, of course, are specific references to aspects of foreign affairs—to treaties, to war, to ambassadors, to duties, imposts, and excises, to commerce with foreign nations—from which it can perhaps be implied

NICHOLAS deB. KATZENBACH is a partner in the law firm of Riker, Danzig, Scherer, Hyland & Perretti and is on the board of directors of the Council on Foreign Relations. Mr. Katzenbach has held several positions with the U.S. Department of Justice, including U.S. attorney general, and was under secretary of state. He served for many years as senior vice-president and general counsel for IBM Corporation. In addition to having been a Ford Foundation fellow, Mr. Katzenbach has served on the faculties of Yale Law School, the University of Chicago Law School, and Stanford Law School.

that foreign affairs is the domain of the federal government. But the specifics are, when compared to the whole, quite sparse.

If one accepts that all the powers of a sovereign nation rest with the federal government without worrying too much about how that came about, it remains difficult to determine just how these powers are divided among its branches when only a few are specifically mentioned. What is reasonably clear is that, on the most important matters, Congress was to have a necessary voice: war, treaties, tariffs, and commerce. And the powers specifically given to the president seem, on their face, to be ceremonial: to receive foreign ambassadors.

Of course, from the outset, it has been the president who has taken the leadership. To find anything in the Constitution itself which would endorse or justify this leadership is a semantic stretch. Various justifications doctrinally—"commander-in-chief," "executive power," the "Constitution as a whole"—scarcely reach as far as the president has. The practicalities of foreign affairs probably do. The Constitution has not gotten in the way of this development. But presidential leadership does not mean that, on *any* foreign affairs development, the president can both *propose* and *dispose*. He may, in the short run, do so to the enormous frustration of Congress (even where they agree); it is clear that, formally or informally, Congress (and the people) must support presidential initiatives where any issue persists over even a relatively short time.

This brief introduction is designed to set a tone. We are talking about procedures—all government is procedure—with respect to a subject matter as to which the founding fathers were vague—perhaps wisely. The details of the relationship between the president and Congress (the Court has not, and probably should not, play the arbitral role it has in domestic matters) have been left to the political process—to the judgment, wisdom, and political moxie of the moment. By doing so they did not do away with dispute as to power or role or policy. They were, it seems in retrospect, pretty neutral—admittedly leaving it to the political passions of the moment.

But those passions have been either blunted or frustrated, depending on viewpoint, a constitutional approach quite consistent with the notion of separation of powers.

Historian Thomas Macaulay's view that our Constitution "is all sail and no anchor" as applied to foreign affairs is both inapt and irrelevant. Whether we are all sail and no anchor, or all anchor and no sail, depends very little on the Constitution, but almost entirely on public opinion. Where there is consensus—as in World War II—there has been little attention paid to constitutional niceties. Where the country is divided—as in arms control or with respect to Vietnam—appeals to constitutional prerogatives are of little avail.

The constitutional scheme of separating powers by allocating the legislative power to Congress, the executive power to the president, and the judicial power to the courts does not easily fit the formulation and execution of foreign policy. Foreign policy is not simply a matter of enacting and executing laws—though the enactment of legislation may be crucial to particular foreign policy objectives. And it is not possible to conduct—"execute"—foreign policy without at the same time "making" it. We are left with a system in which it cannot be doubted that *all* the power is in the hands of the president and Congress, and, when exercised concurrently, it is not open to question save in its intrusion on individual rights and protections. Less certain is what the president or the Congress can do without the other. Inevitably, this leads to a premium on who has the initiative. And here the president has—and always has had—great advantages. John Jay pointed out in *The Federalist Papers* these great inherent strengths: the unity of the office, its capacity for secrecy and speed, its superior sources of information. Even more important was the need for other nations to look to a source to determine the view, or even the commitment, of the United States. Clearly, this has always been, and indeed had to be, the president. Jefferson put it succinctly: "The transaction of business with foreign nations is Executive altogether."

But to point out the leadership that the president enjoys (or suffers) is not to minimize the role of Congress. It is hard to improve on Professor Edward Corwin's analysis of thirty years ago:

> Despite all this, actual *practice* under the Constitution has shown that while the President is usually in a position to *propose,* the Senate and Congress are often in a technical position at least to *dispose.* The verdict of history, in short, is that the power to determine the substantive content of American foreign policy is *divided* power, with the lion's share falling usually to the President, though by no means always.

From a constitutional viewpoint, Justice Robert Jackson probably expressed most clearly the parameters of presidential action. When the power he asserts is pursuant to an expressed or implied congressional authorization, it is at its maximum. When he acts without such authority he can rely only on his own independent powers, but he may be acting in the "twilight zone," where the president and Congress possess concurrent powers. But where he acts against the express will of Congress, his power is least because he must rely on his own exclusive constitutional powers treating Congress as without authority in these circumstances.

Perhaps nothing illustrates the point better than the two explicit provisions of the Constitution, the power of Congress to declare war and the power of the president to make treaties with the concurrence of two-thirds of the Senate. It seems to me significant that the Constitution, consistent with the congressional supremacy it espoused in domestic matters, made sure that on such fundamental policy matters as war and treaties the dominant voice was Congress and not the president. Distrust of the monarchy went at least this far. But to say that these were matters for legislative concurrence is to limit executive power, not to replace executive initiative.

The War Power

The use of military force on any important scale is surely the fundamental and ultimate foreign policy question that a nation can face. And the founding fathers had no intention of allowing the executive to make such a decision on his own. One of the difficulties then and since is simply that force is not the option of only one side to a controversy. A second is that force, or the threat of force, need not amount to the full-scale "war" which the members of the Constitutional Convention surely had in the forefront of their minds. A "Declaration of War" in the late eighteenth and nineteenth centuries was a formal act which carried with it a massive change of legal relations with both the enemy and neutrals. It was not a step lightly taken nor an easy one from which to disengage. For this reason, states often used some measure of force without declaring war, and thus, there grew in international law a good deal of learning as to "undeclared wars," "acts short of war," "policy actions," and so forth. Unless that use of force was against or threatened the interests of a major power, a declaration of war seldom resulted.

It would be a mistake to read international law into the Constitution to the extent of relegating Congress to the purely formal role of declaring war. But at the same time, international law and practice were not then or now wholly irrelevant. Congress recognized from the outset a right of self-defense; indeed, the word "declare" was substituted for the word "wage" largely for this reason. And, despite the unhappiness of many members of Congress with Vietnam, the 1972 War Powers Act permits the use of armed forces in the face of an armed attack on the United States or its armed forces, to protect American nationals pending evacuation, or pursuant to other statutory authority. If they are to continue in hostilities for more than thirty days, there must be explicit congressional approval.

There is value to the War Powers Act, not because of what it says so much as simply because it asserts explicitly congressional control while recognizing realities. The huge powers of the executive during war or major hostilities can be heady, and it is probably useful to remind presidents from whence their authority comes. There is, of course, no need for the Congress to "declare" war in order to wage it. Neither the wording nor the caption of a congressional resolution has any magical significance. What is important is not what it is called but only that the Congress clearly authorizes the use of armed force—which, I believe, is what the founding fathers intended.

The War Powers Act did not have any substantive significance. The law it stated was the law before it was enacted, with the exception of the specificity of the thirty-day provision. It is hard to make the case that presidents have waged wars without congressional authorization, or that their occasional acts of self-defense and protection of nationals have not had congressional support. Vietnam stands out as the only war in which very substantial public opinion turned against continued participation and which therefore raised unprecedented political problems. For that reason it is worth a brief look.

In the first place, Vietnam illustrates how the United States, largely under presidential leadership but certainly with congressional knowledge and acquiescence, can drift toward war without the public and perhaps even the political leaders fully appreciating that fact. Each step down the slope was conceived as the last one—until the next. Even when President Lyndon Johnson asked congressional approval of the Tonkin Resolution—as broad an authorization of the use of military force as any declaration of war could possibly be—there was little concern that the United States was embarking on a long, expensive, and bloody war. Surely much of the reaction in subsequent years about the resolution was not truly aimed at presidential arrogation of power or even that Congress was misled. It was merely that they never would have approved the resolution had they known what would happen.

Vietnam, and Korea to a far lesser extent, became unpopular wars as public support waned when easy victory was denied. And even the acquiescence of Congress is no guarantee of support over the long haul. This is a problem for presidents and a problem for Congress as well. It stems from the complexity of foreign affairs and the global role of the United States.

So long as we have U.S. troops stationed around the world,

the potential for engagement either as a result of attack or as part of mutual defense exists. Anytime the safety of U.S. troops is threatened, there is the possibility of quick response. Once engaged—and the immediate public opinion response will almost surely be supportive of engagement—it may well be difficult, militarily and politically, to disengage. It will be the president who will have been dealing with the escalating foreign policy crisis and, in all probability, the president who will have taken the initial response.

The problem for the Congress is that, once the emotions and prestige of the United States are invoked, it has little choice but to back the president, and Congress can find its role as a rubber stamp annoying and frustrating. What is clear and irritating is that the Congress is not being asked to make the same decision the president made, because by his very action he has foreclosed other options. Whatever one thinks of dispatching U.S. forces to Vietnam, the Dominican Republic, Lebanon, or Grenada, the choice of the Congress is different—in effect, a decision to withdraw them in the context of a response already made.

But one need not postulate an actual attack. Arguably, that existed in the form of terrorism prior to the 1986 raids on Libya, though that seems somewhat questionable. But one cannot rule out the threat of force or the justification for preemptive attack. The Cuban Missile Crisis presents a clearcut case where, despite the gravity of various courses of action contemplated, there was no adequate and secure mechanism for consultation with Congress and securing in advance congressional authorization. To have attempted to do so almost certainly would have denied military choices to the United States and would have escalated the crisis.

In sum, the president has a great capacity to present *faits accomplis* to Congress. The Congress knows this, does not like it, and, especially if things go wrong, may accuse the president of exercising his powers beyond their constitutional authority. But, at the same time, one should remain conscious of the fact that presidents, having made up their minds as to the wisest course of action, are loathed to be second-guessed by Congress. From the president's viewpoint, *faits accomplis* are not all bad.

What is true in terms of repelling minor attacks on U.S. troops wherever they may be stationed or protecting U.S. citizens in foreign countries (which, historically, is almost invariably a pretext for using force to change or support a foreign government for political reasons) is obviously true in terms of response to a nuclear attack. Here the time element once again effectively prevents congressional consideration of the response save in advance of such an attack.

Insofar as the founding fathers intended that the Congress should retain control over the power to use military force in any major way, the Constitution has been adhered to quite faithfully. But the president has from the outset always had the initiative, the ability to act quickly and to speak with a single voice. At times, this fact frustrated Congress and did perhaps tend to dissipate its authority. Given the United States' position in world affairs coupled with a shrinking world, the tilt toward the presidency is more important than in the past. But, from a constitutional viewpoint, there appears to be no satisfactory cure—if, indeed, a cure is needed.

Treaties

Along with the power to declare war, the founding fathers saw the treaty-making power as most important. Once again they preserved a key role for Congress, this time the two-thirds vote of the Senate necessary for ratification. The House was excluded essentially for two reasons. First, it was perceived that there was a need for speed and secrecy, and the sheer numbers of the House would impede those objectives. Second, it was believed more appropriate for representatives of the states than representatives directly elected by the people to advise the president with respect to weighty matters of international negotiation.

Neither of those reasons is pertinent today, and there is substantial sentiment for giving the House a formal role. It already has a substantial voice, and it can, by virtue of its various committees and its appropriations role, play an important part. Many treaties are not self-executing and require legislation in which both houses participate. And economic matters have, by tradition, been left to executive agreement and subsequent legislation.

Today, it is generally accepted that, from a constitutional perspective, an executive agreement with legislation implementing it has the same force and effect internationally and within the United States as a treaty. Thus, as a constitutional matter, the president may have more options than would appear at first glance from the text. Nonetheless, by practice if not law, certain kinds of agreements are felt to be more suitable for classification as treaties. While a two-thirds vote is always difficult to achieve, there may be circumstances where such a convincing affirmation of an international commitment is important to the achievement of foreign policy goals. And the Senate may, as a matter of prestige, insist.

In the contemporary world, the extent of the relationship of the United States with other nations is well beyond anything the founding fathers could have possibly imagined. These relationships are orchestrated by the president through the Department of State—although today even the Department of State and, to a degree, our ambassadors, have lost track of all of them. We interact with others through a multitude of international organizations, through defense, intelligence, treasury, law enforcement, and other specialized channels, and through a host of private organizations. Even if all those who act in these channels are scrupulous in declining to make any final agreements on behalf of the U.S. government, they can and do agree to do things that are within their own governmental authority and competence. Thus a massive flow of informal commitments and expectations unavoidably occurs, which Congress, through a variety of committees, loosely monitors as part of its oversight function. From a constitutional viewpoint, none of these are "treaties," few are executive agreements, but all are important pieces of our foreign policy commitments.

The founding fathers may have believed that, through giving the Senate its role in the treaty process, it would be playing a dominant role in our foreign relations. Again, events and technology have overtaken the allocation of power, and once again the president, through his inherent advantages, plays a dominant role. But perhaps it is not so dominant as first appears. The Senate, and indeed the Congress, can and do defeat executive initiatives—sometimes with traumatic impact on our foreign relations. Versailles is the classic example, but various arms control agreements come to mind as well.

The fact that treaties are often reserved for matters conceived to be of particular importance, the two-thirds requirement, and the rules of the Senate as to debate combine to make the treaty provision sparingly used. Both houses of Congress are accustomed to dealing with specific legislation, to "marking up" and amending proposed legislation, not simply to approving something written and negotiated by someone else. Language that is broad and general is worrisome; ambiguities should be clarified, and so forth. They are convinced that, whatever the terms of the treaty, it could have been better drafted and better negotiated. And there is rarely any political plus at home in a vote for ratification—although rarely a political negative either.

Thus while the treaty provisions are rarely invoked today because of the time-consuming efforts involved, to the extent they reflect, as they do, a constitutional need for substantial concurrence between the Congress and the executive on the most important foreign policy commitments, they serve their intended purpose. To a degree, this fact is concealed by the fact that as part of the legislative and appropriations process, Congress gets involved in almost all foreign policy decisions without necessarily labeling them as such. Indeed, the committee system makes it too likely that a committee will advertently or inadvertently undo, from a foreign policy viewpoint, the work of another. While "reservations" and "understandings" are relatively sparingly used in treaty ratifications, controversial foreign affairs legislation such as foreign aid programs is too often riddled with prohibitions and requirements which are ill thought-out, of dubious constitutionality, and which unnecessarily damage legitimate foreign policy objectives. But these are congressional shortcomings, not constitutional ones. And there would be little support for giving the president more authority than he already has.

The "Foreign Affairs" Power of the President: Commander-in-Chief and Chief Executive

When the president acts by executive order, he must state his authority. In the field of foreign affairs, he most frequently invokes his powers as chief executive and as commander-in-chief. Both are questionable sources of presidential authority, but both have achieved some respectability and a largely undefined scope.

The constitutional debate centers on whether the president's designations as commander-in-chief and as the repository of executive power were in themselves grants of authority above and beyond the specific grants in the Constitution. This debate has gone on from the time the Constitution itself was ratified. Alexander Hamilton stated it, and James Madison attacked him for seeking to import monarchical prerogatives where they had no place. And the matter remains conceptually unresolved and unblessed by the Court. The problem is the one Madison expressed: "If this power incorporates the powers of the Crown it goes much too far; no one can imagine the Convention to have adopted something so massive without discussion or debate—particularly an authority so at odds with the common desire to hold down executive power." Yet without it one is hard put to infer from other constitutional grants the broad foreign affairs power the president enjoys.

Much of this power does stem from his position as president—a position that has no competition as the voice of the nation as a whole—and from his control over representatives of the United States abroad once they have been confirmed. As early as 1800, John Marshall, in the House of Representatives, characterized the president as "sole voice of the nation in its external relations, and its sole representative with foreign nations"—a characterization often quoted and never seriously doubted. From his position as sole representative, he has conducted our foreign relations with broad and effective claims to speak for the United States on all matters great and small.

Excepting those matters where Congress has explicit powers under the Constitution, it is difficult to define the scope of this authority. The Monroe Doctrine and the Open Door Policy are examples. Presidents have, on their own authority, admitted undersea cables and electric current from Canada, and have excluded aliens. It is much less certain that they could have done these and other acts like them in the face of a law or congressional resolution to the contrary.

The rather large expansion of the president's unilateral power came as a result of the Civil War and the two world wars of the twentieth century. In each of these situations, the president was able to combine his power as chief executive with his power as commander-in-chief in a realistic context.

It is difficult to read the president's designation as commander-in-chief of the armed forces as anything more than just that. There is no reason to infer a grant of power independent of congressional control save in the day-to-day command matters that would support, in civilian circumstances, a claim of interference with the president's duty to faithfully execute the laws. But it has been broadly used, often in conjunction with his exercise of national self-defense or to protect U.S. persons and property abroad. It was invoked by President John F. Kennedy in the Cuban Missile Crisis to "quarantine" Cuba, and hostilities in Korea and Vietnam began on sole presidential authority. It has been used to proclaim neutrality—as Washington did in the war between England and France—and by Roosevelt to avoid Congress's neutrality policy to aid Hitler. The latter, including the exchange of destroyers for bases, surely was extreme.

Where there is no congressional prohibition and where the president is confident of broad public and congressional support, there are few practical limits to his exercise of this power. Accordingly, it stands in stark contrast to the president's limited domestic powers absent a prior act of Congress. While in times of crisis presidents have occasionally invoked broad powers, they have usually quickly sought congressional ratification and enabling legislation. But in foreign affairs they have been more inclined to act on their own authority, although in many instances one could find implicit or explicit congressional support in subsequent appropriations or substantive legislation.

There are several reasons why, without explicit constitutional authority, the president has been able to exercise such broad authority. First, few such exercises create fact situations which would permit the Supreme Court to act; and where they do exist, the Court is far more reluctant to interfere in foreign affairs than in domestic ones. So our authority—our "law"—tends to be based on what presidents have said and done and gotten away with. Second, the words and acts have taken place in a context where there is broad public support. While members of Congress and others often have suggested a lack of constitutional authority, not being opposed to what in fact was done has left them relatively ineffective in their efforts to preserve formal prerogatives. Third, as earlier noted, the fact of the president's action changes the decision that Congress would have to make. To repudiate presidential action has consequences in and of itself—consequences which would never have arisen had the president not acted. Fourth, and clearly related, when the issue involves controversy or conflict with other nations, it is often important that Americans speak with a single voice. There is a reluctance stemming from patriotic feelings to be vocal in criticizing the president's conduct of foreign policy, particularly in crisis situations. This reluctance may be substantially less today than a decade ago, and one suspects that as foreign affairs increasingly affect domestic welfare and politics, what the president can do unilaterally may be subjected to increasing scrutiny. The congressional reaction to past abuses by the CIA suggests as much.

From a constitutional perspective, foreign affairs have never been viewed in the same way as domestic activities. The concept that the role of the executive was to faithfully execute congressional policy may be an oversimplification, but it is one that has had no application in foreign affairs. One cannot meaningfully talk about Congress legislating foreign policy and the president executing it—although Madison at one time suggested that the Constitution had this as its basic concept. But to say this does not mean that the Congress cannot take a bigger role in the future than it has in the past. And it may well seek to do so.

The fact that the Congress cannot enact a sensible and comprehensive foreign policy prescribing, as in domestic legislation, the limits and requirements of executive action does not mean it cannot express itself on particular subjects. It may be that the nature of foreign policy requires a broad executive discretion, but this does not mean that Congress cannot and should not play a useful role. What that role is and how Congress will fit into an almost exclusive presidential arena remains to be seen. The Constitution certainly does not prevent it.

The fact that in foreign affairs the president has acted so often unilaterally does not mean that the authority is exclusively his. The design of the Constitution would suggest that Congress is to have a role in important matters and that the power is more often concurrent than exclusive. For example, the president can station troops abroad based on his own authority (assuming appropriations). But it is very doubtful he could do so in the face of a congressional prohibition. Constitutionally, Congress can curb the president, if it desires to do so.

In addition, Congress can invoke more rigorously its oversight capability, and, should it wish to do so, it will almost certainly gain a stronger voice. A combination of these two approaches has been taken with respect to activities of the CIA.

Intelligence Gathering and Covert Activities

It is hard to conceive any peacetime activity more difficult to deal with constitutionally than the use of agents to engage in covert political activities. Since George Washington's administration, presidents have exercised authority to appoint agents without congressional approval (often paying them from a nonaccountable contingency fund). But the institutionalization of covert intelligence gathering and other activities on a large scale is a relatively recent governmental phenomenon growing out of the World War II activities of the Office of Strategic Services and brought together under the legislation creating the Central Intelligence Agency. Thus, while in a very general sense Congress has authorized certain activities and funded them by largely covert appropriations known to only a few, until recently the paramount requirement of secrecy has inhibited any serious congressional participation with respect to specifics. The delegation of authority to the president coupled with his own claimed executive prerogatives have given him the sort of virtually unlimited discretion more appropriate to conducting war than foreign policy.

As part of what might almost be termed a renaissance of congressional power fueled by the Vietnam War and the Watergate scandal, the activities of the CIA were examined in the mid-1970s by the committee chaired by Senator Frank Church. The hearings themselves revealed many theretofore secret activities, and a picture emerged—perhaps an unfair one—of an agency extensively operating with little executive and virtually no congressional supervision. Given the extreme need for secrecy—and perhaps the fact that secrecy tends to breed secrecy—that conclusion is not itself surprising. Clandestine activity is by definition clandestine, and, as the founding fathers themselves recognized, in confining treaty ratification to the Senate with fewer members, foreign policy has always involved a fair dollop of secret doings and confidences.

The conclusion of the Church committee that Congress should exercise greater oversight was, in the then political atmosphere, not surprising. And the use of Select Senate and House Committees to do so creates a constraint that supplements legislative prohibitions on specific activities. It is probably too early to determine whether this mechanism can work and whether such explicit oversight is a technique useful in other circumstances.

It is difficult to square clandestine activity with an open and democratic society in any event. It is equally difficult to imagine a successful foreign policy without preserving confidences and without intelligence acquired in covert ways. Yet it seems clear that these are all part of making, as well as executing, foreign policy.

It remains to be seen whether select committees to oversee intelligence activities will be a satisfactory solution to this dilemma. Clearly, it serves as a restraint on presidential power and should curb excesses. Equally clearly, the demands of secrecy prevent a broader policy-making mechanism. But, even accepting this compromise, problems will remain. The 1986 revelations as to the Iranian and contra activities of the National Security Council suggest that the executive has been avoiding the bite of oversight by concealment. And one may be skeptical of how much candor there will be when lives as well as policy are endangered by leaks in a city where leaks are a recognized technique of political infighting.

Finally, it must be recognized that any form of congressional oversight over clandestine activities will tend to curb executive initiatives both good and bad—no matter how one defines "good" and "bad." The effect is likely to be a substantial diminution over time of all such activities, a result which will be welcomed by some and deplored by others.

Conclusion

If one espouses the view that foreign policy in a democracy should, like other governmental policies, be a matter for public determination, the constitutional framework as it has evolved over two centuries is about as satisfactory a distribution of power between Congress and the president as is possible. While it is undoubtedly true that the president has taken the initiative and that he has often both claimed and exercised enormous power, he has done so in circumstances where, with very rare exceptions, he has had the support of public opinion, has not ignored explicit congressional resolutions, and has had the informal backing of a clear majority of both houses of

Congress. Presidents have been constitutionally arrogant in their verbal claims of unconstrained power where the Constitution is silent (as it usually is), but their actions have recognized the need for congressional support. It seems clear that no president could long sustain an unpopular course of foreign policy.

The Constitution is silent on most powers, and where it is specific, the Congress is given a significant role. From this—and from history—one could and probably should conclude with Justice Jackson that the exercise of unilateral presidential authority demands at least silence on the part of Congress. Thus it is open to Congress to assert far more influence and far more checks on the president than has historically been the case.

But it is hard, if not impossible, for Congress to take the initiative, and it is equally hard to formulate in anything more than the most general terms what a foreign policy should be. And where the president takes the initiative, the congressional decision is not, as we have seen, the same decision the president made. Being coerced by events to support the president is a constant irritant to Congress and more so because it is not the role it plays in domestic policy making.

This situation is not the fault of the Constitution. Indeed, wise presidents have seen that American foreign policy is most effective, and their own leadership most acclaimed, when their actions are perceived as enjoying wide bipartisan support. It is certainly open to Congress to do far more than it customarily has. If, in doing so, conflicts with the president occur, our influence abroad will correspondingly diminish with the doubts inherent in uncertain commitments. If, on the other hand, cooperation rather than conflict results, the constitutional scheme will have worked the will of its authors.

4

The Beast that Might Not Exist: Some Speculations on the Constitution and the Independent Regulatory Agencies

STEPHEN L. CARTER

The Nature of the Beast

The two centuries of government under the U.S. Constitution have been characterized by a remarkable and continuous growth in the scope of activities over which the federal government exercises its power. This tendency, itself controversial, has both fueled and masked a second, arguably more important, evolution in the *manner* in which the government exercises its power. The high school civics image—legislation by the Congress, enforcement by the executive, adjudication by the courts—might never have been an accurate picture of the way the government operates, but such truth as it might once have carried has been buried in the post–New Deal avalanche of administrative regulation.

A 1979 graduate of Yale University Law School, STEPHEN L. CARTER is now professor of law at that institution, specializing in constitutional law, contracts, intellectual property, and legal control of science and technology. He served as law clerk to Supreme Court Justice Thurgood Marshall and to U.S. Court of Appeals Judge Spottswood W. Robinson, III. Mr. Carter has written numerous articles in scholarly publications on various aspects of constitutional law.

The generic term "administrative agency," which refers to any government regulatory body created by statute, gives a clue to the ideological transformation that the rise of regulatory government represents. Prior to the late nineteenth century, the federal government only rarely intruded into the realm of the market. Government in general was viewed as a public servant, one preferably neither seen nor heard except in time of national emergency; most of society was ordered in accordance with private decisions and private preferences, and the role of the government was simply to create an atmosphere in which this private ordering could flourish. The rise of progressive politics around the turn of the century suggested a fresh consensus, in which the unequal power that some could apply in the market was itself viewed as an evil, and government became a protector, expected occasionally to intervene to right the most outrageous of wrongs that an unregulated market could not prevent.

The experience of the Great Depression led to a revolutionary change in the progressive consensus—the suspicion that in many, perhaps most, instances, the free market was itself a problem. Too much private power held too much unchallenged sway; the play of market forces was harming people, who now believed they had a claim to official protection; only government scrutiny and regulation could set matters right. As historian David Potter once put it, "Franklin Roosevelt . . . on the domestic front shifted the emphasis from freedom as immunity to control, to freedom as immunity from social privation." This sharply different consensus was reflected in the New Deal and its obsession with governance through a device that theretofore had been used but rarely, and generally without controversy—the administrative agency.

As the name suggests, an administrative agency exists in order to administer. The thing that is administered is generally some aspect of the economy, some set of relations that in a previous century would have been left to regulation by the action of private capital in the marketplace. The word "administer" is an evocative one, conjuring images of experts poring over mysterious charts and volumes of exhibits before deciding on the best answer. Not the politically popular answer, not the answer most desired either by those with the most money or by those with the most votes, but the answer that some policy science—perhaps economics, perhaps sociology, perhaps ecology—shows to best effectuate the statutory scheme supplying the agency's mandate. In this vision, direct political control has failed; leaving the problem to practical politicians has resulted in runaway disaster; it is time to hand the reins to those best qualified to deal with the problem.

In our own era, a relatively intrusive scheme of federal intervention in the economy, along with squadrons of regulatory agencies to keep the scheme operating, has become ubiquitous. So commonplace is administrative government that one raises doubt about its legitimacy only at peril of being dismissed as a dangerous radical. The existence of federal agencies to monitor everything from the cleanliness of the water supply to the fairness of collective bargaining to the integrity of Wall Street's deal makers is simply a part of the status quo. When the morning news carries a report that the Consumer Product Safety Commission has ordered the recall of some children's toys, only a few sheltered academics and a worried toy manufacturer are likely to think, "Why should some bureaucrat nobody ever voted for be able to do this?" Most people probably respond instead, "Those toymakers, they'll do anything for a buck. It's a good thing they got caught before another child got hurt."

And yet in the political theory underlying constitutional government, the end simply cannot justify the means. The entire point of a written Constitution is to limit the power of the government to do as it pleases, when and how it pleases. So one need be neither a friend of the marketers of unsafe toys nor an enemy of children to consider it worth the effort to think about the place of regulatory agencies in the constitutional scheme. Legions of legal and political theorists have picked over this question, some of them in great and intriguing detail. My purpose here is less to retrace ground already covered than to summarize some of the most important arguments, and to speculate about the constitutional and practical political consequences of the highly rarefied academic debate.

The Beast that Might Not Exist

Although each of the three branches of the federal government encompasses agencies designed to assist the branch in its work—the Office of Technology Assessment and the Congressional Budget Office, for example, are under the control of the legislative branch, and the Administrative Office of the United States Courts is controlled by the judicial branch—the agencies that matter are those with a *public* administrative role, those capable of making judgments that touch the relations and rights of people outside of the government, those agencies, in short, with authority to enforce the law. Of the agencies with enforcement authority, many fall within the executive branch and are therefore under the ultimate control of the president. The Environmental Protection Agency and the Occupational Safety and Health Administration are perhaps the most controversial of these. The other agencies with enforcement authority are those that fall outside the executive branch and, in fact, outside the direct control of any politically accountable officer of the federal government. These *independent* agencies—the Securities and Exchange Commission and the National Labor Relations Board are familiar examples—are, as a rule, answerable only to the commissioners who run them and, in some circumstances, to the federal courts.

All of the administrative agencies, both those that are within the executive branch and those that are not, should look at least a little bit suspicious to those familiar with the political theory underlying the structure of government set forth in the U.S. Constitution. The first and most obvious difficulty is that those who wrote and ratified the Constitution envisioned a republic in which those who made the laws would be accountable, through some political process, to the people in whose name they govern. The particular structural feature through which this ideal was realized was the requirement that laws be made by the legislature, one house of which comprised the elected representatives of the people themselves. Advocates of independence for administrative agencies insist that direct political control will hamper the agency's ability to do its job; that a politically accountable agency will act in a political, rather than a managerial, fashion, and, consequently, that bad policy will be made. The agency, in this theory, must be insulated at least from the direct control of the volatile Congress, and possibly from that of the president as well, and therein lies the difficulty for theory. The greater the insulation wrapped around the agency, the deeper the difficulty, for the insulation is intended to repel the chilly blast of public opinion that liberal democratic theory would seem to require.

A small corner of this debate has already had an honored, if not honorable, place in constitutional theory and history. If the Constitution requires that policy judgments be made in the most representative branch of the federal government—the legislature—and if the legislature delegates to an agency, even an executive agency, not only the authority to implement policy choices but the power to make them, isn't the legislature acting unconstitutionally?

Once upon a time, a majority of the justices of the Supreme Court apparently thought so. In 1935 the Court twice ruled regulatory statutes unconstitutional because of the breadth of the delegation of authority to an agency. These two cases, *A.L.A. Schechter Poultry Corporation v. United States* and *Panama Refining Company v. Ryan,* are often considered to mark the end of one of the darkest ages of constitutional history, the era in which the courts threw prudence and reason to the winds in their zeal to protect laissez-faire capitalism from the ravages of governmental intrusion. Only the popular assault to judicial independence culminating in President Franklin Roosevelt's court-packing plan, so popular mythology teaches, caused the justices to reverse their field. The judicial retreat that saved either the New Deal or authority of the Court or both is generally taught to constitutional law students as a good thing, however deplorable the means for bringing it about.

It is useful, however, to remember just how broad a delegation of authority the cases involved. The provision of the National Industrial Recovery Act at issue in *Schechter,* for example, authorized the president to promulgate "codes of fair competition" upon application of industry trade associations. The president, not the Congress, decided which forms of competition were fair and which were unfair. Even Justice Benjamin Cardozo, usually a strong supporter of the New Deal, was forced to concede in a concurring opinion: "This is delegation running riot," because under the act, "anything that Congress may do within the limits of the commerce clause for the betterment of business may be done by the President." And indeed, it is difficult to resist the image of a powerful and popular president demanding of the Congress: "Give me the power I need to do what I must do"—and of the Congress responding: "Do what you will." It is this vision of a legislature that has abdicated its responsibility to legislate that largely drives the critics of broad delegations of authority.

This nondelegation doctrine has long been a staple of political theory, and, notwithstanding its post–New Deal quiescence in the courts, has within the past two decades received increasing attention from political scientists, constitutional lawyers, and judges. In 1969 Theodore Lowi argued in *The End of Liberalism* that far from being brushed aside as though a dead letter, the rule of *Schechter* should be revived and enforced with gusto. Only "clear standards of implementation," he contended, should save a delegation of authority to an administrative agency. John Ely in *Democracy and Distrust,* his controversial monograph on judicial review, has written that the broad and standardless delegation of vaguely defined authority to an administrative agency is

wrong, not because it isn't "the way it was meant to be" . . . but rather because it is undemocratic, in the quite obvious sense that by refusing to legislate, our legislators are escaping the sort of accountability that is crucial to the intelligible functioning of a democratic republic.

And Justice (later Chief Justice) William Rehnquist later suggested that some of the provisions of the Occupational Safety and Health Act, because they are open to more than one interpretation with sharply differing consequences depending on the interpretation chosen, represent a standardless delegation of precisely the sort with which *Schechter* was rightly concerned.

A conclusion that regulatory agencies are unconstitutional, because they operate under charters granting them too much discretion, would shake the foundations of administrative government as America, in the post–New Deal era of federal activism, has come to know it. Mindful of the dramatic change that an adverse judicial ruling would work in the way the nation is governed, defenders of the regulatory state have sharply disputed the constitutional case against the agencies. The first step in this response is often to remind the critic of the policy considerations that make it undesirable that all decisions be made in ways that are susceptible to direct political manipulation. These policy considerations, which are clearly nontrivial, fall roughly into two categories: concerns about *efficiency* and concerns about *effectiveness*.

The efficiency concerns are responsive to the practical difficulties of lawmaking, and the practical impossibility of legislating in detail all the matters that fall within the purview of the post–New Deal activist state. Simple majoritarian models have long advanced the proposition that democratic governments should determine their goals through the aggregation of private preferences. Legislatures, however, have proved cumbersome tools for counting preferences or for turning preferences into policy. The lowest cost solution, on this model, is a scenario in which the Congress explains clearly and concisely the policy that it wishes to implement, but delegates to an agency the discretion to micromanage that implementation. By delegating the power to cope with a problem, the Congress saves its own time and energy for the broader task of setting policy in all the many areas that demand its attention.

The effectiveness concerns deal with a point that has troubled theorists since the Enlightenment suggested the desirability of divorcing government from God: how a society determines the best means of pursuing its ends. Some of the goals the society decides to pursue, so advocates of the independent agencies insist, are better undertaken by expert managers than by politicians. These goals might, for example, require scientific or other expert judgments that would only be distorted were the agency's rulemaking to be deflected by partisan politics. In this vision, expert agencies are better able to find the best rules than the Congress would be, and independent expert agencies are best of all.

Having explained the policies underlying the delegation of some lawmaking authority, the defenders of the agencies might then proceed to make the constitutional case. A common route is to begin by dismissing nondelegation as an archaic formalism, something that stands in the path of necessary institutional reform. In this vision, the Congress and the president, working together in the legislative process, have the best sense of the nation's problems and of the paths to their solution; the courts might have some role of policing these paths along the very edges, but should, aside from the most egregious violations, permit the reform to continue. If the reform in question requires a delegation of authority, then the judicial concern should be to ensure only that a means exists for checking abuse of that delegation.

Until recently, one of the preferred means of retaining a legislative check on the abuse of delegated power was the legislative veto, and it is easy to see the charm of that device as a matter of political theory. The agency is nominally independent of the Congress, and perhaps of the president as well, and thus is free to propose the rules it considers best. If the Congress does not block them, the rules will go into effect. Because the efficiency justification for independent agencies proposes that legislation is cumbersome, the Congress will, by hypothesis, use the veto only rarely, the threat of it perhaps a bit more often. Because, moreover, the congressional role is limited to a potential vote of "no," the Congress is not indulging any rulemaking of its own. So in theory, under the legislative veto, expert managerial rulemaking would continue, with an occasional disapproving prod from the most representative branch.

Unfortunately for the theory, the Supreme Court in 1983

pronounced the legislative veto unconstitutional *(Immigration and Naturalization Service v. Chadha)*. Some supporters of administrative government have decried this judgment as another archaic formalism, which perhaps it is, although a substantial case against the veto exists. In any event, the decision is there, and it poses a significant practical obstacle for those trying to demonstrate how broad delegations of power can be made consistent with democratic theory.

My colleague Jerry Mashaw has attacked the delegation problem from a different direction, presenting an attractive argument that some delegations of substantial lawmaking discretion might actually heighten governmental responsiveness, instead of leaving the lawmaking process less responsive to voter preferences. Professor Mashaw's case proceeds from the single insight that the transaction costs of legislating are relatively high, those of regulating relatively low. Put otherwise, an administrative rule is more readily modified than a congressional statute. Were the Congress to enact highly specific laws, narrowly channeling agency discretion, there is no reason to think that the laws would be easily changed simply because voter preferences shifted, unless, of course, the shift were passionate and overwhelming—and perhaps not even then. Presidents and their administrations, however, are more sensitive to rapid changes in the public mood, and an agency under executive control, more easily than one bound by an intricate and detailed statutory mandate, can move along with that mood.

The point is an interesting one, made more troubling, perhaps, by its empirical assumption that the executive branch really is more responsive to public mood than the Congress, as well as by its implicit rejection of the insistence of classical liberal theory that law should bind the sovereign rather than empowering him. These, however, are in the nature of quibbles, and Mashaw's argument might work for agencies within the executive branch. It does nothing at all to salvage the quite different role played by independent agencies beyond the direct control of the president. Mashaw's position might provide more ammunition for those who insist that all federal agencies must be under ultimate presidential control; it does little to arm those who want the agencies to remain independent and to retain substantial discretion.

To be sure, one might accept the claim, occasionally pressed, that theory aside, the executive branch possesses so much influence over the independent agencies that they *are*, as a practical matter, under effective presidential control. No one insists that the evidence arrayed to support this claim is unambiguous, but if the president really can exercise de facto control over the independent agencies, then a delegation of authority to an independent commission might effectively represent a delegation to the president. But if that is so, then those theorists who support the independent agencies precisely because they are not subject to political direction are supporting something mythological; similarly, those who rail against the independence of the agencies from political control are struggling to tame a beast that does not exist.

And yet because so many advocates of administrative government insist on independence as an ideal, and because the hypothesis that the independent agencies are under political control is practically untestable, it is worth taking the constitutional analysis a few more steps. As will be seen, the courts in the post–New Deal era have turned a deaf ear to the larger claim of administrative illegitimacy. But there are enough small defeats for administrative government, and there remains a sufficiently substantial stumbling block in political theory, that it is still too early to conclude that the legitimacy of the administrative state has been established for once and for all.

Surrounding the Beast on All Sides

Although the New Deal experience and some recent setbacks continue to rankle, the defenders of the administrative state have so far been generally successful. Since its use as a weapon against the New Deal in 1935, the nondelegation doctrine has languished. In that same year, the Supreme Court gave explicit recognition to the authority of the Congress to establish administrative agencies that are formally beyond the control of the president. This judicial approval of the independence of administrative government can be traced to the Supreme Court's 1935 decision in *Humphrey's Executor v. United States*. In *Humphrey's Executor*, the justices sustained a congressional statute restricting the president's authority to dismiss members of the Federal Trade Commission. The Court acknowledged that the commission was a peculiar body, one that acted "in part quasi-legislatively and in part quasi-judicially," and that it could not "in any proper sense be characterized as an arm or an eye of the executive." The congressional power to establish an agency independent of the executive branch and to vest it with authority to promulgate and enforce regulations, the justices concluded, "cannot be well doubted." There was little more analysis than that; the Court seemed to consider the matter of congressional authority self-evident. Certainly, the Federal Trade Commission was not the only independent regulatory agency in 1935. There were at least a dozen others, and the federal courts had frequently reviewed cases involving these agencies without questioning their constitutional legitimacy.

Paradoxically, *Humphrey's Executor* was handed down on the same day that the same Court, in *Schechter Poultry*, endorsed the nondelegation doctrine. The paradox might, however, be more apparent than real, for the theory on which agencies are permitted to act independently can supply a criterion for judging whether their independence involves too much discretion. In other words, one may perfectly well conclude that yes, the Congress may establish administrative agencies independent of direct political control, and no, the Congress may not do so unless it supplies the agency with a highly specific mandate.

The more important aspect of *Humphrey's Executor* is the paucity of argument supporting its judgment in favor of agencies independent from the executive branch. Later opinions have not filled the gaps, and some might even cast a degree of doubt on the thrust of the decision. In *Bowsher v. Synar* (1986), for example, the case in which the Supreme Court struck down the "automatic" budget-cutting provisions of the Gramm-Rudman-Hollings deficit reduction measure, the majority focused on the delegation to a congressional employee—the comptroller general—of what the justices apparently considered a power that should be exercised by an executive branch officer. The officer had to be in the executive branch because, in the Court's analysis, he was executing the law:

The Comptroller General must exercise judgment concerning facts that affect the application of the Act. He must also interpret the provisions of the Act to determine precisely what budgetary calculations are required. Decisions of that kind are typically made by officers charged with executing a statute.

The irony of this analysis is that the Congress could plainly have undertaken to do itself what it had delegated instead to a legislative branch agency. Had the Congress cut the budget, the presentment process would have offered the president the opportunity to veto. Or the Congress could apparently have delegated the budget-cutting authority, but only to the executive branch. The implication of the analysis (although it remains unstated) is that delegation to a wholly independent agency might have been impermissible.

"Implication" and "might have been" can hardly constitute a rejection of the message of *Humphrey's Executor,* but the *Bowsher v. Synar* language does suggest a line of reasoning that should give pause to the supporters of the independent agencies: yes, the justices seemed to say, some powers can be delegated, but that is not the end of the inquiry. The identity of the delegate may prove as important as the nature of the delegated power.

If that is so, then perhaps the beast is at last surrounded, and political theory can again go to work, this time not on regulatory agencies generally, but with particular emphasis on those that are established outside of any branch of the federal government. These independent administrative agencies, each created by statutory mandate, represent a perplexing hybrid of

government functions which, under the high school civics tri-
chotomy already mentioned, might be thought to be the prerogative of the three branches established by the Constitution.
Many of these agencies create new law, through the issuance
of regulations; they may enforce the laws (including the laws
that they themselves have created) in administrative proceedings; and they frequently interpret the law, when deciding
whether their own regulations have been violated. In other
words, the agencies perform functions that seem legislative,
executive, or judicial in nature, and yet are designed to be
independent of all three branches.

This description, oversimplified or not, matters a great deal,
because the political theory reflected in the 1787 Constitution
has a second facet, too, one potentially far more dangerous to
the independent agencies than is any aspect of the nondelegation doctrine. This is the vision of the separation of powers as
a *system* of checks and balances, as a richly conceived, painstak-
ingly designed set of interlocking powers and blockades
against power intended to limit the ability of any branch of the
federal government to arrogate to itself too much authority,
and, just as important, to restrict the scope of governmental
intrusion into the sphere of private autonomy. It is textbook
Locke and Montesquieu, and textbook Madison as well, that
the principal safeguard against government oppression is the
dispersion of governmental authority among different
branches, and the establishment of a structure permitting the
branches to check and balance each other's efforts to act.

It is "too great a temptation to human frailty apt to grasp
at Power," wrote John Locke in a much-quoted line of his
Second Treatise, "for the same Persons who have the Power of
making Laws, to have also in their hands the power to execute
them." In *The Spirit of Laws,* Baron de Montesquieu added that
there was no liberty unless "the government be so constituted
as one man need not be afraid of another." This meant that
there would be no liberty "when the legislative and executive
powers are united in the same person" or "if the power of
judging be not separated from the legislative and executive
powers." And he concluded:

Miserable indeed would be the case, were the same man, or the same power whether of the nobles or of the people, to exercise those three powers, that of enacting laws, that of executing the public resolutions, and that of judging the crimes or differences of individuals.

In all of this, the concern is no longer with the political accountability of the lawmaker, but with the practical checks on the possibility that the government will become tyrannical. The political theory of the framers of the Constitution was deeply imbued with the same concerns. Thus, in *Federalist Paper No. 47*, James Madison was simply stating a truism of his time when he concluded that "the accumulation of all powers, legislative, executive, and judicial, in the same hands, whether of one, a few, or many . . . may justly be pronounced the very definition of tyranny." In *Federalist Paper No. 51*, he went further, answering the challenges of those who held that the separation of powers in the Constitution was inconsistent with the argument that separation alone was not a sufficient check on the possibility of tyranny: "Experience has taught mankind the necessity of auxiliary precautions." The "auxiliary precautions" to which he referred were at once straightforward and ingenious: "The constant aim is to divide and arrange the several offices in such a manner as that each may be a check on the other—that the private interest of every individual may be a sentinel over the public rights." In short, the ideal constitution would not only separate the powers of government but also provide for each of the branches to check and balance the operations of the others.

The U.S. Constitution may not be an ideal one, but it is adorned with provisions designed to effectuate the system of checks to which Madison made reference. To take just a sample of some of the more important ones: judges are nominated by the president and confirmed by the Senate, but once in office can decide all cases "arising under" the Constitution, and can be removed from office only on impeachment and conviction. No money can be taken from the Treasury except according to law, and all legislation must pass both houses of the Congress and be presented to the president, who may cast a veto, which may, however, be overridden by majorities of two-thirds in each house. The Congress alone may declare war, but the president is the commander-in-chief, although only of the armed forces which the Congress creates, the appropriations for which may not be for a period of longer than two years. Strung together this way and read quickly enough, the checks and balances sound almost like a Rube Goldberg contraption, so peculiar are they in their interlocking complexity. And like Rube Goldberg's inventions, the system of checks and balances may look peculiar and operate oddly, but in the end, it does seem to work.

All of this is well known, and yet it is worth emphasizing because it recalls an aspect of the separation of powers that is often curiously absent from policy debate: the role of checks and balances in preventing tyranny. And considered against this background, the potential difficulty with the independent administrative agencies is clear: they fit only uncomfortably into the carefully developed scheme for a system of checks and balances. They are not under the direct control of any of the three branches. They make law through the regulatory process, and courts owe deference to the law that the agencies make. They interpret the law through the adjudicatory process, and courts owe deference to the interpretations that the agencies offer. They often enforce the law, too, and judicial review of agency enforcement decisions is tempered by the deference to the agency's regulations and to its interpretation of its own regulations. The degree to which the agencies preserve their independence from the rest of the federal government is aptly illustrated by the name of a case decided a few years ago in the United States Court of Appeals for the District of Columbia Circuit. The case was styled *United States of America v. Federal Communications Commission.* Sometimes, it seems, even the executive branch has no recourse against the agencies other than to sue them; for the deity the agencies worship is often neither politics nor checks and balances nor accountability, but simply expertise.

Supporters of the independent agencies respond to arguments of this nature in a number of ways. One is to note that the courts are always available to ensure the fundamental fairness of agency procedures—that all parties are heard—and to make certain that the agencies act in accordance with their statutory mandates. Another is to emphasize what are called the "informal" checks on the operation of the agencies. The commissioners who run them may not be removable, but they do resign or retire and their terms do expire, and thus they are replaceable, often quite quickly. When new commissioners are needed, the president nominates them and the Senate must usually confirm them. The agencies rely on the Congress for their budgets. And when these and other checks are laid out in a line, so the argument runs, it is plain that the agencies are accountable.

This argument, in form if not in substance, is similar to the claim discussed previously, that even the independent agencies are finally accountable to the president. And like the claim of accountability to the president, it is not so much wrong as irrelevant. The temptation to conclude that the separation of powers difficulties are overcome once accountability is shown is a dangerously seductive one, for the argument is simultaneously difficult to refute and quite beside the point. The argument assumes that the classical vision of checks and balances supposed the need to protect against the tyranny of a government that could not be called to account by the governed. The argument ignores the crucial desire to protect against the tyranny inherent when one branch of government, whether ultimately accountable or not, attained either too much authority or authority of too many kinds.

So, for example, an elective monarch, as some antifederalists insisted the Constitution would create, would be accountable at the end of his term, but he would be a tyrant nevertheless because of the scope and kinds of authority that would be concentrated in him. James Madison, in *The Federalist Papers*, was at pains to demonstrate the likelihood that no one branch would have the opportunity to gather to itself too much power, even though the political theory of the time strongly suggested that each branch would try. Thus to argue that the agencies are finally accountable does nothing to refute the claim that they are inconsistent with a political theory demanding, as a crucial bulwark against tyranny, a system of balanced and separated powers. An agency later called to account for what it does may nevertheless be acting simultaneously as legislature, executive, and judiciary (albeit within the sphere assigned it by the Congress), and this admixture of powers is precisely the "miserable case" to which Montesquieu made reference.

One response—probably quite a weak one—might be to suggest that this analysis seriously misreads the political theory background against which the framers designed the American Constitution. Those who wrote and ratified the Constitution might have been aware, for example, that when in 1696 the House of Commons proposed creation of a Council of Trade to be appointed by Parliament rather than by the monarch, John Locke, much involved in the issue of trade at the time, made no objection. In fact, there is apparently no evidence that any of the opponents of the council argued that it violated the fledgling notion of separation of powers then fast gaining currency. How then can Locke be cited as author of a political theory that would make such a council impermissible?

The easy answer is also probably the correct one. It is a serious analytical error to suppose the actions of the proponent of a theory to be necessarily consistent with the theory. Locke had a very strong motive for not speaking out, as W.B. Gwyn suggested in *The Meaning of the Separation of Powers:* he knew that he was to be appointed to a royal commission on the same subject, and must have realized how self-interested his criticism would appear. And as for the rest, Professor Gwyn has an answer for that, too: "To argue that it was a violation of the separation of powers to allow the two houses of Parliament to appoint executive agents might strengthen the opposition's case that the presence of numerous royal office holders in the House of Commons was such a violation." Besides, the Council of Trade example comes too late in the day, for the Supreme Court has ruled that officers with authority to execute the law cannot constitutionally be appointed by the Congress. In sum, once one concedes the propriety of seeking to learn whether independent agencies might fit snugly into the political theory underlying the Constitution—once one agrees that originalism is wise—the difficulties with administrative government are evident.

The obvious route for supporters of the agencies to take, then, is to seek to save administrative government by challenging originalism itself as a strategy for understanding the meaning of today's Constitution. The line of argument is a familiar one. It typically begins with what is supposed to represent an irrebutable intuition from quite a different field of constitutional endeavor: surely no one would seriously put the case, so the argument runs, that we should turn back the clock to the Reconstruction Era and hold that the Fourteenth Amendment does not prohibit segregated schools now because it did not prohibit them then. The next step might be in the nature of *reductio:* it would be patently ridiculous to hold, for example, that because the framers did not envision that one could possibly exist, the Air Force cannot be constitutional. And then there is the leap to serious theory: there are troubling theoretical questions about whether it is possible to know in any detail what consensus the framers might have shared on the issues that confront us today. Given all of this, the argument might conclude, why would anyone believe that the answer to any constitutional question posed by administrative government is to be found in the history of the drafting and ratification of the Constitution itself? Why not seek the more sure ground of contemporary debate over public policy?

These challenges to constitutional interpretation guided by an understanding of preconstitutional history and theory are weighty, and in some circumstances they may be decisive, but here they are unconvincing. It may be true that employing a strict originalism—trying to replace our own world with the one the framers knew—would have led to a morally repugnant result in the school desegregation cases. But that fact, if it is a fact, simply illustrates the difficulty in using originalist premises to interpret the open-ended constitutional clauses intended to protect individual rights. These clauses are generally phrased in terms so broad and high-minded ("the equal protection of the laws," "cruel and unusual punishments") that it is not easy to argue, even on originalist grounds, that those who wrote them intended to freeze for all time a specific set of prohibitions and no others. Thus, rejecting an interpretive approach that would limit the reach of the individual rights clauses by the imaginations of their authors might be a very sensible notion. The structural clauses setting forth the scheme for the operation of the federal government, however, are comparatively rich with detail. It is difficult to read through the structural provisions and come away with any conclusion other than that the authors had in mind specific referents and tried hard to spell them out. So the different natures of different constitutional clauses might be enough to lead to the conclusion that different interpretive approaches are appropriate.

Even one who insists on enforcing the original understanding need not always embrace results that are morally repugnant (segregation is permissible) or patently ridiculous (the Air Force is not). In this connection, in *Taking Rights Seriously,* Ronald Dworkin some time ago suggested a useful distinction between the "concept" and the "conception" that lie behind the constitutional language. The concept is the broad value choice that the language reflects; the conception is the concrete image that the authors possessed of the way the value choice would work out in practice. Thus those who wrote and ratified the Fourteenth Amendment shared a conception that racially segregated schools did not entail oppression of the sort with which they were concerned; but their broad concept of ending racial oppression was sufficiently flexible to account for changes in society, and thus in the nature of oppression, over time. Similarly, those who wrote and ratified the 1787 Constitution shared a conception in which the armed forces traveled on land or on water; but their broad concept of permitting the nation to defend itself was sufficiently flexible to account for changes in technology, and thus in the nature of warfare, over time.

The final objection points to the difficulty in discerning an original understanding. From a historian's perspective, the sources are woefully inadequate, and law still has much to learn from hermeneutics about the difficulties a modern reader will necessarily have in comprehending the world view of someone who studied, pondered, drafted, or voted in a sharply different world. Courts and commentators (and many politicians as well) are fond of referring to "the intent of the framers" as though they envision a glossary of constitutional meanings that emerges unambiguously as people of good will ponder the text and its history. But a discoverable intent of that sort is a beast that definitely does not exist.

In short, there are things that originalism cannot do. But there are also things that it can do. We can never form a complete picture of the world the framers knew, but we can gain a reasonable vision of the political theory that drove them (although even on that, there is controversy at the margins), and at least with respect to the structural clauses detailing the operation of the government, we can build a relatively clear image of the most important checks and balances that they tried to build into the Constitution's structure. We can know no part of their intentions completely, but we can say with confidence that they did not, for example, envision that legislative enactments would have the force of law if not presented to the president for veto—or that they did not envision a president who was less than thirty-five years old. Thus a study of their political theory may be both reasonable and possible, notwithstanding the difficulties that reading causes for proponents of independent administrative government.

The biggest problem with rejecting even a moderate originalism, however, is that it isn't clear what should be put in its place. The proponents of administrative agencies rarely contend that what they want is total deference by the courts to all congressional judgments on what institutional forms are necessary to effectuate national (read congressional) policy, but their arguments do sound very much as though that is where they end. Some have suggested arbitrary stopping points—Justice Byron White, for example, has argued that the proper question is whether the statute under review leaves in place some "real" checks and balances, without regard to whether they are the same checks and balances contemplated by the

Constitution. That solution, however, strays dangerously close to an abdication of any claim of constitutionalism in favor of a theory turning on whether the judge likes or dislikes the proposed institutional form.

Bruce Ackerman has proposed a strategy that seeks to avoid both the worst aspects of originalism—in his view, a rejection of administrative government—and the worst aspects of the alternative—a lack of standards to guide adjudication. In his 1983 Storrs Lectures at Yale, he suggested the possibility that the Supreme Court was right in the first third of the century in restricting the power of the government to intrude upon the domain of market forces, and was also right in later years to permit that intrusion. For Professor Ackerman, the key to harmonizing both trends is the same one that justifies adherence to the Constitution in the first place: the idea that on rare occasion, political consciousness is so stimulated that dialogue reaches a level at which the people self-consciously seek to make over their own world and the rules that govern it.

This higher level, the level of constitutional politics, was reached at the time of the American Revolution and led after a decade to the American Constitution. That Constitution, Ackerman argued, provided in Article V for amendments to itself as a way of recognizing the possibility that eras of constitutional politics might recur. The Civil War and the series of amendments adopted in its wake represented one recurrence. The dramatic changes in popular consciousness leading to the New Deal, Ackerman insisted, represent another recurrence of constitutional politics. The 1936 presidential election, he contended, was essentially a referendum on the Court's treatment of government regulation of the economy, and regulation won. The rapid judicial retreat thereafter, and the subsequent rise of the administrative state, simply recognized the change in the Constitution—the structural constitutional amendment, as he called it—that the people implicitly ratified when they overwhelmingly swept Franklin Roosevelt back into office.

Some formalists are no doubt troubled by Ackerman's desire to do with Article V anything other than what the plain words of the article seem to imply should be done, but that is not the relevant difficulty with his quite clever effort to meet originalist critics on their own ground. The more important problem with his theory is that it provides no useful rule of recognition—no way in which an observer can tell whether a particular election, or even rise of passion and subsequent legislative initiative, represents politics that rise to the constitutional level. Liberal theory insists on rules for recognizing law in order to distinguish it from power grabbing. Ackerman's approach does not close off the possibility that administrative government is no more than the power grab that liberal theory condemns.

And yet there is a deeper implication to the analysis that Ackerman suggests, an implication that might suggest a way of resolving the constitutional controversy without suggesting what that resolution ought to be. Ackerman's theory proceeds, in a sense, from the Constitution's preamble, from the notion that here, for the first time in history, was a government purporting to take the entirety of its authority from "We, the People." Lawyers, judges, and theorists may read the Constitution and discover one truth; the people of the United States of America may read it and find something very different. The Constitution and the notion of government under law are central to American social and political iconography. As Pulitzer Prize winning historian Michael Kammen has noted, the point is not so much that we worship constitutionalism as that we rely on it; the Constitution contributes, perhaps more than anything else does, to our sense of a shared nationhood. Thus the hidden issue in the debate over administrative government, and in other constitutional debates as well, may be this one: whose Constitution is it?

The Beast in Its Lair

The conclusion one reaches on the constitutionality of administrative agencies depends, of course, on how one reads the Constitution, and as with the reading of any document, a variety of interpretive methods is available. I have mentioned only two. First, the interpreter may take the view that at least with respect to the separation of powers, the courts should try to enforce some vision of the political theory reflected in the understanding that those who wrote and ratified the Constitution might have shared on the way in which the federal government might operate. Second, the interpreter might take a more deferential stance toward federal statutes, preferring to permit an evolution in the relationships among the branches of the federal government, in order to enable the government to respond to the necessities of the day.

Neither of these positions is absurd, and each possesses its practical and theoretical problems. But regardless of which view a participant in the debate might prefer—and there are many besides the two that I have discussed—it is vital to understand the limitations of constitutional theory. In such a nation as ours—one in which the Constitution and how it is interpreted really matter, and one in which the notion of constitutionalism is so central to nationhood—proponents of any position would do well to realize that a judicial ruling based on their favorite theory, even a ruling by the Supreme Court, is not a victory but only a first step on a long path toward establishing (not discovering) constitutional meaning.

Constitutional law is neither an endlessly flexible mechanism for implementing the most persuasive recent theory of government operations nor a magic time machine capable of remodeling our world to resemble more closely a rather fuzzy snapshot of some earlier age. Too many theorists try to make it one or the other or even both, without pausing to consider the role that the Constitution and constitutionalism play in American culture, self-conception, and nationhood.

The Constitution can be, but need not be, a document for lawyers and judges alone; it can be, but need not be, no more than a frozen image of the way that the government should operate; it can be so many small things, and that is all that it will be, unless we, the people in whose name the Constitution speaks, choose to make it more. By cherishing constitutionalism as we do, we, the people, do make it more. We place debates over constitutionality at the center of our moral discourse, and in so doing, we profess a faith in the possibility that our fundamental law will realize our ideals. Our fundamental law shapes us, but it is shaped by us as well.

Thus while the Constitution, however construed, will inevitably shape our society, we, the people, and our values, can shape the Constitution, too. Academic lawyers and cloistered judges may lean against the wind of change, but as the Supreme Court discovered when it tried in the first third of this century to withstand the force of public demand for the government to place limits around the worst excesses of laissez faire, the wind is finally strong enough to flatten its opposition into dust. The Supreme Court that tried to declare that state governments violated the due process clause when regulating the hours that individuals could work, or that some commercial establishments were of too local a character to be touched by the federal power to regulate interstate commerce, finally was forced to retreat, its decisions consigned to the special oblivion reserved for bad law.

Yet the decisions of that earlier era were not bad law because they were wholly insupportable in logic; they ended up on the junk heap of constitutional history because they tried to place barriers in the path of winds of change that blew with too much power. Put otherwise, those decisions finally became bad law because bad law was what the people of the United States wanted them to be. In this sense, Professor Ackerman is surely correct: time and public awareness and insistence *can* change the meaning of the Constitution, if not in ways that would satisfy the formalist, at least in the sense that the courts must seek fresh interpretive paths if they are to survive with the public respect they will need for the next battle. Constitutional courts, more than other courts, must be eternally vigilant against spending their efforts refighting the last war rather than girding for the next. This surely is what Justice Robert Jackson had in mind in 1952 when, faced with President Harry Truman's claim that peril to the nation's security permitted him, as commander-in-chief, to seize the steel mills from their owners to prevent a strike, he concurred in the Court's conclusion that the president had exceeded his powers, but also added a cautionary note:

> I have no illusion that any decision by this Court can keep power in the hands of Congress if it is not wise and timely in meeting its problems. A crisis that challenges the President equally, or perhaps primarily, challenges Congress. If not good law, there was worldly wisdom in the maxim attributed to Napoleon that "The tools belong to the man who can use them." We may say that the power to legislate for emergencies belongs in the hands of Congress, but only Congress itself can prevent power from slipping through its fingers.

If the public demands action, so Justice Jackson seemed to say, then it will in the long run matter very little that the Court forbids the president to answer the demand. For if the Congress cannot bestir itself to act instead, and if the demand continues and increases in pitch, sooner or later the president will respond, and given time, even the Court will accommodate itself to the fresh reality.

This dialogic vision of judicial review can be a frightening one; it suggests that the courts are moved by considerations other than their best judgments about what the Constitution "really means"; it suggests, too, that law is largely politics, which is not liberal democratic theory, but nihilism.

And yet the vision is not nihilistic and it need not frighten. It can instead reassure all of us—all of we, the people—about the responsiveness of the institutions of our government. It can also help liberate us from the crutch of turning constantly to the Constitution and to the courts to implement the latest fashion in political theory or moral philosophy. Liberalism rests at bottom on dialogue, and on a faith in people—a faith that they will govern themselves wisely, in accord with the dictates of conscience and the results produced by reason. Too great a reverence for a judicial review that proceeds wholly in ignorance of the demand for change would cast a long shadow over that faith.

This does not mean that the justices should simply approve whatever a majority of the people prefer, or that they should capitulate at the first sign of opposition. It does suggest, however, that all who read the Constitution, no matter how diligent and sincere their search for the truest or best meaning, should recognize the complexity of interpretation and the indispensability of public trust. Interpretation of the Constitution is an activity that takes place in a larger world than the hushed, wood-paneled chamber of the judge. The courts and the people, wrote the late Alexander Bickel in *The Morality of Consent,* carry on "an endlessly renewed educational conversation," and the wisdom or folly of a proposed interpretation of a constitutional clause is the principal subject matter. Over the short run, courts may restrain foolish or oppressive majorities from acting on the passion of the moment. But if over the longer term, we, the people, continue to reject what the courts command, it is somewhat silly and finally elitist and antidemocratic to insist that the courts, and not the rest of us, should of right prevail.

Our Constitution, finally, will be what we make it, and our government, finally, will do what we demand of it. What is sometimes treated as a dark, dirty secret—that many, perhaps most, lay people develop judgments on constitutionality based not on analysis but on personal preference—may perhaps be something to be paraded, a source of civic pride. Something so central to nationhood as the Constitution surely belongs to everyone, and not just the physical document, but the language and its interpretation as well should ultimately be considered as the property of all. The Constitution is not endlessly malleable, but it is flexible enough to accommodate most broadly shared points of view on most of the major issues of the day. A conclusion that administrative agencies must all be in the executive branch is at least as defensible, in logic and in constitutional history, as one that the Congress may make them independent of direct political control. No matter what the Supreme Court might have said half a century ago in *Humphrey's Executor* or much more recently in *Bowsher v. Synar,* the issue is not settled because the justices have spoken; in the educational conversation about the proper scope of administrative government, they must take their turn and listen to the response.

Thus to ask what the political theory underlying the Constitution commands on the degree of independence that regulatory agencies might possess is to ask a question that leads down useful paths, but is ultimately not quite to the point; in the long run, it is far more important to know what shape it is that we, the people, want our government to have. We have tracked the beast of administrative government to its lair, and we have discovered that this beast, like so many others that we imagine or create, exists only if we want it to.

5

New Federalism: State Constitutions and State Courts

SHIRLEY S. ABRAHAMSON
DIANE S. GUTMANN

Introduction

In 1984 John Minor Wisdom, senior judge, U.S. Court of Appeals for the Fifth Circuit, commented, "It is striking indeed that so many . . . [who] write on the subject of 'Civil Rights and Federalism' have focused on the growing role of

SHIRLEY S. ABRAHAMSON is justice of the Supreme Court of the state of Wisconsin and has taught at the University of Wisconsin Law School. Justice Abrahamson is a member of several American Bar Association committees, a fellow of the Wisconsin Academy of Sciences, Arts and Letters, and a member of the Council of the American Law Institute. She has published widely on state constitutional law, among many other topics.

DIANE S. GUTMANN is a graduate of Tufts University and the University of Pennsylvania Law School. She served for two years as an attorney for the federal government before going into private practice in Madison, Wisconsin, where she specialized in civil and appellate litigation.

The authors wish to thank Diana Balio, Sharon Ruhly, and Joel R. Wells for their assistance in the preparation of this chapter.

the *states* in protecting civil rights, in some cases going beyond Supreme Court guidelines."

For a long time, few people seemed aware that protection of individual liberties could lie in the state constitution—and not solely in the U.S. Constitution. In the 1970s, state courts gradually reawakened to their legitimate authority to construe the rights that their state constitutions provided independently of the U.S. Supreme Court's construction of analogous rights in the federal Constitution. When a state court construes the state constitution in the same way that the U.S. Supreme Court construes the federal Constitution, or when a state court goes beyond the Supreme Court in the protection of human rights, there is no inherent conflict between nation and state. Conflict does arise when state standards fall short of federal standards.

Federal Court of Appeals Judge Skelly Wright recently declared himself an "enthusiastic new convert to 'federalism'" and applauded "state judges who have resumed their historic role as the primary defenders of civil liberties and equal rights." Federalism has been a perplexing idea from its very inception. At the Constitutional Convention one of the framers expressed his confusion with the as yet not fully developed idea of federalism when he said, "I cannot conceive of a government in which there exist two supremes." Although the Constitution explicitly makes the federal government supreme, the idea that the states remain in some sense sovereign or autonomous has retained vitality throughout our history.

As James Madison recognized in *Federalist Paper No. 37,* no mathematical formula can tell us how to allocate power between the national government and the state governments. History shows us that the allocation of authority between the states and the national government shifts over time. The tension between pressures for state autonomy and pressures for national supremacy is fundamental to federalism. This tension has led at times to conflict and at other times to dialogue and accommodation.

Some commentators use the term *new federalism* to refer to

a new relationship between federal and state courts and between the federal and state constitutions. New federalism refers to the renewed willingness of state courts to rely on their own law, especially state constitutional law, to decide questions involving individual rights. In new federalism, the federal Constitution establishes minimum rather than maximum guarantees of individual rights, and the state courts determine, according to their own law (generally their own state constitutions), the nature of the protection of individual rights against state government. New federalism also includes the potential for greater deference by federal courts to state court proceedings and decisions.

Federal and state courts work out their relationship with each other as they work out the relationship between the federal and state constitutions. The balance between state autonomy and national supremacy is vividly illustrated in the context of the protection of civil liberties, and we shall discuss this aspect of the relationship of federal and state constitutions.

First we examine the historical background of the relationship between federal and state courts. Then we turn to the experience of both court systems in the protection of civil liberties. Finally, we attempt to assess the impact on both court systems of incorporation, that is, applying many portions of the federal Bill of Rights to the states through the Fourteenth Amendment. We look first at increased state court interpretation of state bills of rights, then at the U.S. Supreme Court reaction in *Michigan v. Long* (1983) to the increased role of the state courts in the interpretation and application of the state and federal bills of rights.

The System of Dual Governments

Dual Governments: Federalism

The states predate the Constitution and its predecessor, the Articles of Confederation. During the months preceding independence, colonists debated the uniformity of state constitutions but rejected uniformity in favor of each state's calling a convention to draw up its own constitution. This individuality reflected a political reality that manifested itself in such incidents as the response of New Jersey soldiers to George Washington's attempt to get them to swear allegiance to the United States: "New Jersey is our country."

At the time of the Constitutional Convention in 1787 in Philadelphia, the states were an independent and somewhat fractious lot loosely bound together by a central "government" backed only by the force of persuasion. Protective of state autonomy, the people waited nervously for the results of the convention, unaware that the delegates were laboring over an entirely new constitution in apparent disregard of the mandate to meet "for the sole and express purpose of revising the Articles of Confederation."

The idea of unqualified state "sovereignty" lost some of its luster under the Articles of Confederation, but state sovereignty was to survive—albeit somewhat redefined—the framing and ratification of the Constitution.

A proposal at the convention that the existing governmental foundations be swept away in favor of a purely national government was not well received. The framers built the Constitution on the foundation of the states, rather than attempting to lay an entirely new foundation. The Constitution assumes the existence of states (mentioning them at least fifty times), state judiciaries (at least three times), and state constitutions (at least once). In structure and conception, the Constitution drew heavily on the constitutions of the states. As John Adams declared, "What is the Constitution of the United States, but that of Massachusetts, New York and Maryland! There is not a feature in it which cannot be found in one or the other."

Thus the document that emerged at Philadelphia presupposed two levels of government, each with its own constitution and governmental structure, each existing simultaneously in the same geographic territory, and each deriving its powers from and governing the same people. The states remained autonomous entities under the Constitution, instead of being reduced to mere administrative subdivisions of the central government. Like the people, the states retained whatever powers were not delegated to the central government. James Madison wrote in *Federalist Paper No. 45:*

The powers delegated by the proposed Constitution to the federal government are few and defined. Those which are to remain in the State governments are numerous and indefinite. . . . The powers reserved to the several States will extend to all the objects which, in the ordinary course of affairs, concern the lives, liberties, and properties of the people, and the internal order, improvement, and prosperity of the State.

Although the states retained autonomous status, the United States was constituted as more than a federation, more than a league or an alliance between nations. The government established by the new Constitution acted on the people directly as well as on the states, in contrast to the Articles of Confederation, which were concerned only with relations between the states.

As Madison described it, the Constitution "is, in strictness, neither a national nor a federal Constitution, but a composition of both." Alexis de Tocqueville put it aptly many years later: "Evidently this is no longer a federal government, but an incomplete national government, which is neither exactly national nor exactly federal; but the new word which ought to express this novel thing does not yet exist." The Constitution established a hybrid national-federal government in which the national government was not to swallow up the states and the states were not to undermine the national government. The Constitution encased two political communities within one system, creating the potential for conflict as well as the potential for fruitful collaboration and dialogue.

A classic description of our federalism in this century comes from Justice Hugo Black. He described it as

a proper respect for state functions, a recognition of the fact that the entire country is made up of a Union of separate state governments, and a continuance of the belief that the National Government will fare best if the States and their institutions are left free to perform their separate functions in their separate ways.

The concept of federalism, observed Justice Black, requires neither "blind deference to States' Rights" nor the centralization of control over every important issue. Rather, each government must be sensitive to the legitimate interests of the other. Anxious though the national government may be to vindicate and protect national rights and national interests, it must do so in ways that will not impede legitimate state activities.

As we shall elaborate further, federalism and individual rights have been intertwined in American constitutional history from the very beginning. The framers strove to bestow upon the national government authority to deal with national problems, while safeguarding state autonomy and individual liberty. As Madison wrote in *Federalist Paper No. 51:*

In the compound republic of America, the power surrendered by the people is first divided between two distinct governments, and then the portion allotted to each subdivided among distinct and separate departments. Hence a double security arises to the rights of the people. The different governments will control each other, at the same time that each will be controlled by itself.

With the division of powers between the national and state governments and the separation of powers, the framers of the Constitution, according to John Quincy Adams, gave us "the most complicated government on the face of the globe."

Dual Courts: Judicial Federalism

In attempting to tell the story of the dual court system in condensed form, we begin with the ending. This country has two independent but interrelated judicial systems: state and federal. The framers and Congress provided for a complex and intricate system of two sets of courts with overlapping jurisdiction. They did not attempt to simplify the dual judicial system by apportioning federal adjudicative powers solely to the federal courts and state adjudicative powers solely to the state courts. Rather, both the federal and state courts apply federal and state law.

Before exploring the interaction between state and federal

courts as an aspect of our federalism, we will trace the origins of the dual system of courts. The dual judicial system grows out of the tension between two contending principles: national supremacy and state autonomy.

The federal judiciary seems so natural and inevitable now that it may be difficult to imagine a time when its establishment and existence were controversial. We have been schooled to think of constitutional governments as necessarily composed of three branches: the legislative, the executive, and the judicial. Our national government would seem unbalanced without a judiciary.

Yet in order to comprehend the original understanding of the role of the federal judiciary, we must realize that a federal judiciary was not at all inevitable. There was no national judiciary under the Articles of Confederation except for a national appellate tribunal to decide maritime cases. While not very controversial during the drafting process, the establishment of a federal judiciary became intensely controversial during the ratification process. The establishment of the federal judiciary was perceived as a threat to state autonomy. The resistance to this perceived threat did not succeed in blocking the establishment of a federal judiciary, but it did succeed in influencing its structure and jurisdiction.

The cornerstones of the present-day federal judicial system are Article III of the Constitution and the Judiciary Act of 1789. Our discussion will focus on the forces that went into shaping these important texts, particularly as revealed by the records of the Constitutional Convention, the ratification debates, and the congressional deliberations of the Judiciary Act of 1789.

The Convention: Article III. If we were to look to the records of the Constitutional Convention for information on the original understanding of the role of the federal judiciary and its relationship to the states, we would find surprisingly little on the subject. What controversy there was concerning the federal judiciary centered on the form it would take, not on whether it should exist at all.

The convention quickly decided to establish a federal judiciary separate from the existing state judicial systems, adopting Edmund Randolph's resolution "that a National Judiciary be established." The reason for this quick assent, Alexander Hamilton later explained, was that the framers were convinced that a national judiciary was an essential part of a government. This conviction must have rested in part on the belief that all properly formed governments have three branches. The national government would rely on the national judicial system to uphold federal laws (especially when the national and local policy were at variance) and to provide a more uniform system of justice than the state courts could. As Tocqueville later put it, "The object of creating a Federal tribunal was to prevent the state courts from deciding, each after its own fashion, questions affecting the national interests, and so to form a uniform body of jurisprudence for the interpretation of the laws of the Union."

Although the framers were willing to limit state autonomy in order to ensure that the laws and the Constitution of the national government would be fairly and uniformly applied, they balked at setting up any federal courts other than the Supreme Court. Many feared that lower federal tribunals would unacceptably infringe on state autonomy and the integrity of the state judicial system. John Rutledge urged that

the State tribunals might and ought to be left in all cases to decide in the first instance, the right of appeal to the supreme national tribunal being sufficient to secure national rights & uniformity of Judgmts: that it was making an unnecessary encroachment on the jurisdiction of the States and creating unnecessary obstacles to their adoption of the new system.

Some delegates viewed creating a national system of courts as expensive and as a possible impediment to the states' ratification of the Constitution if the states feared that lower federal courts would encroach on the jurisdiction of the state courts. Madison and other delegates, however, favored a provision in the Constitution creating lower federal courts with final jurisdiction.

After Rutledge's motion against lower federal courts carried, James Wilson and Madison urged that "there is a distinction between establishing such tribunals absolutely and giving a discretion to the Legislature to establish or not establish them." They proposed the compromise that the convention adopted: the national legislature would be empowered to institute lower federal courts. In the end, therefore, because the framers were unable to reach a conclusion on the issue of lower federal courts, they decided to leave the matter to Congress.

To summarize what emerged from the convention concerning the judiciary, Article III of the Constitution expressly provides that the federal judicial power encompasses both the states and individuals as litigants. Furthermore, the federal judicial power, like the legislative and executive powers, is an enumerated power. The listed categories of cases which federal courts could hear may be viewed as restrictions on federal invasion of state judicial power. The federal judicial power of the United States extends to "all cases in law and equity arising under the Constitution," a broadly worded grant of jurisdiction, and to laws of the United States and to diversity jurisdiction, that is, to suits between citizens of different states. Diversity jurisdiction was accepted without debate at the convention and without explanation of its purpose, although debate on this provision was extensive during ratification and has been intermittent ever since. Hamilton explained in *The Federalist Papers* that because state courts could not be supposed to be impartial in cases pitting a citizen of their state against a citizen of another state, diversity jurisdiction was properly in the federal courts.

The text of the Constitution clearly evinces concern for the independence of the federal judiciary, perhaps because the framers were aware that many state judges depended on state legislatures. This concern is evident in the method of judicial appointment (the president with the advice and consent of the Senate), the protection of judicial tenure (during good behavior), and the prohibition on diminishing judicial salary during continuance in office.

One issue the Constitution did not address directly, however, is the relation of the federal courts to the state courts.

The Supremacy Clause. A mechanism was needed to settle disputes over the respective spheres of state and federal judicial power, i.e., to ensure that the states did not undermine the national government and that the national government did not usurp state powers. To address that need, the framers adopted Article VI of the Constitution, the supremacy clause. The supremacy clause provides that the Constitution, laws, and treaties of the United States are the supreme law of the land, superior to state constitutions and state laws. State judges are bound by oath to support the Constitution and are "bound [by the Constitution], any thing in the Constitution or Laws of any State to the Contrary notwithstanding." The supremacy clause makes the Constitution enforceable in all the courts in the land.

Madison, in *Federalist Paper No. 44*, vividly portrayed the need for the supremacy clause, stating that without it

the world would have seen, for the first time, a system of government founded on an inversion of the fundamental principles of all government; it would have seen the authority of the whole society everywhere subordinate to the authority of the parts; it would have seen a monster, in which the head was under the direction of the members.

In contrast to the constitutional mechanism to prevent the states from undermining the national government, the Constitution did not expressly provide a mechanism to thwart a central government's "natural tendency" to destroy state governments. While scholars still debate the original understanding of the framers, the federal judiciary has had this power since *Marbury v. Madison* (1803).

The framers did not try to resolve with finality the tension they had set up between national supremacy and state autonomy in the judicial sphere. Future generations would have to work that out by adjusting and readjusting the relationship between state and federal courts. As Hamilton said in *Federalist Paper No. 82*, "Time only can mature and perfect so compound a system, liquidate the meaning of all the parts, and adjust them to each other in a harmonious and consistent WHOLE."

Ratification. The need for a federal judiciary, which had seemed so self-evident to the framers at the convention, became the center of controversy during the ratification debates. Some antifederalists feared the breadth of federal judicial power and argued that state courts were adequate. In fact, the antifederalists prophesied the demise of the state tribunals should the Constitution be ratified. According to George Mason, "The Judiciary of the United States is so constructed and extended as to absorb and destroy the Judiciaries of the several States."

In contrast to the gloomy picture painted by the antifederalists, some passages of *The Federalist Papers* paint a rosy picture in which the state and federal courts function as kindred systems and parts of a whole. Hamilton interpreted the Constitution as permitting state and federal courts concurrent jurisdiction, with both state courts and federal courts deciding questions of state and federal law arising in cases within their respective judicial powers.

According to Hamilton, the state courts would retain the jurisdiction they had, except where state jurisdiction was expressly prohibited. The state courts were not, according to Hamilton, divested of their "primitive jurisdiction" except for appeals. Furthermore, except where expressly prohibited, the state courts would have concurrent jurisdiction in all cases arising under the laws of the union. Hamilton reasoned that the supremacy clause demonstrates the framers' assumption that state courts could adjudicate issues of federal law.

Hamilton concluded, however, that in instances of concurrent jurisdiction, the Supreme Court's appellate jurisdiction would extend to decisions of the state courts as well as the federal courts. Indeed, Hamilton saw a need for federal appellate jurisdiction over state courts. He claimed in *Federalist Paper No. 81* that state judges could not be "relied upon for an inflexible execution of national laws" because, in all states, judges were to some degree dependent on the state legislatures through selection, salary, or term, and might not stand up to them. Hamilton found no impediment to permitting appeals from state courts to inferior federal courts. "The evident aim of the plan of the convention is," wrote Hamilton, "that all the causes of the specific classes shall, for weighty public reasons, receive their original *or* final determination in the courts of the union."

The prospect of a national court with ultimate authority to determine the final meaning of the supremacy clause was a frightening one for the antifederalists. Not only was the federal government deemed supreme, it was also empowered to decide what this supremacy meant. Federal courts were charged with the important responsibility of limiting the supremacy of the federal government and protecting state autonomy.

The Judiciary Act of 1789. Article III was not self-executing, and on September 24, 1789, the first Congress adopted "an Act to establish the Judicial Courts of the United States." The Judiciary Act of 1789 is weighty evidence of the true meaning of the Constitution, according to the U.S. Supreme Court, because it was passed by the first Congress assembled under the Constitution, many of whose members had taken part in the convention. Furthermore, the act set forth, to a large extent, the basic structure of the federal courts as we know it today.

The Judiciary Act of 1789 established the Supreme Court, which has existed continuously ever since, although the number of associate justices has changed. More significantly, the act resolved the controversy over lower courts: Congress established them. After a vigorous debate reminiscent of ratification, Congress decided that federal trial courts were necessary. The act set up two tiers of trial courts: district courts (at least one per state) and three circuit courts. The circuit courts, composed of two Supreme Court justices and one district court judge, were the weak spots in the system and were later abolished; separately constituted circuit courts of appeal were ultimately established.

Congress did not confer on the federal courts the full judicial power granted by the Constitution. Surprisingly, the act did not grant the federal trial courts jurisdiction over "federal question cases," that is, cases arising under the Constitution or laws of the United States in private civil litigation. The prevailing view was that state courts were the appropriate forums for the enforcement of federal law and that federal courts should be available to citizens who might be victims of bias in sister state courts. Accordingly, Congress granted diversity jurisdiction to the lower courts, concurrent with state courts, and authorized the removal of diversity actions from state court to federal court.

Federal district courts did not obtain "federal question" jurisdiction until 1875. Until that time, federal question cases, in the absence of diversity jurisdiction, could only be brought in state courts.

To ensure state court autonomy and a final determination by a federal court for all cases raising federal issues, the 1789 act provided for Supreme Court review of state courts' final judgments or decrees in matters of federal concern in three categories of cases in which the state court held *against* a federal claim:

1. where the validity of a treaty, statute, or authority of the United States is drawn into question and the state court decides against its validity;
2. where the validity of a state statute or authority is challenged on the basis of federal law and the state court decides in favor of its validity;
3. where a state court construes the U.S. Constitution, a U.S. treaty, statute, or commission and decides against a title, right, privilege, or exemption under any of them.

The Supreme Court could not review state court decisions favorable to a claim of federal right until 1914, when Congress granted this review power to the Supreme Court. This amendment was prompted largely by a New York Court of Appeals decision holding a state workers' compensation law in conflict with the due process guarantees of both the federal and state constitutions.

During Reconstruction and thereafter, Congress broadened federal jurisdiction largely at the expense of state courts. Federal removal jurisdiction was expanded. The writ of habeas corpus empowered lower federal courts to test the legality of confinements by reviewing the judgments of state courts, even after they had been affirmed by the state's highest court. Thus state criminal defendants could challenge their convictions in lower federal courts and ultimately in the U.S. Supreme Court. Within this dual judicial system, federal courts have a significant impact on state courts and cases.

The Dual Court System. The United States still has the dual system of courts it had initially. State courts retain the authority they possessed before the Constitution, plus the power to hear questions of federal law. In the Constitution and the Judiciary Act, the state courts appeared to be the primary guarantors of federal constitutional rights and in many instances actually have been the ultimate ones. Congress gave federal courts, existing side by side with their state counterparts, limited jurisdiction. The ability of federal courts to decide matters of state law was restricted to state law issues arising in cases in which federal jurisdiction was independently established.

Thus only the basic parameters of the relationship between federal and state courts were set by the Constitution and the Judiciary Act. Much was left to be worked out in practice. We now turn to examine how this relationship has developed with respect to the federal and state constitutional protections of civil liberties.

Federal and State Constitutional Protections of Individual Liberties

Although it initially lacked a bill of rights, the Constitution did not ignore the subject of individual liberties altogether. It guaranteed jury trial in criminal cases, freedom from both federal and state ex post facto laws and bills of attainder, and freedom from state laws impairing the obligation of contract.

Missing, however, were the traditional clauses of a bill of rights found in many state constitutions protecting such individual liberties as freedom of religion, freedom of speech and press, and freedom from unreasonable searches and seizures or compulsory self-incrimination. Thomas Jefferson viewed the absence of a bill of rights securing the people's liberties against governmental power as a major obstacle to the acceptance of the Constitution. The champions of ratification, recognizing their political error, promised to amend the Constitution. The first session of the first Congress drafted a bill of rights in the form of a series of amendments, ten of which were approved by the required number of states by December 15, 1791.

The federal Bill of Rights now protects individual liberties against the federal and state governments, while the state constitutions protect against the state government and sometimes against action by private persons. It has not always been so. We shall trace the development of the dual constitutional protections that limit state governmental action against individuals.

The Federal Bill of Rights

Despite the presence of bills of rights in so many state constitutions, the delegates, with the notable exception of George Mason, seemed uninterested in appending a bill of rights to the Constitution. Mason objected: "There is no Declaration of Rights, and the laws of the general government being paramount to the laws and constitution[s] of the several states, the Declaration of Rights in the separate states are no security." Until Mason raised it, James Wilson said, the issue of a bill of rights had never "struck the minds" of the delegates.

To many of the delegates, the guarantees of individual liberty in the state constitutions appeared to be enough, in part because the federal Constitution, unlike a state constitution, established a government of limited, enumerated powers. Roger Sherman apparently expressed the consensus of the convention when, in response to a question about the need to preserve the right to trial by jury, he said, "The State Declarations of Rights are not repealed by the Constitution; and being in force are sufficient."

During the ratification process, the people were unpersuaded by federalist arguments against inclusion of a federal bill of rights in the Constitution: the state declarations of rights would adequately protect individual liberty; the state declarations of rights would wither away if a federal bill of rights were established; and the enumeration of rights in a federal declaration of rights might prejudice those rights not enumerated. The popular clamor for a bill of rights was so great that several states agreed to ratify the Constitution only on the understanding that a bill of rights would be added. The Constitution was ratified without a bill of rights, but Congress immediately took up the issue.

Abiding by promises made during ratification, James Madison, initially a staunch opponent of a federal bill of rights, supported the Bill of Rights in Congress. Arguing before Congress that fundamental rights should not depend on the "too uncertain" hope that the limited powers of the national government enumerated in the Constitution would be interpreted to protect individual liberties, Madison claimed that state declarations of rights would not be sufficient. Echoing Mason's argument at the convention, Madison noted that while a state bill of rights might protect an individual's rights from state interference, it might not prevent the national government from interfering with those same rights. Besides, some states had no bill of rights and bills of other states were defective.

Although Madison's arguments in favor of a bill of rights restraining the national government prevailed, his proposal to have the federal bill of rights impose specific restraints on the state governments failed. Madison's proposed amendment XIV provided: "No State shall infringe the right of trial by Jury in criminal cases, nor the right of conscience, nor the freedom of speech or of the press." Although some states had no bill of rights, and although Madison reasonably argued that "if there were any reason to restrain the Government of the United States from infringing upon these essential rights, it was equally necessary that they should be secured against the

State Governments," amendment XIV did not pass. A federal constitutional protection against state infringement of individual rights would have to wait until well after the adoption of the Fourteenth Amendment after the Civil War.

The Separate and Distinct Spheres
of State and Federal Constitutions

The challenge after the ratification of the Bill of Rights was to reconcile its existence with the existence of state bills of rights. The Supreme Court responded to this challenge by confining the Bill of Rights to national governmental action. In *Barron v. Baltimore* (1830), an owner of a wharf sought compensation from the city of Baltimore under the Fifth Amendment to the Constitution for destroying the commercial use of his property in making street improvements. The Supreme Court concluded that the owner had no Fifth Amendment protection, calling the issue a matter "of great importance, but not of much difficulty."

Overlapping Spheres of the Two Constitutions:
The Reconstruction Amendments and the Process of
Incorporation

Reconstruction dramatically changed the scope of the Bill of Rights and changed the relations between the court systems. Adopted in 1868, the Fourteenth Amendment expressly limits states' interference with civil liberties. It is reminiscent of Madison's proposed amendment XIV, but Madison's proposal was restricted to certain specific rights; the language of the Fourteenth Amendment is more open textured.

Section 1 of the Fourteenth Amendment prohibits the state from making or enforcing any law that abridges the privileges or immunities of citizens of the United States; deprives any person of life, liberty, or property without due process of law; or denies any person within its jurisdiction the equal protection of law. The last section of the amendment empowers Congress to enforce the amendment by appropriate legislation.

Between 1866 and 1877 Congress took steps to enforce the Fourteenth Amendment by adopting several major civil rights statutes that created new federal rights and remedies modifying existing state law. Congress also increased federal judicial jurisdiction. It opened the lower federal courts to civil rights claims, and, as we described previously, in 1875 to all cases founded on federal law. Thus litigants could bypass state courts in federal question cases. Finally, Congress authorized the lower federal courts—as opposed only to the Supreme Court—to supervise or supersede the state courts in their implementation of federal law by habeas corpus, removal, and injunction.

The first test of the limits of the postwar restructuring of federal-state relationships came in the *Slaughterhouse Cases* (1873). The Fourteenth Amendment provides that no state shall abridge "the privileges and immunities" of citizens of the United States. In the *Slaughterhouse Cases* a group of butchers challenged as a denial of one of the protected privileges and immunities a Louisiana statute granting a monopoly of the slaughtering trade to a private corporation. The Court declared the claim was not a federal right or privilege but rather a state right or privilege not within the ambit of the Fourteenth Amendment.

The Supreme Court construed the Fourteenth Amendment as extending against the states only those rights that were national in character: the right to travel, the right to petition for redress of grievances, the right to use the navigable waters of the United States, and other similar rights. This list of national rights remained short since the Supreme Court refused to hold that the other guarantees enumerated in the Bill of Rights were among the privileges and immunities of citizens of the United States.

While the Supreme Court read the privileges and immunities clause of the Fourteenth Amendment narrowly in the *Slaughterhouse Cases,* the Court later applied many of the first eight amendments to the states through the Fourteenth Amendment's due process clause, rather than the privileges or immunities clause. This application of the first eight amendments to the states through the Fourteenth Amendment is known as incorporation.

In 1897 the Court held that the Fourteenth Amendment proscribed the taking of private property for public use without payment of just compensation. It was not until 1925, in *Gitlow v. New York,* that the Court suggested in dictum that the rights guaranteed by the First Amendment are among the fundamental personal rights and liberties protected by the due process clause of the Fourteenth Amendment against the state government.

Thus from 1787 to 1925 the Bill of Rights offered individuals little or no protection in their relations with state and local governments. The state constitutions provided those protections. During that period, however, the states' records in preserving individual rights were uneven within a state and among the states. For example, the states' records were good in appointing counsel for indigent criminal defendants at public expense. In 1859 the Wisconsin Supreme Court, as a matter of its own state constitutional law, required counties to appoint counsel for indigent felons at county expense. It was not until 1963, 104 years after the Wisconsin Supreme Court had acted, that the U.S. Supreme Court required a state, as a matter of Fourteenth Amendment due process, to provide counsel in state felony trials. By the time the U.S. Supreme Court imposed this requirement, most states appointed counsel at public expense, as called for by state constitutions, state laws, or state practice. In *Gideon v. Wainwright* (1963) the U.S. Supreme Court brought only a few laggard states into line.

In other areas of individual rights, the states' records are poor. Many have argued that the failure of the states to provide better protection for individual rights created a void— one that the Supreme Court felt compelled to fill.

Incorporation after 1925

After 1925 the incorporation of the enumerated guarantees of the first eight amendments into the Fourteenth Amendment gained momentum, and the pace accelerated during the

1960s. The incorporation doctrine partly nationalized individual liberties, and the doctrine coincided with technological, economic, and social changes that tended also toward nationalization.

Because many of the first eight amendments deal with the criminal process, the incorporation doctrine involves, to a large extent but not exclusively, a defendant's criminal procedural rights. The Fourteenth Amendment, for instance, now applies to the states the guarantees of the Sixth Amendment, including the rights to obtain a speedy trial, to have a public trial, to have an impartial jury, to confront one's accusers, to have compulsory process for obtaining witnesses in one's behalf, and to have the assistance of counsel. The Fourth Amendment right of freedom from unreasonable searches and seizures, including the federal exclusionary rule, which since 1914 has required federal judges to exclude illegally seized evidence from the trial, has been fully binding on the states since 1961. The Court made the Fifth Amendment prohibition of double jeopardy and the rule against compulsory self-incrimination fully binding upon the states as well. This privilege against self-incrimination became the basis of *Miranda v. Arizona* (1966), requiring police to give warnings before custodial interrogation. Those rights in the federal Bill of Rights that are not incorporated in the Fourteenth Amendment remain dependent on state law.

The Supreme Court also expanded certain rights afforded by the Constitution as it was extending them against the states through the Fourteenth Amendment. The Court expanded not only the procedural rights of the criminal defendants but also other civil liberties. For example, several decisions of the 1960s expanded First Amendment protections, thereby barring state required prayers in public schools and limiting the extent to which public officials and public figures could avail themselves of state libel laws.

The incorporation doctrine gave prominence to the Constitution as a protection against invasions of individual liberties by either the state or national government. The combination of incorporation and expansion of rights increased state judges' obligations to apply federal law in state cases.

State courts, of course, were not total strangers to federal law. The two systems have always influenced each other, both directly and indirectly. Federal courts had always applied and developed state law, and state courts had always applied and developed federal law. As Justice John Harlan wrote in the 1884 *Robb v. Connolly* decision, "Upon the State courts, equally with the courts of the Union, rests the obligation to guard, enforce, and protect every right granted by the Constitution of the United States. . . ."

Nevertheless, the incorporation of much of the Bill of Rights through the Fourteenth Amendment, as well as the extension of the reach of federal law in general, made the state courts partners with the federal courts in the enforcement of federal law to an unprecedented extent. Working out the terms of this new partnership is one of the main challenges in adjusting federal-state court relations in the postincorporation period.

State Courts: The Separate and Distinct Sphere of the State Constitution

State Constitutions Disappear

In the 1960s, as a result of incorporation, the states suddenly found that there was a floor, a minimum, of federally protected liberties, which the state court was bound to provide (though some scholars still argue for a rollback of incorporation). The state courts suddenly found themselves routinely applying federal constitutional law, especially in state criminal cases that inevitably made up a large portion of their workload. For many states, the federal "floor" had been set far above where the state "ceiling" was or might have been. The U.S. Supreme Court went faster and probably further than many of the state courts were willing to go. The state courts, some reluctantly, followed the lead of the U.S. Supreme Court. Under these circumstances, the state bills of rights had little to add to their federal counterparts, and the state bills began to lose their significance in state cases. As the federal constitutional guarantees grew, state courts' reliance on state constitutional protection of individual rights diminished considerably. The danger against which some of the antifederalists had warned, the atrophy of state constitutional protections of individual liberties, seemed to have become a reality.

There was even discussion that state bills of rights were no longer necessary and need not be included in revisions of state constitutions. A countertrend became noticeable, however, as Professor Vern Countryman, Professor Hans Linde (now Oregon Supreme Court justice), and others began urging a greater reliance on state constitutions. In 1968, during the Warren Court's expansive protection of individual liberties, Professor Countryman emphasized the importance of the state bill of rights. Because not all federal rights are applicable to the states and because the Fourteenth Amendment reaches state but not private action, Countryman argued, our society must continue to look to state bills of rights. At about the same time, Professor Linde was arguing that, as a jurisprudential matter, state courts should determine whether there had been a deprivation of a state constitutional right before determining whether there had been a deprivation of a federal constitutional right.

State Constitutions Reappear

The 1970s produced changes that brought state constitutions into the foreground once again. Justice William Brennan, writing in the *Harvard Law Review* in the spring of 1977, pointed out what he and others saw as two significant changes in the Supreme Court and its attitude toward individual rights. First, they perceived (although others did not) a retrenchment in the Burger Court from an aggressive position in protecting individual rights against both state and federal encroachments. Second, they saw a conscious barring of the federal courthouse door by procedural devices designed to limit adjudication of claims against state action.

In the 1970s, Justice Brennan and others began urging state
courts to look to their own constitutions and to become a new
"font of individual liberties."

Both before and after Justice Brennan's article, several state
courts began to examine and rely on their own constitutions.
A state court's decision to rely on its own constitutional law in
deciding cases involving individual rights does not necessitate
a particular result in the case. Many state courts have adopted
the U.S. Supreme Court's interpretation of a federal constitutional provision as the interpretation of an analogous state
constitutional provision. Other state courts have taken interpretive stances independent of the Supreme Court. On occasion some state courts have interpreted a bill of rights provision more restrictively than the analogous federal provision.
Of course, in this event the greater federal protections take
precedence. From 1970 to the mid–1980s, state courts interpreted the state constitutions as according individuals greater
protection than the federal Constitution in more than 300
cases. In 1976 Justice Stanley Mosk of the California Supreme
Court could write, "I detect a phoenix-like resurrection of
federalism, or, if you prefer, states' rights, evidenced by state
courts' reliance upon provisions of state constitutions." After
the Civil War, the emphasis was on supremacy of national law.
In the 1970s there was a growing movement in the direction
of state autonomy and a new federalism.

A Place for a State Bill of Rights

The question state courts now face is whether state bills of
rights have a place in the postincorporation era. Proponents
assert that state court reliance on state constitutions is a sound
process of decision making, regardless of the result reached in a
particular case. Our federalism, they urge, is based on the dual
concepts of strong states and a strong national government,
and there are historical and doctrinal bases for state courts to
turn to state law rather than to federal law to decide cases in
state courts. Furthermore, there are practical reasons for state
court reliance on state constitutions. State courts handle the

bulk of legal business in this country and develop expertise in areas that they confront day in and day out. Being closer to the people and to the practical problems of administration of the state justice system, a state court may, for example, be better able to draw bright lines as to search and seizure of an automobile than a federal appellate court. The state court applying state law can achieve stability of law; state law need not shift with the changes in the decisions of the U.S. Supreme Court. Finally, if a state court's interpretation of a state constitutional provision differs from the federal court's interpretation of a similar federal provision, there will be a continuing dialogue on the issue. Dialogue is healthy for the system.

There are many critics of new federalism. Some assert that power should rest with the national government. Others classify themselves as states' rightists but reject new federalism as result-oriented and not grounded in legal doctrine or legal principles; to these critics, the new federalism is a theoretical device used instrumentally to enlarge protection of individual rights.

Other critics are civil libertarians who assert that new federalism is a means for the national government to retreat from ensuring civil liberties and civil rights. They are concerned that it will be harder to persuade fifty state courts than one U.S. Supreme Court of the correctness of their position. Other critics fear that state judges cannot handle the task of protecting civil liberties and that, accordingly, neither the federal nor state courts will tend to the job of protecting individual rights if new federalism prevails. These critics claim that state judges will be susceptible to local political influences or timorous in deciding the tough individual rights cases. They worry that moving the arena of individual rights from the national capital to the state capitals puts the constitutional issues closer to the state legislature and the public, who will become hostile to state judges. They are concerned that elected state judges may have trouble resisting the popular and political pressures that could threaten individual rights. There is concern that if the people are unhappy about a state court decision, they will amend the state constitution, which in many states may be relatively easy to do.

Working out the proper relationship between state and federal bills of rights is one of the state courts' major tasks in the postincorporation era. The state courts' approach to the two bills of rights in turn affects the relationship of state and federal courts. The state courts—as we shall discuss later—have been given the responsibility to shape their own role in the federal system and to adjust their relationship with the federal courts.

The State Court's Identity Crisis

When a claim is raised under both the federal and state bills of rights, a state court is being asked to wear two hats: that of a "quasi-federal court," subordinate to the Supreme Court, interpreting the U.S. Constitution and also that of a state court rendering the final interpretation of the state constitution.

State courts disagree about how best to integrate their two identities. The struggle to resolve this identity crisis can be seen in the different approaches the state courts have taken in addressing their bills of rights.

Since the 1960s and despite the growing attention to new federalism, state courts frequently don only the federal hat, making little or no reference to the state constitution. One explanation may be that lawyers do not present the state law issues to the state court. Nevertheless, the number of cases in which state courts look to state law is growing.

Some state courts decide the state constitutional claim first, reasoning that the state constitution is the first guardian of an individual's rights. These courts reach the federal question only if they find that no state constitutional right has been violated. In that way, a state court can forge its identity as a state court without falling below federal standards. Taking this "primacy of state law" approach means that the state court has chosen the posture it will adopt with respect to the federal courts: it will adjudicate state claims first.

Other state courts examine the issue under both the federal and state constitutions. Using this "dual reliance" mode of analysis, the state court always looks to both state and federal law, even if the defendant's challenge would succeed, in the court's opinion, on the federal or state ground alone. Thus the court dons both its hats, even though the federal hat may be superfluous if the court decides the state claim is successful.

Finally, many state courts use the "interstitial" method. The court considers the federal constitutional issue first, turning to the state constitution only when it fails to find that a federal constitutional right has been violated. Implicit in this approach is the state court's decision to forge a new identity for itself only in the interstices of the Bill of Rights. Courts using this approach are opting to define their role as primarily parallel to that of a federal court in the protection of individual liberties and relegating the state bill of rights to a secondary position behind the federal Bill of Rights. Some commentators find this approach a realistic and modern one in view of the domination of the federal Bill of Rights in constitutional litigation in the last half of the twentieth century.

The aura of the supremacy clause looms over the state court when it is confronted with both bills of rights in this postincorporation era. The state court may not easily discern the countervailing principle of state autonomy in the shadow of national supremacy. The supremacy clause, exercised repeatedly in the past few decades to bring state courts up to minimum federal requirements, has become what some have referred to as the "sprawling supremacy clause," spilling over the borders of its text to exert an influence even where it is not directly applicable.

Supremacy of federal law does not require a state court to apply the federal Bill of Rights first nor to render its bill of rights identical to the federal Bill of Rights. It does prohibit state courts from denying a federal right. The choice of approach is emphatically the state court's. It must define its own identity and the role of the state constitution in this postincorporation era, both in terms of when it chooses to rely on state law and in terms of how it approaches the interpretation of state law.

State Court Interpretation of State Bill of Rights

When a state court dons its state hat, it must decide how to interpret the state bill of rights. There is no one answer to this question. We must expect as an incident to our federalism that fifty states would answer in diverse ways.

State court interpretation of a state bill of rights is still a new area with many unexplored frontiers. We will not discuss all the issues that arise when a state interprets its own bill of rights, but instead we focus on how federalism affects and is affected by the interpretive process.

When state courts set out to interpret a provision in the state bill of rights, they must remember that in their capacity as interpreters of the state constitution they are not being disloyal to the U.S. Supreme Court or the supremacy clause when they choose to examine their own constitution and question Supreme Court precedent. The state court should not confuse its federal with its state duties or its federal with its state identity. As each member of the U.S. Supreme Court has said at one time or another in recent years, state courts are free to interpret their state constitutions differently than the Supreme Court interprets the federal Constitution.

Having freed itself of the influence of the supremacy clause, however, the state court need not ignore the decisions of the U.S. Supreme Court. State court interpretation of the state bill of rights occurs in a federal context. The twin contending principles of national supremacy and state autonomy enter into the state court's approach to its interpretive task.

The principle of national supremacy entails a concern largely for national uniformity in the interpretation of one right or a set of rights. The state court may conclude that interpretation of the state constitution should follow the federal Constitution in a particular case or subject area because of its principled belief that national uniformity is a paramount consideration. State courts, for instance, often cite a need for uniform rules for law enforcement officers as a reason for interpreting a state constitutional right having to do with criminal procedure to be coextensive with the corresponding federal constitutional right. Just as federal courts at times defer to the states, so must state courts at times defer to the federal courts.

The principle of state autonomy includes the state's freedom to foster or respond to state distinctiveness. States can draw their own conclusions about the meaning of their state constitutions. This is the multifaceted aspect of federalism, which does not require a monolithic conformity to a single court's answer to a question of textual interpretation. Even if there were one correct answer to questions of textual interpretation, the Supreme Court would not be deemed always to have a monopoly on the correct answer. The freedom to foster state distinctiveness has often been described as the laboratory function of the states. States are able to experiment, and the nation can then profit by using what succeeds and avoiding what fails.

States do in fact have characteristics that distinguish them from the nation as a whole and from other states, and state courts interpreting state constitutions must confront that distinctiveness. State constitutions are different kinds of documents than the federal Constitution, sometimes with a different text and always with a different history. The texts of state constitutions tend to resemble each other more than they resemble the federal Constitution. State courts must also take into consideration the conditions and history in the state, including the original understanding surrounding the state constitutional provision in question. That state constitutions are more easily changed than the federal Constitution is also a factor that may influence a state judge's approach to interpretation of the state constitution. This factor may be seen either as giving a state court more interpretive freedom or as limiting the state court's interpretive freedom.

A good example of a state court responding to state distinctiveness can be found in the free speech area, where a few state courts have concluded that the free speech provision in their state constitutions restrains private action as well as state action. The Supreme Court of California, for example, held that the California Constitution protects those collecting signatures for a petition in a privately owned shopping center. The textual differences between the state clauses and the federal clause have played a role in these decisions. While the First Amendment reads, "Congress shall make no law . . . abridging the freedom of speech, or of the press . . .," many state constitutions contain a seemingly more affirmative right to free speech, such as, "Every citizen may freely speak, write and publish his sentiments on all subjects, being responsible for the abuse of that right; and no law shall be passed to restrain or abridge the liberty of speech or of the press." State courts, it should be emphasized, have also disagreed among themselves about the significance of this textual variation.

The twin contending principles of national supremacy and state autonomy have played out differently in different state courts. Some state courts have given conclusive weight to federal precedent, apparently adopting in perpetuity all existing or future U.S. Supreme Court interpretations of the federal constitutional provision as the governing interpretation of the parallel state provision. Other courts give great but not controlling weight to interpretations of a parallel federal provision. Still other courts treat U.S. Supreme Court opinions much as they would those of sister states or lower federal courts—as decisions deserving of whatever weight the reasoning and intellectual persuasiveness of the opinion warrants. Thus dissenting and concurring of U.S. Supreme Court justices take on a new significance, opening lines of communications between federal and state systems and thereby promoting the dialogue that is a central virtue of federalism. Finally, at other times, state courts put aside the extensive federal gloss on the Constitution and make an in-depth, fresh analysis of an analogous state constitutional provision. The Vermont Supreme Court wrote, "One longs to hear once again of legal concepts, their meaning and their origin. All too often legal argument consists of a litany of federal buzz words memorized like baseball cards."

As state courts begin to share once again in the responsibility for deciding how far constitutional protections of civil liberties extend, they may be drawn into the national debates about how to interpret a constitutional text. Each of these approaches has been commended and criticized, and each has an important impact on the relationship between state and federal courts and on the state court's definition of its own place in a federal system. Regardless of whether the state court reaches the same result as the U.S. Supreme Court, the process it goes through in order to reach the result is the major determinant of the state court's self-definition. When a state court goes through a process of evaluation and reflection in order to render its interpretation of the state constitution, it is investing the idea of state autonomy with meaning, even if it ultimately chooses to follow the lead of the Supreme Court.

The state courts' interpretation of the state bills of rights may be viewed as state courts building a separate sphere, thus nurturing the idea of state autonomy necessary to the maintenance of the tension essential to our federal system. As Justice Black pointed out in his description of our federalism, there is a national interest in having effectively functioning states.

Federal Courts: *Michigan v. Long,*
The Adequate and Independent State Ground

The U.S. Supreme Court does not have a responsibility to review a state court interpretation of state law and will not do so unless an interpretation somehow implicates issues of federal law. In other words, if a state judgment rests on adequate and independent state grounds, the Supreme Court will not reach either the state or the federal issues in the case. While some commentators assert that neither the Constitution nor federal statutes requires this position, the adequate and independent state ground doctrine is the generally accepted and traditional test for reconciling the respective claims of the state for independence of state law and of the national government for review of interpretations of federal law.

The genesis of the adequate and independent state grounds

test as a way of determining which state court decisions are subject to Supreme Court review lies in *Murdock v. City of Memphis* (1875). Seventy years later, the Supreme Court more clearly explained its position in *Herb v. Pitcairn* (1945). The doctrine is premised on the Court's respect for the independence of state courts and the Court's desire to avoid issuing advisory opinions, that is, opinions that discuss and answer legal questions unnecessary to the resolution of the case. The Court explained:

This Court from the time of its foundation has adhered to the principle that it will not review judgments of state courts that rest on adequate and independent state grounds. The reason is so obvious that it has rarely been thought to warrant statement. It is found in the partitioning of power between the state and federal judicial systems and in the limitations of our own jurisdiction. Our only power over state judgments is to correct them to the extent that they incorrectly adjudge federal rights. And our power is to correct wrong judgments, not to revise opinions. We are not permitted to render an advisory opinion, and if the same judgment would be rendered by the state court after we corrected its views of federal laws, our review could amount to nothing more than an advisory opinion.

Complications arise when the state court opinion is ambiguous about whether the court relied on federal or state law. Determining whether an independent and adequate state ground exists is no easy task. Until 1983, when presented with an ambiguous state court decision, the Supreme Court could exercise one of several options. It could dismiss the case. It could vacate the decision and send the case back to the state court to clarify the grounds. It could order a continuance and direct the petitioner to obtain clarification from the state court. Finally, the Court itself could determine which constitution the state court relied upon.

In 1983 in *Michigan v. Long*, the Court admitted that it "had not developed a satisfying and consistent approach for resolving this vexing issue" and adopted a new approach to the independent and adequate state grounds test, concluding that its prior "ad hoc method of dealing with cases that involve

possible adequate and independent state grounds is antitheti-
cal to the doctrinal consistency that is required when sensitive
issues of federal-state relations are involved."

The Holding

Michigan v. Long involved the constitutionality of a protective police search of an automobile for weapons. During the
search of the trunk, the police found seventy-five pounds of
marijuana; the defendant moved to suppress the evidence.
Citing the Michigan Constitution twice, but otherwise relying
exclusively on federal law, the Michigan Supreme Court held
"that the deputies' search of the vehicle was proscribed by the
Fourth Amendment to the United States Constitution and art.
I, sec. 11 of the Michigan Constitution."

Writing for the five-member majority, Justice Sandra Day
O'Connor stated that the Court was unconvinced that the
Michigan decision rested upon independent state grounds.
More important, the Court announced a new approach to its
use of the adequate and independent state grounds doctrine
in state cases in which the grounds for the decision are ambiguous. The Court would "accept as the most reasonable explanation that the state court decided the case the way it did
because it believed that federal law required it to do so."

In other words, the Court set forth a presumption that the
state decision rested on federal grounds. If the state court
wanted to avoid this presumption, it

need only make clear by a plain statement in its judgment or opinion
that the federal cases are being used only for the purpose of guidance,
and do not themselves compel the result that the court has reached.
. . . If the state court decision indicates clearly and expressly that it
is alternatively based on bona fide separate, adequate, and independent grounds, we, of course, will not undertake to review the decision.

The Court's justification for imposing the plain statement
requirement was to protect the integrity of both federal and
state lawmaking. To the extent a state court decision is based

on federal law, federal review is required for doctrinal coherence, and for uniformity of federal constitutional law. State court systems and the federal courts develop and interpret federal constitutional law. Indeed, state courts turn out a larger body of criminal law cases than the federal courts. Justice O'Connor viewed the mixed federal-state opinions as threatening the federal system with a deluge of unauthoritative elaboration on federal law. The *Michigan v. Long* rule promotes uniformity by enabling the Court to review more state court decisions, because the Court now reviews decisions that are or *may* be based on federal law. The Supreme Court thus fulfills its role as the final arbiter of federal constitutional law.

Commentators assert that the *Michigan v. Long* presumption apparently rests on the Court's belief that the Constitution is the primary law in the state courts for protecting civil liberties. They say that the presumption relegates state constitutional law to a marginal role such that state judges may ignore it altogether and render judgment exclusively under federal law. The effect of the presumption is that the U.S. Supreme Court treats state courts as functional equivalents of federal courts unless the state courts expressly deny equivalency in a particular case. In this sense, *Michigan v. Long* nationalizes state courts when their decisions are based on federal and state grounds. The Court will presume that state court decisions resolving federal and state issues rest on the resolution of the federal issues in the case. State courts will be presumed "federal forums," unless they plainly state that they are not so acting.

In summary, in the interests of "efficiency," "uniformity," and "justice," and out of "respect for independence of state courts," the Court requires that state court opinions contain a "plain statement" that their judgments rest on adequate and independent state grounds if the state courts do not wish to invite Supreme Court review. The judicial presumption, therefore, is that a state court's decision does *not* rest on adequate and independent state grounds, and a state court must clearly rebut that presumption if it wishes to insulate its decision from federal review.

Michigan v. Long also seeks to protect the integrity of the state. If a state court plainly says that it is relying on state law, the Supreme Court will not review its decision. The Court reaffirms the state court's opportunity to be the final arbiter of its own law and to divest the U.S. Supreme Court of jurisdiction to review. As Justice O'Connor explained in a speech, a state determines whether to "grant or withhold jurisdiction to the Supreme Court by the choice and articulation of the grounds for the state court decisions." Furthermore, *Michigan v. Long* appears to encourage state courts to function more effectively by considering separately their functions as "federal courts" and as state courts. As author of the majority opinion in *Michigan v. Long,* Justice O'Connor stated the goal as facilitating justice and judicial administration, not thwarting state constitutional development.

One effect of *Michigan v. Long,* therefore, is to shift the burden to the state courts to decide just how far they are going to be nationalized. If a state court feels it important to assert the state's autonomy by interpreting its constitution independently—not necessarily differently, just independently—then the court itself must ensure that its decisions are based on adequate and independent state grounds. Essentially, state courts must begin to develop their own philosophy of federalism from the state perspective.

Nonreviewability is the U.S. Supreme Court's acknowledgment of state autonomy. Reviewability is the affirmation of national supremacy.

The Dissent

Justice Blackmun concurred in the judgment of the Court but did not join the Court in fashioning the new presumption. The dissent of Justices Brennan and Marshall focused on the merits, urging that the search and seizure violated the Fourth Amendment. Justice John Paul Stevens viewed the case as raising "profoundly significant questions concerning the relationship between two sovereigns—the State of Michigan and the United States of America." He argued that historically the presumption was that adequate state grounds are independent unless it clearly appears otherwise. He favored retaining this policy of federal judicial restraint, thereby husbanding the limited resources of the Supreme Court. Justice Stevens expressed the belief that "a policy of judicial restraint—one that allows other decisional bodies to have the last word in legal interpretation until it is truly necessary for this Court to intervene—enables this Court to make its most effective contribution to our federal system of government."

Moreover, Justice Stevens reasoned that the Court has an interest in a case only when state standards fall short of federal standards and an individual has been deprived of a federal right. He believed the Court should not be concerned when the state court interprets federal rights too broadly and overprotects the individual. Justice Stevens complained of a "docket swollen with requests by States to reverse judgments that their courts have rendered in favor of their citizens."

Some commentators take issue with Stevens's contention that the majority's presumption of reviewability is not supported by any significant federal interest. They point out that cases that grant rights to the citizen against the state government affect important government functions that protect all of us and that Supreme Court review ensures that state courts will not hamper state officials by imposing erroneous federal constitutional requirements on them. Other commentators assert that the majority's presumption serves the federal interest in having effectively functioning states, because it eliminates a "dysfunction" caused by incorporation. According to this dysfunction viewpoint, where a state court decision that erroneously relies on federal law to restrain state action goes unreviewed, because a state ground was also cited for the decision, there would be an error in the system that everyone would seem powerless to correct. The Supreme Court could not correct it because it could not review it. It would be beyond the reach of the state legislature as well.

The majority and dissent in *Michigan v. Long* agree that state courts may constitutionally develop an independent body of civil liberties law and that if no federally guaranteed rights are abridged in the process, state courts may apply state law to the exclusion of federal law. *Michigan v. Long* does not signal a change in the rule that state constitutions may provide more protections for the individual than those provided in the federal Constitution. It does remind the states that when they act like federal courts and interpret federal rights, they are potentially subject to review as a federal court.

The disagreement between Justice Stevens and Justice O'-Connor is thus not whether to adopt a clear rule for determining whether a state decision is independent, but what that rule should be.

The Aftermath

Michigan v. Long has engendered a large body of literature that ranges from praise for the decision to condemnation of the "plain statement" rule to questioning the constitutional, theoretical, and functional bases of the adequate and independent state doctrine.

The proponents of the decision support it as a workable, practical way for handling state decisions that fail to state clearly whether they rest on federal grounds or independent and adequate state grounds. They conclude the U.S. Supreme Court ought to promote its federal lawmaking role and ought not to renounce its power to interpret federal law in favor of the nonauthoritative state court readings of federal law. They view *Michigan v. Long* as promoting the U.S. Supreme Court's maintaining uniformity and supremacy of federal law.

To its admirers, *Michigan v. Long* furthers federalism because it delineates clearly the respective spheres of state and federal law and possibly enhances the ability of state courts to experiment in developing principles of constitutional law suitable for that state constitution and that state's people. They see the case as attempting to encourage states to construct their own inviolable sphere of state law. Some commentators conclude that the plain statement will be a burden only to those state courts that were purposely ambiguous in grounding their decision in federal and state law to evade Supreme

Court review and to insulate the decision from the state political process.

Other commentators are more skeptical. They question whether *Michigan v. Long*, which was decided in the name of federalism, really encourages federal judicial interference with state courts' constitutional discretion. The detractors of *Michigan v. Long* view it as an artificial attempt to impose federal law on state courts. They suspect the case is not based on a neutral principle of federalism but rather is a means of constraining civil liberties protection. They view *Michigan v. Long* as masking the Court's substantive goal of keeping state courts from interpreting their constitutions generously.

These commentators conclude that although in theory *Michigan v. Long* preserves the state court's ability to interpret its own constitution, in the real world the decision hinders state courts from developing state law. These writers argue that the state political climate might prevent state judges from interpreting state law more broadly than federal law. They say a state court opinion that benefits a minority or runs against majoritarian preferences places a state judge, who is often an elected official, at risk. The detractors reason that a state judge who holds that state and federal law together compel an unpopular result is taking a safer political course than a judge who holds that state law gives greater rights than federal law. Moreover, these commentators point out that the people of the state can respond to an unpopular state court interpretation by amending the state constitution. Indeed, some states have amended their constitutions to require state courts to harmonize their interpretation of the state constitution with federal precedents. Putting a new twist on the old fear that state judges are "dependent" rather than independent and are not on a par with federal judges, some believe that state courts whose interpretations of the state constitutions will be subject to review by state legislators and the electorate will not be as receptive to claims that a constitutional right has been denied as would be a federal court that is independent from other branches of government and from the electorate at large. Thus, the argument goes, state courts will either interpret their constitutions restrictively or risk Supreme Court review so that federal law will take the blame for the increased protection of civil liberties.

Regardless of which view one takes of *Michigan v. Long,* the U.S. Supreme Court has itself made a plain statement. If a state court wishes to insulate its decision from Supreme Court review, it must express clearly the state law grounds for its decision and must, of course, not deny any federal right.

The advent of incorporation has required a readjustment of the relations between federal and state courts. Incorporation affects each system. It threatens the federal system with a loss of control over federal law, and it threatens the state system with nationalization. In *Michigan v. Long,* the Supreme Court apparently tried to stave off both these threats. The measure of its success will be seen in future state and federal court decisions involving civil liberties.

Impact on Federal and State Courts

Michigan v. Long will be felt in federal district courts and circuit courts of appeals as well as in state courts. As we said earlier, federal courts may apply state law and thus function as state courts. In *City of Mesquite v. Aladdin's Castle, Inc.* (1982), for example, the U.S. Supreme Court remanded a case to the Fifth Circuit Court of Appeals to decide whether its opinion declaring a city ordinance violative of the constitutional guarantees of due process and equal protection rested on Texas law or federal law. The Supreme Court held that it would not decide this novel federal constitutional question if Texas law provided independent support for the court of appeals' judgment.

Similarly, in 1985 the Ninth Circuit Court of Appeals set aside a city ordinance prohibiting the solicitation of donations in public areas used by a municipal stadium. The court began its analysis by stating that the challenge was based on both the federal and California constitutions and that if the California Constitution provides independent support for the claim, there is no need for a decision of the federal issue. There is no certification procedure in California for the federal court to ask the state supreme court to declare the state law issue. The Ninth Circuit decided the state law question, holding the ordinance violative of the California Constitution, and did not reach the federal question.

It is too early to judge the long-term impact of *Michigan v. Long* on state and federal courts. We can say, however, that many state courts remain unaffected by *Michigan v. Long*, and their decisions are like their pre–1983 decisions. Many still do not refer to state constitutions. Those that do often make no effort to separate the state and federal grounds upon which the decision is based. At the same time, a growing number of state high courts have been relying on their own constitutions. If a state court adopts federal interpretations as the interpretation of the state constitution, however, the state ground may not be sufficiently independent of federal law to insulate the decision from review.

If federal and state courts respond to *Michigan v. Long* in the future by increased reliance on state law, the number of cases in which the Court can articulate its views of federal constitutional law may be decreased. In this eventuality, *Michigan v. Long* may achieve disparity between federal and state interpretations of similar constitutional provisions.

We discussed previously the various approaches state courts take to decide federal and state constitutional claims. *Michigan v. Long* does not mandate any approach, although scholars are divided on whether Justice O'Connor's and Justice Stevens's opinions represent a debate over the interstitial and primacy approaches, which in turn represent different views toward federalism. For the present, however, hopes and fears will abound with regard to *Michigan v. Long*. Some will continue to fear that federal review of state court decisions that do not make clear whether they rest on federal or state grounds will become "advisory" in a new sense—that the U.S. Supreme Court will be advising the states how to construe their state constitutions. Such advice is not unprecedented. In a case predating *Michigan v. Long*, Chief Justice Warren Burger criticized the Florida Supreme Court's construction of the Florida

Constitution, saying that it was not rational law enforcement and suggesting that the people amend the state's laws or constitution to override state court opinions that extend individual rights.

Others will continue to hope that the presumption of reviewability will force state courts to make clear the grounds of their decision and interpret their state constitutions. In that case, the Supreme Court may also receive some unsolicited commentary, favorable or unfavorable, on its own opinions, such as that found in some recent state court opinions.

Perhaps such spirited mutual advice is not totally unwelcome in a federal system of which one of the chief virtues is the dialogue between the national and the state governments.

Conclusion

Federalism will continue to mean different things to different people. From the time the framers adopted the term *federal,* which is derived from *foedus,* meaning treaty or alliance, there was confusion and disagreement about what it meant. The term federal was coopted by the proponents of the Constitution to refer to their quasi-national form of government. As political analyst Garry Wills puts it, "By a kind of preemptive verbal strike, the centralizers seized the word and cast the original federalists in the role of antifederalists."

The term was born through a process of redefinition, and it has been continually redefined since that time. The genus federalism already includes a wide variety of species: dual federalism, cooperative federalism, interactive federalism, classical federalism, and dialectical federalism, to name just a few. We will not attempt to classify "new federalism" within any of these categories.

New federalism represents an attempt to reinvigorate the idea of federalism by reviving the idea of state autonomy, an idea which some had declared dead during the incorporation period. The meaning of state autonomy and the proper role for states remain unsettled: state courts, among other institutions, will play a role in resolving these unsettled issues as they decide whether and how to apply the protections of civil liberties in their state constitutions. In this respect, new federalism is a return to the preference of the framers for a monolithic system tempered by pluralism.

New federalism is not an attempt to return to the nullificationist vision of the role of states. The proponents of new federalism do not suggest that state courts be the sole guardians of individual liberty or that the U.S. Supreme Court retreat from applying the Bill of Rights to state action. As Justice Brennan said, "One of the strengths of our federal system is that it provides a double source of protection for the rights of our citizens. Federalism is not served when the federal half of that protection is crippled." The difficulty is to work out a system in which federal and state protections can coexist. The fundamental puzzle, as law professor Paul Bator notes, is to determine what the appropriate criteria are for deciding which questions the federal Constitution should be deemed to have made a matter of uniform national policy.

State court approaches to the questions of when and how to interpret their state bills of rights will tend to define their relationship with the federal courts. As *Michigan v. Long* seems to indicate, state courts will have substantial freedom in determining the extent of their autonomy as long as their decisions do not violate federal law. Thus the great challenge for state courts in the postincorporation era is to ground their decisions both in the protection of individual liberties and in the principles of federalism.

6

The Constitution and the Nationalization of American Politics

MARK TUSHNET

The Political Basis of Federalism

The framers of the Constitution believed that federalism—the system of dividing governing authority between the states and the nation—was central to their scheme of creating a system of government that was powerful enough to defend the nation against external threats and internal disorder, but not so powerful as to threaten the valued liberties of the citizenry. Yet, though the assumption that states would be important permeates the Constitution, the document as written actually says rather little about how the balance between national and local authority was to be sustained. Perhaps the closest it comes to such statements is the enumeration of the powers that Congress would have. Although the

MARK TUSHNET, professor of law at the Georgetown University Law Center, received a J.D. and M.A. from Yale University in 1971. After serving as a law clerk to U.S. Supreme Court Justice Thurgood Marshall, Mr. Tushnet taught at the University of Wisconsin from 1973 to 1981. He is the author or coauthor of several books and articles on constitutional law and history.

enumeration implied that Congress lacked power to act on subjects not listed, the terms actually used to describe Congress's powers were obviously susceptible to substantial expansion.

James Madison's discussion of federalism in *The Federalist Papers* explains why the framers were relatively unconcerned about the Constitution's failure to spell out the protections afforded local power. For Madison, the political process was sufficient to guarantee that states would continue to deal with "all the objects which, in the ordinary course of affairs, concern the lives, liberties, and properties of the people." Madison described formal and informal aspects of politics that protected the role of the states. The formal aspects of the constitutional system made the states "constituent and essential parts of the federal government," as when state legislatures elected the Senate and prescribed how presidential electors would be chosen. Less formally, there would be far fewer employees of the national government than of local governments, so that political organizations would focus on building power bases in cities and towns. Voters would have "ties of personal acquaintance and friendship" with local officials; because those officials would regulate "the more domestic and personal interests of the people," the voters would become "familiarly and minutely conversant with them." Further, the members of the House of Representatives would be "chosen very much under the influence" of the people "whose influence . . . obtains for themselves an election into the State legislatures." Indeed, many officials of the national government would serve first as local officials, and would carry localistic "prepossessions" into the national sphere. Madison concluded that politics was sufficient to guarantee that state and local power would not be subordinated to "ambitious encroachments of the federal government."

In 1985 *Garcia v. San Antonio Metropolitan Transit Authority* upheld federal regulation of the wages paid to employees of state and local governments, over the objection that such regulation unconstitutionally intruded on the interests of those governments. Justice Harry Blackmun's opinion for the Court

squarely endorsed Madison's view that the "basic limit" on
national authority is "the built-in restraints that our system
provides through state participation in federal governmental
action." A vigorous dissent by Justice Lewis Powell chided the
majority for its "myopic" and "unrealistic" assessment of the
operation of the political process. Some of Justice Powell's
concerns were overstated, for he failed to acknowledge that he
was urging the Supreme Court to advance the cause of "democratic self-government at the state and local levels" by overturning the democratically chosen course of the people in
their capacity as national citizens. Nonetheless, the force of
Justice Powell's dissent cannot be denied. He noted that the
Seventeenth Amendment had eliminated the role of state
legislatures in selecting the Senate, and argued that "the weakening of political parties on the local level, and the rise of
national media" had made Congress "increasingly less representative of State and local interests, and more likely to be
responsive to the demands of various national constituen-
cies."

More broadly, the rise of the national party system and the
mobility produced by citizens taking advantage of the opportunities provided by economic dislocation—local growth and
decline distributed differentially across the nation—have undermined the Madisonian confidence in the vitality of state
and local governments. Yet this seems somewhat paradoxical.
The Constitution was designed to promote individual liberty,
which in one of its forms is precisely the association of like-
minded people in political parties. It was also designed to
provide the framework for economic growth, which produces
the dislocations that weaken the citizenry's ties to particular
localities. Did the Constitution contribute to the weakening of
federalism, one of its own central institutions?

The Constitutional Framework and
the Weakening of Local Authority

The general structure of the Constitution made it unlikely
that Madison's vision of strong local governments supporting

and constraining the national government would be realized over the long term. The Constitution's economic and political structures provided powerful incentives for actions that produced the centralization that Justice Powell decried.

The Economic Structure

The framers of the Constitution regarded economic growth as a primary goal of the social order. Growth would ensure domestic tranquility by providing all citizens with a material stake in order; it would promote political stability by making citizens independent of people who might otherwise use economic coercion to control the citizens' votes; and it would provide the basis for national self-defense. But experience had convinced the framers that the benefits of growth might not be achieved if local governments were free to advance their local economic interests at the expense of the interests of the citizens of the entire nation. The Constitution reflected that experience in three ways.

First, and perhaps most important in the short run, the states were expressly prohibited from enacting the most prevalent forms of protectionist legislation. This prohibition made it easier for goods to flow across state lines to localities where they could be used most productively. It also signaled the value the Constitution placed on free trade as an instrument of growth, helping to discredit, in the political arena, protectionist proposals that might be constitutionally permissible.

Second, the framers authorized Congress to regulate interstate commerce. The Supreme Court under John Marshall interpreted this power broadly, though Congress did not exercise its powers extensively until the late nineteenth century. But even in 1824, when Justice William Johnson expressed concern about his colleagues' expansive interpretation, he agreed that Congress obviously had the power to override protectionist state laws (*Gibbons v. Ogden,* 1824).

Third, for about a century after the adoption of the Constitution, its interpretation was shaped by a sense, never fully adopted by the Supreme Court but always affecting its decisions, that Congress's power to regulate interstate commerce, at the least by displacing protectionist laws, necessarily implied that states completely lacked power to adopt such laws. Again, this view of the Constitution was probably more important in affecting public debate, providing arguments against the adoption of protectionist laws, than in restraining the enforcement of whatever laws managed to be enacted.

Taken together, these aspects of the constitutional structure created the framework within which vigorous economic growth could occur. The dynamics of development produced substantial mobility in the United States. People were displaced by economic changes that reduced the returns on their customary activities, and opened up opportunities elsewhere. Americans became what some historians have called a "restless" people. Mobility was enhanced by some ingrained assumptions about the constitutional structure. For many years, both Congress and the states exercised some power over immigration, but the general course of public policy encouraged essentially unrestricted immigration. The right of the people to move freely from one state to another was so readily assumed to be fundamental that the Supreme Court, in recognizing a constitutional right to interstate mobility, found it unnecessary "to ascribe the source of this right . . . to a particular constitutional provision" (*Shapiro v. Thompson,* 1969). In the twentieth century, Congress enacted restrictive immigration laws, as part of the more general processes that have made the national government the primary locus of governing power. The constitutionalization of the right to travel also makes it more difficult for states to sustain distinctive policies, as we will see in more detail below.

The ties to locality, and the intimate knowledge of local politicians that Madison had assumed would exist, weakened as economic development proceeded. In addition, economic growth went together with territorial expansion and population growth. Together, these various types of growth made it increasingly difficult to sustain the localism that Madison believed to be an important counterweight to the centralizing tendencies of the national government.

The development of the modern regulatory state in the twentieth century both responded and contributed to the nationalization of politics. Economic growth in a federal system meant that social problems attendant upon growth could frequently be resolved only by the national government. National politics naturally became the focus of public attention, and the national government's gradual accretion of policy-making roles made state governments seem increasingly less important. Thus the economic growth that the Constitution was designed to promote indeed did undermine some of the Constitution's premises.

The Political Structure

Similar centralizing tendencies were inherent in the political structure of the Constitution. The president and vice-president are elected on a nationwide basis. Though the framers believed that the electoral college would be the forum for discussion of and choice among candidates, it rapidly became merely the forum for ratifying the voters' choice. Once that occurred, presidential candidates needed the support of political organizations that crossed state boundaries—national political parties consisting of fairly stable alliances among state and local political groupings. Second, the Constitution delegated to state legislatures the responsibility for developing rules for electing members of the House of Representatives. Early in our history, legislators exercised that responsibility by using single-member districts rather than at-large or proportional representation systems. Single-member systems encourage the development of only two parties: because the winner takes all, people are reluctant to "waste" their votes on a candidate who is unlikely to obtain a majority in the district; candidates are therefore likely to come forward only if they believe that they have near-majority support at the outset, and only two candidates can have that kind of support. A national two-party system developed in response to these institutional arrangements, though such a system was also rooted in fundamental characteristics of the American political culture, such as the relatively broad range of agreement on many issues of public policy among most of the politically active citizenry. And, once again, such a system has powerful centralizing effects.

Paradoxically, federalism itself can contribute to centralization. The states are independent of each other, except to the extent that they cooperate in Congress. Often one state wishes to develop an innovative program—increasing the social welfare benefits available to its residents, for example—but is deterred from doing so out of fear that the increased costs associated with the program will lead businesses to locate in other states. Historically, the problems of child labor and unemployment compensation placed states in this dilemma. The response is obvious: the states that wish to avoid this "race to the bottom" can secure national legislation that imposes the regulations they desire on unwilling states (see *Steward Machine Co. v. Davis,* 1937). In the service of local innovation, then, centralization may occur.

The right-to-travel cases mentioned earlier illustrate how this can occur by judicial as well as legislative action. The Court invalidated local laws denying public assistance to otherwise qualified people who had recently moved to the state. A state with a relatively generous policy might find itself flooded with new residents demanding assistance. It could respond either by reducing its benefit levels or, more significantly for this discussion, by seeking national legislation that would require other states to increase *their* benefit levels. The incentive to convert local policies into national ones is strong.

This sort of outcome is consistent with another aspect of Madison's discussion of federalism. As we have seen, he defended national power against criticism that it undermined the states, by emphasizing that the states would constrain national power through their political action. Madison also thought that it was affirmatively desirable that states retain substantial power. One of the framers' concerns was to ensure that people in charge of the national government not use their offices to advance their personal goals rather than the goals sought by their constituents. Madison stated that the "federal and State governments are in fact but different agents and trustees of the people." If the federal agents overreached their "due limits" and attempted "ambitious encroachments of the federal government on the authority of State governments," a "general alarm" would sound, to which all the state governments would respond. Thus federalism was for Madison a means by which the people could secure what they desired. As a constitutional matter, it was irrelevant whether they secured it from the states or the nation, so long as ambitious overreaching could be avoided.

Finally, we must consider that federalism was transformed by the Civil War and the Reconstruction Amendments that ratified the war's outcome. A strong theory of states' rights had provided the best constitutional defense of slavery, and the defeat of the Confederacy was a defeat for such a theory. In the course of fighting the war, Northerners came to understand that national power could be deployed effectively on behalf of widely valued goals, thus allaying earlier concern that national power was necessarily inefficient and oppressive. After the war, continuing Southern resistance to the new social order created by emancipation showed Northerners that concerted national action was sometimes not merely convenient but essential. These experiences received their constitutional expression in the Reconstruction Amendments, which are important for the present discussion less for their precise legal meaning than for the fact that they endorsed a shift in the primary locus of governing authority to the national government.

The Role of the Supreme Court

So far, we have examined how the constitutional structure had a dynamic that encouraged political centralization and weakened the localism that Madison believed would resist it. Constitutional doctrine as articulated by the Supreme Court played a relatively small part in this centralization until recently. In its early years, the Court did discourage state economic protectionism, but its endorsement of broad congressional power to regulate interstate commerce meant little until Congress chose to exercise that power.

The Court might have invoked ideas about the framers' intent to inhibit the development of a national two-party system, but it did not—which may be its major contribution to that development. Madison's *Federalist Paper No. 10* dealt with the problem of "faction"—for present purposes most readily understood as "narrow interest groups." Madison argued that a sound system of government had to "break and control the violence of faction" in order to promote "the permanent and aggregate interests of the community." Elections would prevent minority factions from obtaining power. Madison was more concerned with majority factions, which, again in modern terms, might be thought of as coalitions of interest groups. He noted that such coalitions had to be assembled, and found the solution to the problem of majority faction in devices that would impede the coordination of factional interests: "The majority . . . must be rendered . . . unable to concert and carry into effect schemes of oppression." For Madison, the primary obstacle to coordination lay in the creation of an "extended" government, that is, one with a "greater number of citizens and extent of territory." After all, "the smaller the compass within which [members of a majority] are placed, the more easily will they concert and execute their plans of oppression." An extended territory made it harder for such a faction "to discover [its] own strength, and to act in unison," because of the simple difficulties of communication, and because of the more subtle problem that "where there is a consciousness of unjust or dishonorable purposes, communication is checked by distrust."

Madison summarized his argument by saying that "the influence of factious leaders may kindle a flame within their particular States, but will be unable to spread a general conflagration through the other States." This argument loses much of its force once a national party system, especially a national two-party system, develops. It is precisely the function of such a system to allow party leaders in different states to coordinate their schemes easily. A Supreme Court infused with modern

ideas about its role in preserving the constitutional scheme
could readily have found unconstitutional the development of
national party systems. For example, it might have insisted
that the electoral college perform its intended deliberative
role.

The Supreme Court under John Marshall and Roger Taney
was, for better or worse, not such a Court. Its contribution to
the dynamics of the Constitution was to stay out of the way.
Its legacy may have been the weakening of the political constraints on the exercise of national power.

The Modern Court and the
Nationalization of Politics

Until the 1940s, the nationalization of American politics was
propelled by the economic and political elements described
above. The Constitution provided the structure for those elements; the Supreme Court did little other than refrain from
interfering with them. More recently, however, the Supreme
Court has invoked the Constitution in a variety of ways to
regulate the operation of the national political system. The
Court's actions have contributed to the nationalization of politics in two ways. First, as this section will describe in some
detail, many of the Court's doctrines enhance the power of
national political parties at the expense of local authorities.
Second, and probably more important, the very fact of Supreme Court action nationalizes the political process: by enforcing national norms of constitutional law against state and
local governments, the Supreme Court treats the political system, and the political parties, as necessarily national. Thus
recent developments embody a double movement. National
political parties are strengthened while local parties are weakened, and national institutions, especially the Supreme Court,
are strengthened, while local governments are weakened.

Weakening Local Parties

Patronage. Political patronage systems in the past contributed to the development and maintenance of strong local parties. As Madison understood, local politics deals with matters that affect people's daily lives, but it has proven difficult to ensure sustained attention to local politics between elections. Patronage systems allow those who are elected to develop a political organization that will persist during these dull periods. They provide people with jobs, and therefore a motivation to support the organization beyond simple agreement with the policies it espouses; that additional motivation may lead them to publicize the policies more vigorously to uncommitted voters. Since the Jacksonian era, patronage systems have been an important part of the party system.

Patronage has been weakened in two ways. Civil service reformers, concerned about what they saw as the corruption and inefficiency of patronage-dominated local governments, successfully urged legislatures to create professional civil service systems. These systems require that merit be used in choosing public employees, and limit the role that political considerations can play. Most civil service systems bar public employees from participating in politics. For example, the federal Hatch Act prohibits federal employees in the civil service from taking "an active part in political management or in political campaigns," such as by serving as an officer in a political party or by soliciting funds for a political party. The Supreme Court upheld the Hatch Act in 1973, writing that the interests in "administering the law in accordance with the will of Congress, rather than . . . [that] of a political party," and in avoiding the appearance of political justice, were "obviously fundamental" (*United States Civil Service Commission v. National Association of Letter Carriers,* 1973).

Civil service systems are legislative products that weaken patronage. The Supreme Court itself has held that the free speech clause of the First Amendment prohibits parties that win elections from dismissing nonpolicy-making employees who supported the losing side (*Elrod v. Burns,* 1976; *Branti v. Finkel,* 1980). These decisions deprive local political parties of one of the resources they could use to attract supporters. According to the Court, patronage-based dismissals interfered with public employees' freedoms of belief and association. It rejected the arguments that patronage dismissals were needed to guarantee efficient support of the victorious party's program, and that they were necessary to preserve party politics.

The lower federal courts have responded to the Court's antipatronage decisions with unrelenting hostility, perhaps because the judges on those courts, closer to local politics, understand that patronage is an important mechanism of support for party systems. The Court was undoubtedly right in saying that patronage was not necessary, in any strong sense, to guarantee democratic responsiveness and the party system. Yet its holdings may overlook the utility, if not the necessity, of patronage. In weakening patronage systems, the Court may have contributed to the overall weakness of government, making it difficult for any government to accomplish its goals. At the same time, it may have enhanced the power of the national bureaucracy, which may perhaps be better placed to implement national programs on its own, without having to rely on local agents of the sort previously made available by strong patronage systems.

We should not overestimate the Supreme Court's contribution to weakening patronage. Civil service systems were adopted by legislatures, and the Court went along; civil service is undoubtedly a more important factor in the decline of local parties than the Court's antipatronage interpretation of the First Amendment. But the effects of these legislative and judicial programs are clear.

Reapportionment. For Madison, local control over drawing district lines was one of the formal mechanisms by which local governments would control the national one. By apportioning representation according to a variety of criteria—population, the economic importance of an industry to a state, and the

like—local politicians could strike deals and thereby enhance
the importance of local politics. Farmers who received representation disproportionate to their numbers would use the
state legislature to obtain programs they favored, thereby
reinforcing their localist attachments. But politicians would
have to apportion in ways that responded to the interests of
locally important groups, all of whom would then see state
governments as particularly important to them.

The Supreme Court's reapportionment decisions since
1964 have complex effects on the local political process, but
overall they, like the patronage decisions, have modestly weakened that process. The Court has enforced a rule of strict
equality of population in apportionment for the House of Representatives (*Karcher v. Daggett*, 1983). It has allowed somewhat larger deviations from strict equality in apportioning
local legislatures, particularly where the deviations result from
attempts to respect pre-existing political boundaries (*Mahan v.
Howell*, 1973). These decisions impose limits on the deals that
local politicians can make, substantially confining them to
trading on a pure population basis.

Such limits actually could strengthen local political organizations. Deprived of the currency of interest representation,
politicians might well use reapportionment to promote their
parties' interests within the bounds set by the requirement of
population equality. The Supreme Court endorsed one form
of political apportionment in *Gaffney v. Cummings* (1973), which
upheld a plan designed to place Democrats and Republicans
in the state legislature in numbers roughly proportional to the
statewide strength of the parties. But *Davis v. Bandemer* (1986)
disapproved political gerrymandering that would "consis-
tently degrade a voter's or a group of voters' influence on the
political process as a whole." As Justice Sandra Day O'Connor's dissent pointed out, this standard, or any other designed
to identify impermissible political gerrymandering, drives in
the direction of proportional representation. Because proportional representation has been so widely rejected in the American political system, *Davis* is unlikely to have significant effects
on apportionment, except insofar as it further discredits the

influence of politics on apportionment. Even that effect, however, contributes to the Court's message that local politics is less important than Madison thought. When such a message is sent often enough and in so many different ways, people may come to believe it.

The Voting Rights Act. The Fifteenth and, later, the Nineteenth Amendments altered the original allocation of authority to control voting by barring states from denying the right to vote on the basis of race and sex. Once these changes in the Constitution had been made, amendments prohibiting poll taxes and setting the voting age at eighteen seemed less significant in their implications for the Constitution's structure.

The Supreme Court invalidated a number of statutes that were designed to impede black voting: literacy tests that exempted voters whose parents or grandparents had been eligible to vote before the Civil War (*Guinn v. United States,* 1915), racial gerrymandering (*Gomillion v. Lightfoot,* 1960), and discriminatory administration of tests requiring that voters interpret the Constitution (*Schnell v. Davis,* 1949). Demonstrations in the South and lobbying in Congress convinced Congress that the goals of the Fifteenth Amendment would never be realized through the case-by-case processes of litigation. As a result, Congress enacted the Voting Rights Act of 1965. Among other things, the act barred the use of literacy tests in states where voter registration was so low as to suggest that large numbers of blacks were being unconstitutionally excluded from the franchise. It also prohibited the affected states from altering their voting practices until the Department of Justice or a federal court had determined that the new practices would not discriminate against blacks.

Initially in effect for five years, the Voting Rights Act was extended in 1970 and 1975. The ban on literacy tests was extended to the entire nation and made permanent; the "preclearance" requirement was extended indefinitely in 1982. The act's effects were dramatic. Black registration in the South grew rapidly, as did black influence on many statewide and some local elections there. The numbers of black elected officials in the South rose from near zero to the hundreds. The Supreme Court assisted this development in a series of decisions that gave the act a relatively broad interpretation, applying it to local decisions to reapportion, change the form of local government, and alter a city's borders by annexations that affected the racial make-up of the city.

Southern states attacked the act on constitutional grounds as soon as it was enacted. They argued that its provisions went beyond Congress's power to enforce the Fifteenth Amendment "by appropriate legislation," and that it unconstitutionally deprived states of their right to organize their polities as they chose. At the outset, the Court rejected these challenges easily enough. The history of racial discrimination in the South was so well known that the Court readily treated the act as providing remedies for prior discrimination that would effectively prevent its recurrence.

The expansive interpretations of the act, its extensions in 1970 and 1975, and its apparent successes raised new questions, however. The act applied when state laws "abridge or deny" the right to vote. It was easy to see that a test that was deliberately made more difficult for blacks than whites to pass abridged the right to vote. And, if a city annexed a suburb precisely in order to ensure that the city's black population would not become large enough to influence elections in the city, it was similarly easy to find an abridgement of that right. Where the annexation was not so motivated, though, and merely had the effect of making the black percentage in the city smaller, the gap between the ensuing vote dilution and an abridgement of the right to vote seems too large to some critics.

The Supreme Court held in 1980 that the Fifteenth Amendment itself barred only purposeful discrimination, but on the same day it agreed that the Voting Rights Act prohibited practices that had either the purpose or the effect of reducing black influence on elections (*City of Mobile v. Bolden,* 1980; *City of Rome v. United States,* 1980). When the act came up for renewal in 1981, the Reagan administration proposed that discriminatory "purpose" become the sole standard under the act. Civil rights advocates insisted that the act should also prohibit practices that produced discriminatory "effects." Proponents of the "purpose" standard argued that the only way one could determine that a practice had discriminatory effects was to see whether blacks were elected in proportion to their numbers in the population, and that proportional representation in matters of race smacked of a quota system. Eventually, Congress reached a compromise, adopting a "totality of the circumstances" test that explicitly made relevant the extent to which minorities had been elected to office but also explicitly denied that minorities had a right to proportional representation.

It may be doubted that this compromise is entirely coherent. The Court's 1980 decision established that it *is* constitutional. Developments in this area are consistent with several themes already identified. Pursuing one of the amended Constitution's goals—eliminating racial discrimination in voting practices—has weakened another of its goals—the preservation of state governments as important counterweights to the national one. In addition, the primary impetus for this process has come from Congress. The Supreme Court has, in the main, simply found that what Congress has done is permitted by the Constitution. As we have seen, this too is a Madisonian conclusion: federalism was to be protected by Congress, not the courts.

In the context of the Voting Rights Act, another of Madison's points deserves attention. After arguing that Congress would be sensitive to state and local interests, Madison addressed the question raised by claims that, from one observer's perspective, Congress has not been sensitive enough. Madison responded:

If . . . the people should in future become more partial to the federal than to the State governments, the change can only result from such manifest and irresistible proofs of a better administration as will overcome all their antecedent propensities. And in that case, the people ought not surely to be precluded from giving most of their confidence where they may discover it to be most due.

By noting that when the people perceive a "better administration" in the national government, they must perceive a worse one in the states, we might say that Madison foresaw the Voting Rights Act.

National Control of Party Structure

Smith v. Allwright. A series of cases challenging the exclusion of blacks from Texas's primary elections culminated in *Smith v. Allwright* (1944). The state Democratic party had adopted a rule prohibiting black participation in primary elections. The Court held that this rule was unconstitutional. It wrote that "the place of the primary in the electoral scheme" results from a "delegation of a state function." When such delegations occurred, the party's rules were controlled by the same constitutional restrictions that were applicable to the state itself.

Smith v. Allwright was an understandable reaction by the Court to the system of racial subordination prevailing in the South of the 1940s. Its continuing significance lies in its imposition of constitutional standards on political associations. This imposition subjects those associations to controls not of their own making. Robert Cover, discussing *Smith v. Allwright* in his article "The Origins of Judicial Activism in the Protection of Minorities" (1982), struck a Madisonian note when he cogently stated that "only by protecting the right of . . . groups to associate . . . can one have a community life that is antecedent and superior to the acts of the state. . . . If all political life must pass a test of healthfulness, those who control the testing apparatus have the means to substitute party and state for political society."

The elevation of the national government over party structure was not entirely due to Supreme Court decisions. Notably, the campaign finance innovations of the 1970s were produced by Congress. In a variety of ways, national campaign finance legislation contributed to an overall centralization of party efforts in elections for Congress as well as for the presidency. Presidential campaigns that accept public financing are required to limit the private funds they raise. The Supreme

Court held unconstitutional Congress's attempt to restrict expenditures by supporters of a candidate, if they act independently of the candidate's campaign. Although this ruling reduces the centralization that Congress sought, a more important impetus toward coordination was the effective encouragement of political action committees (PACs) by the 1970s campaign finance legislation. PACs raise money from contributors around the country. By strategically choosing the candidates to whom funds will be distributed, PACs promote the nationalization of politics. In addition, the national parties have developed for congressional elections campaign committees that use sophisticated techniques to coordinate expenditures. The complexity of the campaign finance legislation itself has produced a specialized, nationally oriented campaign finance bar. Finally, the national parties must impose central accounting and similar systems to ensure that local activists do not violate the campaign financing regulations.

These legislative and doctrinal developments have made the party structure subject to national control in many important ways. They have thereby continued the process by which the party system has shifted the locus of political organization from the state and local levels to the national level.

Support of Party Choice against Local Control. The Supreme Court has treated political parties as forms of political association. As a result, it has held that the First Amendment prohibits states from adopting certain regulations of party structure. *Smith v. Allwright* invoked the Fourteenth Amendment's ban on racial discrimination to prevent states from endorsing the party structures adopted by the parties themselves. By nationalizing the rules under which states could regulate the parties, it expanded participation while restricting the states' power to control the parties. The Court's First Amendment decisions, while only arguably promoting participation, have similar effects.

During the 1970s, the national Democratic party changed its rules, so that delegates to its national convention would be seated only if they had been selected by processes such as "closed" primary elections, in which only declared Democrats could vote. This rule conflicted with Wisconsin's longstanding practice of allowing open primaries, in which any voter could walk into a polling place on the day of a primary and decide which party's primary to vote in. Wisconsin sought to require the Democratic party to seat delegates bound by the results of an open primary, but the Supreme Court held that the First Amendment protected the national party's decision (*Democratic Party of United States v. Wisconsin*, 1981). The Court described the party's rule as an effort to ensure rank-and-file influence at the convention and to guarantee that the people who affected the convention's outcome were willing to identify themselves with the party and its chosen candidate. It agreed that parties could "protect themselves" from the inclusion of people whose views "may seriously distort [a party's] collective decisions . . . thus impairing the party's essential functions." Stating in the strongest terms that "a State . . . may not constitutionally substitute its own judgment for that of the Party," the Court dismissed as insubstantial the state's argument that open primaries encouraged voter participation.

The Wisconsin case involved a state effort to regulate the activities of a national party. *Tashjian v. Republican Party of Connecticut* (1986) involved a state effort to regulate the activities of a *local* party. There the state party wanted to hold an open primary, probably to attract moderate adherents to offset the strength of the ideologically committed members of the party who would dominate a closed primary. However, state law required that primaries be closed. The Supreme Court held that the statute violated the First Amendment rights of the party and its members: the state could not compel an unwilling party to hold a closed primary, just as it could not compel it to hold an open one. The open primary was a constitutionally protected "attempt to broaden the base of public participation in and support for" the party's activities, because the party's members were simply deciding that, for some purposes, they wished to associate with nonmembers. The Court rejected the argument that the state insisted on closed primaries to avoid raids by a party temporarily flooding its rival's primaries, because the statute barred *independents* from voting in party primaries. Nor could the state try to "avoid voter confusion" by trying to guarantee that Republican candidates adhere to "what the State regards as true principles"—the voters themselves were the agency to ensure truth-in-labeling.

As the Court stated in *Tashjian*, "the relative merits of closed and open primaries have been the subject of substantial debate since the beginning of this century, and no consensus has emerged." Closed primaries may promote more ideologically coherent parties; open ones may attract new voters excited by the conflicts of a particularly important primary. For present purposes, what matters is the Court's insistence that the decision about which system best promotes democratic values may not be made by the people of a state acting through their legislative representatives, but can only be made by the parties—or more precisely, by the parties' activists.

The Court *has* allowed the states some power to protect the integrity of the parties, but usually, as it said in *Tashjian*, "to prevent the disruption of the political parties from without, and not . . . to prevent the parties themselves from taking internal steps affecting their own process." For example, the Court upheld a "party loyalty" statute that denied a position on the ballot as an independent candidate to someone who had been a registered party member within the year preceding the election (*Storer v. Brown*, 1974). It also allowed New York to require that voters register their party affiliation at least thirty days before the general election preceding a party primary, which could be as late as eleven months later (*Rosario v. Rockefeller*, 1973). The Court did invalidate a similar party affiliation statute where the period of exclusion was twenty-three months (*Kusper v. Pontikes*, 1973). These cases involve state regulations that are consistent with the desires of the political parties. They are important to this discussion only because they illustrate the proposition that state decisions about party structure are subject to control according to the national norms embodied in the First Amendment.

Endorsing the Two-Party System. Justice Powell, dissenting in the Wisconsin case, noted that the two major parties had a

"special status" in the law. *Smith v. Allwright* rested in part on
the judgment that for blacks to be excluded from the Democratic party in the South of the 1940s was for them to be
excluded from politics altogether. This concern has led the
Court to endorse the two-party system as the means by which
politics is conducted in this country. It has done so largely by
upholding legislative attempts to protect the two-party system
against a variety of efforts to use the Constitution to weaken
those legislative protections.

As we have seen, one of the Court's reapportionment decisions upheld a redistricting plan that was designed to produce
a legislature whose membership mirrored the statewide
strength of the major parties. In a sense, this scheme en-
trenched the two-party system, though the difficulties that
third parties have in attracting support, whether statewide or
in particular districts, makes this effect rather unimportant.
More significant doctrinally is a portion of *Buckley v. Valeo*
(1976) that upheld federal financing for the major parties'
presidential campaigns, allowing Congress to provide such
funding for minor parties only if they meet rather stringent
requirements. Once again, the complex details of the legislation are not important here; as illustrations, consider that the
statute provides pre-election funding for the major parties and
only postelection funding for qualified minor parties, and that
it denies any funds to parties that fail to receive 5 percent of
the vote. The Court said that "public financing [was] an appropriate means of relieving major-party Presidential candidates
from the rigors of soliciting private contributions," and that
the 5 percent requirement "serve[d] the important public interest against providing artificial incentives to 'splintered parties and unrestrained factionalism.' " It argued that the different treatment of major and minor parties did not "reduce [the]
strength [of the minor parties] below that attained with public
funding." In addition, the relative position of minor parties
was in fact improved, because major party candidates who
accepted public funding had to accept a ceiling on expenditures. Justice William Rehnquist dissented, calling Congress's

action an effort to "enshrine" the major parties "in a permanently preferred position," which it certainly was.

The Court that made the *Buckley* decision relied on a series of cases in which it examined the restrictions that states placed on the ability of third parties to appear on the ballot. These restrictions typically prescribed the number of signatures that party petitions would have to have, and a time by which the petitions must be filed, before the party could appear on the ballot. The Court has invalidated some of these restrictions and has upheld others. For example, it struck down Ohio's requirement that independent candidates file their petitions in mid-March to qualify for the November ballot (*Anderson v. Celebrezze,* 1983), and upheld a Washington statute requiring that a minor party candidate receive 1 percent of the total votes cast in a primary election for an office, before being placed on the general election ballot (*Munro v. Socialist Workers Party,* 1986).

In the Court's analytical framework, the Constitution permits the states to assume that the two-party system is worth defending in itself. The states may attempt to preserve elections as arenas for "major struggles" by screening out candidates who do not make "some preliminary showing of a significant modicum of support," as the Court put it in upholding a 5 percent petition requirement (*Jenness v. Fortson,* 1971). The reason, it said, was that restricting access to the ballot could "avoid confusion, deception, and even frustration of the democratic process." It should be noted, however, that these dire results ensue from placing *minor* parties on the ballot; the Court simply assumes that the two major parties will be on the ballot, often without going over the same hurdles that minor parties must, and that confusion and deception occur when other parties are added.

Once again, we should note two points. The Court has assumed responsibility for supervising state systems of regulating elections, thus creating a national framework for such regulations. But, second, the Court is willing to tolerate, within that framework, state regulations that provide substan-

tial preferences for the major parties, so long as the states do
not go too far in burdening minor parties. Given the existence
of a national two-party system of relatively nonideological parties, the Court's analytical framework is entirely understandable. Yet it is not irrelevant to my theme that the Court has not
found any tension between the Constitution and the national
party system.

The Constitution and the
Future of National Politics

Three themes in the preceding discussion deserve emphasis
in any attempt to assess the prospects for politics resembling
what the framers contemplated. First, though the nationalization of politics has been endorsed and to some extent assisted
by the Supreme Court, the larger portion of the effects have
resulted from legislative initiatives. For example, compared to
civil service reform, the Court's inroads on patronage have
been relatively minor.

In addition, the transformation of American politics has
been the consequence of economic, population, and territorial
growth far more than it has resulted from deliberate choices
among competing visions of an appropriate form of politics.
The role of the national media in political campaigns and the
rise of PACs merely symbolize the effects of the overall expansion of the scope of politics.

Finally, virtually all the innovations that contributed to the
nationalization of politics seemed sensible when they were
instituted, and most continue to appear to have been worth-
while on balance. *Smith v. Allwright* and the Voting Rights Act
responded to the gross injustices of racial politics in the South.
The patronage systems of classic urban political machines promoted corruption and inefficiency, which civil service reform
remedies to a degree. It could have been expected that modern developments in campaign finance legislation would have
been shaped by the interests of the politicians whom the reformers sought to regulate; nonetheless, those developments
seem to have contributed to a healthy sensitivity to a question-

able degree of interaction between private money and public power.

One consideration ties these themes together. The nationalization of politics resulted from the normal, and at least in retrospect expectable, operation of the political system created by the Constitution. The constitutional framework, not the details of the Constitution or of Supreme Court decisions, is what made a difference. Of course, the difference it made was to undermine substantially the local attachments that played so large a part in the framers' understanding of how the national government could be both powerful and limited.

We might conclude our examination of this topic by considering whether it is possible to retrieve the balanced system that the framers envisioned. This volume's chapter by Shirley Abrahamson and Diane Gutmann suggests one possibility. State governments remain vital sources of legislative innovation; they have initiated antidiscrimination laws, sunset legislation, and other new devices for organizing government and regulating private activity that have been imitated elsewhere and, sometimes, adopted by Congress. Abrahamson and Gutmann suggest that similar innovations might be promoted by increasing reliance by state courts on state constitutions as sources of law. That would indeed make one branch of state government an important center of power. Consider, though, what we might call the underside of judicial review based on state constitutions. That form of review accomplishes something only if the state courts find in their constitutions guarantees that are absent from the U.S. Constitution. Such guarantees allow state courts to displace the judgments made by local legislatures. Often judicial review of this sort will succeed in altering local policy priorities. Sometimes, though, it will generate resistance on the familiar ground that courts should not displace the decisions made by democratically elected bodies. In the present context, there is a natural form that this resistance can take: voters can amend the state constitution, as they have in Florida and California on some criminal justice issues, to insist that their courts apply standards no more stringent

than those required by the national Constitution. Thus revital-
izing state constitutions might lead to greater centralization of
the law in some areas.

Finally, we can consider again the *Garcia* case mentioned in
my introductory comments. Four justices dissented from the
majority's refusal to hold unconstitutional a federal statute
regulating the wages and hours of those employed by state and
local governments. The dissenting opinions of Justices Rehnquist and O'Connor predicted that, as Justice O'Connor put
it, "this Court will in time again assume its constitutional responsibility."

Consider what it would mean to overrule *Garcia.* Justice
O'Connor would thereupon treat "state autonomy as a factor
in the balance when interpreting the means by which Congress
can exercise its authority on the States as States." Justice
Rehnquist did not exactly endorse his earlier formulation that
Congress could not "infringe upon certain fundamental aspects of state sovereignty that are essential to 'the States'
separate and independent existence,' " but, in refraining from
"spell[ing] out further the fine points of [the proper] principle," he did not exactly repudiate it, either.

It is always hazardous to predict how a balancing test will be
applied, but Justice O'Connor's concern for "the States as
States" suggests that merely overruling *Garcia* would do relatively little to revitalize local politics in a way that would have
mattered to the framers. Much the same seems true of Justice
Rehnquist's formulation. We might contrast the issue in
Garcia—the ability of state and local governments to set the
wages and hours of their own employees—with Madison's
statement about those governments in *The Federalist Papers.*
They were important to him, because they would regulate "all
the more domestic and personal interests of the people," "all
the objects which, in the ordinary course of affairs, concern the
lives, liberties, and properties of the people." That describes
not the wages and hours of state employees, but those of the
larger numbers employed in the private sector. Yet even the
dissenters in *Garcia* conceded the power of Congress to regulate private employers.

As an initial matter, one might have thought that what was essential to a state's existence, as Justice Rehnquist put it, was precisely the power to regulate "domestic and personal interests," so as to demonstrate to the citizenry the central role that state governments were to play in the constitutional scheme. Even he would not have gone so far as to deny Congress the power to displace the states in that sphere, which in itself shows how hard it would be to retrieve the system envisioned by the framers. One might pursue the framers' thought that the enumeration of powers in the Constitution—making them, as Madison put it, "few and defined"—was one guarantee of the importance of local government. Doing so would require one to repudiate the entire structure of constitutional doctrine erected at least since *Gibbons v. Ogden* (1824). However much one might quarrel with the details of that structure, though, it is clear that it is indeed faithful to the framers' desire to create a national government powerful enough "to be adapted to the various *crises* of human affairs," as John Marshall said in *McCulloch v. Maryland* (1819).

This leaves us with several conclusions. There is indeed a sense in which the Constitution undermined one of its premises. The overall success of the constitutional scheme meant that federalism could not be sustained in its original form. Nor, as the example of the Voting Rights Act shows, is it clear that we should want to do so. Nonetheless, there is something to be said for the proposition that vital local governments are a democratic good in themselves, promoting citizen participation in the public life of their world, and are important controls on an overreaching national government. If we cannot and perhaps should not retrieve a federalism of the sort the framers envisioned, at least we should understand what we have relinquished, and why.

7

The Influence of Judicial Review on Constitutional Theory

FRANK H. EASTERBROOK

Meaning and Review

Most debate about the role of judges is about the meaning of the Constitution. In an exchange between Attorney General Edwin Meese and two of the justices in 1986, the attorney general proposed a "jurisprudence of original intention." The justices, many scholars, and editorial writers everywhere replied that there is no interesting "intent." What was the framers' intent concerning wiretaps? The proposed constraint on judges' roles being empty, the argument proceeds, courts must draw rules from moral philosophy and enlightened modern opinion. Justice William Brennan proposed that judges engage in "a personal confrontation with the well-

FRANK H. EASTERBROOK is a judge of the United States Court of Appeals for the Seventh Circuit. He is also a senior lecturer for the Law School at the University of Chicago, where he formerly served as the Lee and Brena Freeman Professor of Law. He is an editor of the *Journal of Law and Economics.* Judge Easterbrook has written several books and many scholarly articles. Between 1974 and 1979 he served in the Office of the Solicitor General, ending as deputy solicitor general of the United States.

springs of our society" and derive "solutions of constitutional questions from that perspective." His goal is not interpretation of a text but implementation of a "constitutional vision of human dignity" that does not have any particular source but suffuses the document.

All participants in this exchange shared an assumption about the institution of judicial review. They assumed with Chief Justice John Marshall in *Marbury v. Madison* (1803) that "it is emphatically the province and duty of the judicial department to say what the law is"—or in a more modern version, "it is the province and privilege of the judicial department to say emphatically what the law is." And by judicial review they did not mean the self-denying version of *Marbury*, in which judges must decide what rules apply to the conduct of their own business. They meant the modern version of *Cooper v. Aaron* (1958), one in which no one else may disagree with the judges' conclusions, in which everyone must dance to the judges' tune whether party to the litigation or not. In this vision, there is no effective check on judges other than old age.

It was predictable that the next round would be a challenge to the power of judges to decide constitutional questions. Attorney General Meese proposed that judges' views are working hypotheses about the Constitution, binding on the parties but just suggestive or persuasive for the rest of us. The predictable response was that the attorney general had called for anarchy. He quickly retreated by saying that all he had meant is that although decisions of the Court are absolutely binding, people may ask the Court to reconsider, obeying all the while. The Court remained supreme in role as well as name.

Every constitutional argument today takes *Cooper* as a premise. Judicial supremacy is established. The debate is about the meaning of the commands. This debate has proceeded without regard to the link between the meaning of a document and the uses to which the meaning will be put. One cannot derive meaning without knowing the uses to be made of the meaning. The use influences which treatments are legitimate. Literary criticism may proceed on the basis of modern intuitions and innovative reflections precisely because it is designed to stimulate rather than govern. Philosophical interpretation may invent new worlds and revolutionary ethical systems, because it is meant to furnish a theory of life rather than govern an ongoing state. Constitutional interpretation is more confined; it is a process of holding an actual government within certain bounds. The power to issue *commands* on the basis of interpretation influences the theory of interpretation. Theories of meaning that do not recognize this stand in danger of destroying the basis of review. Whether other officers of government should do as courts say depends on *how* courts decide what to say—and much of judges' interpretive apparatus today derives from theories of meaning that cannot explain why others must obey.

Literary Versus Legal Interpretation

Let me give you an example that does not depend on the peculiar role of judges in a representative political system. Two new schools of literary criticism dominate the literature departments at major universities. One is "deconstruction," an approach to texts designed to bring out the contradictions that are concealed in any person's work. Deconstructors often deny that the deconstructed text has "meaning," because, after all, a contradictory syllogism has no meaning. The intellectual reward lies in the method, not in the power to reveal meaning. A second approach, often dubbed New Criticism, treats literary texts as artifacts. They are to be enjoyed according to the meaning that may be attributed by the reader. The reader's approach will vary with time, place, and experience. The process of generating meaning may be objective and disciplined, as it is for many New Critics, or narcissistic and indulgent, the pure reader-response vision of Stanley Fish's *Is There a Text in This Class?* (1980). In either case, a text is praised to the extent that it facilitates the attribution of evocative or provocative meanings; an interpreter is worthy to the extent that he or she can find these meanings. A text with a single or time-bound meaning will be forgotten, because it no longer stimulates readers' imaginations. New Critics are uninterested in what the writers may have wanted to convey. Readers, not writers, are sovereign. Just as people may find unexpected meaning in a painting, or discover in a photograph something the photographer did not know was in the frame, so interpreters may attribute new meaning to texts.

These methods free readers from the grasp of the authors' desires. The intentional fallacy had long been denounced. Few people today try to pin down the meaning of *Moby Dick* by looking inside Melville's head. You want to know the text, not the author. Modern literary criticism suggests that you need not be tied to the words, either. This is the last step of an approach carelessly attributed to Ludwig Wittgenstein. Words are appeals to readers; words have meaning only to the extent that they conjure up shared understandings; therefore, it is the readers rather than the writers who matter. Any interpreter can suggest a new understanding. If this prevails among a community of readers, it is acceptable.

The more clever the interpreter, the more surprising the meaning, the greater the scholarly reward. Hundreds of people need to write dissertations. Each wants to be novel. And for established scholars, rewards turn either on the ability to propose an unexpected meaning and attract adherents, or the ability to show that no one else can propose *any* acceptable meaning.

This is a productive academic enterprise. Too productive, too trendy. Legal scholars are beginning to use it as a model of constitutional interpretation. Ronald Dworkin's *Law's Empire* (1986) is a bearer of this law-as-literature flag. Dworkin is a New Critic who believes that the text of a legal document should be given the "best" meaning in light of concerns within the domain of moral philosophy. Dworkin uses the objective methods of the New Criticism, employing texts and community rather than the judges' private preferences as the source of rules. Others are not so encumbered. You can find traces of the deconstructive technique in the work of many other legal writers. Its employment is not confined to members of the Critical Legal Studies group. Suppose, though, we were to ask whether modern methods of literary criticism would be acceptable even within the literary world if interpretations were binding.

Suppose the people who chair the departments of English literature at nine universities were appointed as the Board of Literary Arbiters. The board would decide by majority vote which interpretations were acceptable. These would be taught everywhere, and any practitioner of literature who disagreed with the decision would be jailed. If a majority concluded that John Bunyan's *Pilgrim's Progress* was really about Buddhism or priestly homosexuality, or that *Moby Dick* was about the environmental problems of whaling (from whales' perspective), this would become dogma.

If this were the method of settling questions of meaning, we would quickly come up with different and more objective— more "intentional" or "originalist"—theories of meaning. Approaches to meaning that exalt novelty and creativity are acceptable only in a world where they are not the basis of penalties. We give scholars freedom from reprisal based on their ideas. The legal world, however, is one in which ideas govern conduct. Jail and fines are real. An approach to meaning that is useful in a classroom when provoking thought is not useful as a method of governance.

Modern Constitutional Theory

I shall define "modern constitutional theory" as the method that produces meaning for the Constitution by methods designed for literature. I also include theories in which law follows social or ethical philosophy. In general, I refer to any method of generating meaning that boosts the level of abstraction and applies the tools of literary criticism.

Again, an example: the Fourth Amendment says that you need probable cause to obtain a warrant and that all searches must be reasonable. The effect of these rules is to increase privacy. Therefore, the value secured by the Fourth Amendment is privacy. To decide whether a given action is prohibited by the Fourth Amendment, then, we decide whether it is inconsistent with a particular ideal of privacy. We assume that the Constitution supplies an answer; if it is not express then it must be implied. The act of implication follows the principle that the Constitution requires what is just, good, and consistent with principle. Here the principle requires us to define the ideal of privacy. We do not get this ideal from consulting what privacy meant in 1789 or from locating powers of government that allow curtailments of privacy. Text, history, and structure are as unimportant as the drafters' private intent, wealth, and marital harmony. We get the ideal from reason, perhaps informed by hopes for how society should develop or beliefs about how its "better part" has developed. We get the ideal, in other words, from a vision of the future rather than an understanding of our past. The theory of meaning then becomes a method by which the future pulls the present onward, rather than a method by which the experience and decisions of the past serve as anchors. It is not too far off to say that I have in mind by modern constitutional theory those sorts of arguments that would have unsettled Edmund Burke. The expositors include Dworkin and almost all professors of constitutional law at the major law schools. They also include Justice Brennan and a substantial chunk of the federal judiciary.

My thesis: judicial review and modern constitutional theory are incompatible. A theory of meaning that treats a legal text as if it were a poem or appeals to philosophy and hopes for a better future destroys the basis of judicial review. We cannot simply assume review and then argue about meaning. We must choose a theory of meaning that simultaneously allows review. None of the justifications for review works well with modern theories of meaning.

There are three common justifications for judicial review. Remember, what I mean by judicial review is not just that judges must follow the Constitution, but that everyone else is bound by the judges' interpretation. I shall call the three approaches the Hierarchy approach, the Ringmaster approach, and the Positivist approach. (You can tell that I, too, am tainted by modern theory. I've invented fancy titles for old ideas and insist that you indulge my whimsical vocabulary.)

The Hierarchy argument is that there are identifiable rules, with the Constitution at the top of a sequence. The Ringmaster argument is that whatever the rules, all people must play by the same rules; otherwise, there would be chaos. The Positivist argument is that whether or not there was a reason for judges to start issuing orders, they have done so, and obedience works better than the next best alternative. I examine each in turn.

The Hierarchy Approach

Chief Justice Marshall's argument in *Marbury* is the best of the Hierarchical arguments ever made. One of his major premises is that the Constitution is law—the supreme law, binding on all organs of government. Another premise is that these rules are sufficiently clear to be enforceable as law. Marshall gives the ex post facto clause as an example and asks rhetorically whether in case of clear conflict one applies the retrospective criminal law. The third premise is that the Constitution includes a hierarchy—that it is the supreme law and not just on a par with statutes and treaties. Finally, Marshall argues that every public official has a duty, by virtue of his or her oath if not the written nature of the document, to follow the supreme law in event of conflict. Written instruments are meant to have bite, and our Constitution not only is written but also establishes a system of limited government. If there are limits, then there are boundaries to be patrolled. Otherwise ours is not a limited government after all.

Although Marshall does not spell out the argument for other actors' obedience to judicial decisions, his approach fills every need. The Court must follow the Constitution rather than a law because there is no difference between a judge's duty and that of a member of Congress. The judge cannot accept Congress's answer. Congress and the president must follow the Court because the same syllogism that drives the

Court's action drives everyone else's. That is, there are understandable rules. They are laid down in the past and govern us all. To have identified the rule is to have identified the reason why all must obey. The Supreme Court's decision about the content of the rules prevails because of the definition of a rule, given to all of us alike. It is the basis of Alexander Hamilton's statement in *Federalist Paper No. 78* that judges have "neither FORCE nor WILL, but merely judgment"—an argument that Hamilton thought sufficient to support judicial review.

The demonstration was not flawless. Perhaps legislators' views on the constitutionality of their handiwork must be accepted. This is the practice in most other countries with written constitutions. Marshall replied that this would make the legislators rather than the Constitution supreme. A risk, no doubt—but Marshall's own view risks making the judges rather than the Constitution supreme. Why not the executive, which, like the court, stands apart from Congress? Why not whoever must decide the constitutional issue first (or last, as Thomas Jefferson suggested)? The method of deriving meaning does not ineluctably identify the ultimate interpreter. Whoever has the last word is supreme in a sense, and the dangers in giving the last word to Congress do not necessarily mean that judges were given that dangerous word in the original plan. Yet, flawed or not, the argument is the best that has ever been constructed.

Modern constitutional theories deny one or more of Marshall's premises. They deny, for example, that rules laid down in the past have content when applied to today's disputes. Perhaps they deny that rules laid down in the past bind us, even if they have content—perhaps especially if they have content. Why would we want to be ruled by slaveholders from their graves? To deny any of Marshall's premises, however, is to defeat the argument for review.

It is an interesting sidelight that people who deny the power of the past to rule today's affairs rarely deny the power of Article III to rule today's world. That is, they treat the judicial review as handed down by our forebears, not subject to question. I do not know why judicial review should be the only example of an established rule to escape modern scrutiny. Indeed, it is more open to a demand for justification. It cannot be found in the document. It is implied from the choice made in 1787 to have a written constitution. That, too, is part of Hamilton's argument. The judges' duty is "to declare all acts contrary to the manifest tenor of the Constitution void." This assumes that the document has a "manifest tenor." The writers thought it did, surely. We broke from England by having rules—and therefore enforcement of the rules—instead of having only practices and consensus, which are not enforceable by judges because they are always in political evolution.

The argument in *Marbury* depends on the choice to have a written constitution. It depends on a belief that the Constitution is law. Writing means the perpetuation of the ideas of the drafters. Law means rules. The ex post facto clause is there. We know, too, that states may not coin money, and that the president must be thirty-five years old. These govern because of the hierarchy of rules. We do not know that judges have the power to issue orders to other branches. That must be inferred. It must be rejustified constantly. Its scope is uncertain and may adjust to the theory of meaning advanced in the litigation.

That the Constitution is a dead hand is essential to judicial review. That the hand is dead and the words writ do not imply that society is fossilized. Quite the contrary, it ensures that change comes from the will of majorities rather than the will of judges. The fixity of the document does not stop the creation of new rights; it simply designates who, among the living, is authorized to speak for the living. I do not mean to condemn the method of philosophy; there is a powerful philosophy underlying the constitutional rules. It is a political rather than a moral philosophy, however. Locke and Montesquieu, rather than Rousseau, supplied the intellectual foundations for our system of government.

Chief Justice Marshall justified review by reference to the content of the rules at hand. For the next 100 years, judges and scholars such as Joseph Story, Eli Thayer, and Thomas Cooley took the same approach. The character of the rules in a hierarchy of rules supplied the foundation for review. Thus only clearly unconstitutional statutes could be set aside—otherwise, the rule-based quality was missing, and the Court could not supply the essential justification why its decisions must prevail. It is plain that no modern constitutional theory satisfies the criteria for judicial review that appear in *Marbury*. (The Civil War Amendments do not supply what is missing. They gave Congress and the Court power against the states, but there is no clue that they expand the Court's power against Congress or justify innovative theories. Their principal aim, after all, was to get rid of *Dred Scott,* not to enlarge the Court's discretion.)

One can say that a modern approach is "law" in the sense that it calls for reasoning of a certain form. This may be buttressed by a claim that the meaning of the Constitution includes authorization to adapt the rules to modern needs. This line of argument may show why the document is adaptable, but it does not supply the essential underpinnings of judicial review: that there be *one right answer* to a problem, and that the single source of that answer be the judicial branch. Adaptations commonly produce a range of admissible answers, and it is hard to say that choices about the identity of a range and selections within it can come from only one place in the government. An observation that the legal profession accepts some form of reasoning as sufficient to constitute "law" will not carry the day. The legal profession is not demanding obedience of itself. Judges must have a theory of meaning that will appeal to those who will be bound by their decisions, not just a theory that will appeal to those who propose to lay down the rules. The argument for placing the power to decide with judges must come from the Ringmaster approach, not the Hierarchy approach.

The Ringmaster Approach

There were problems with Marshall's argument. One is that no matter the logic, it still teases judicial review from structure rather than language. If review depends on structure, there are

other lines of argument. The Ringmaster argument is that, on
certain fundamental questions, we must speak with one voice.
Judicial review flows from the terror of the alternative—chaos.
So it seemed to Oliver Wendell Holmes, at least in part, for
he opined that the Republic would dissolve if the federal
courts did not have the power to declare state laws unconstitutional. It went without his saying that this meant having judgments obeyed. So it seemed to Learned Hand, whose argument in *The Bill of Rights* (1958) goes:

It was probable, if indeed it was not certain, that without some arbiter
whose decision was final the whole system would have collapsed.
. . . The courts were undoubtedly the best "Department" in which to
vest such a power, since by the independence of their tenure they
were least likely to be influenced by diverting pressure. It was not a
lawless act to import into the Constitution such a grant of power.

Why judges? Hand answers: because judges, free from pressure, will be most faithful to the decisions of the past. It is a
powerful argument. The governing documents are the work of
the past. Our history embodies wisdom exceeding that of tran-
sient majorities. To allow disobedience to judges' assessments
of the claims of the past is to remove that anchor—the
branches doing the disobeying are apt to be those whose judgment is least reliable. This is all very well, but there is a corol-
lary, which Hand acknowledged:

It was absolutely essential to confine the power to the need that
evoked it: that is, it was and always has been necessary to distinguish
between the frontiers of another "Department's" authority and the
propriety of its choices within those frontiers. The doctrine *presupposed that it was possible to make such a distinction,* though at times it is
difficult to do so.

The Constitution, in other words, is a set of boundaries rather
than a set of substantive rules. The vision works to the extent
that those boundaries are discernable.
    There are substantive rules. The First Amendment is a mat-
ter of substance. The substantive rules, however, were designed to ensure that we did not repeat what the framers saw

as the mistakes of England and its governance of the colonies. The substantive rules were seen as complements to a Lockean system of government. They, too, are anchors.

There is a second source of the judges' claims to be Ring-masters: dispassion. They are not elected or disciplined by voters and, therefore, are the most likely to carry out the plan of government (to the extent that it is not supposed to be responsive to the voters—the critical question). But, of course, one could name other scholarly figures in government, the solicitor general and the assistant attorney general for legal counsel being the most familiar. The difficulty with the "expertise" branch of the Ringmaster argument is that it seems disjointed from any particular theory of meaning, and we are trying to make the two work together.

One thing that any version of the Ringmaster argument cannot do is justify novelties. Suppose one can make a powerful moral argument that capital punishment is immoral. Will the Republic fall apart if some states use capital punishment and others do not? If some states permit abortion and others prohibit the practice? If the city of East Cleveland does not allow grandmothers to live with three grandchildren at once? The argument from chaos cannot establish that diversity of practice about debatable moral questions is baleful. Quite the contrary—many visions of utopia entail great diversity of moral views and the power of people to choose their polity. Because people are different, because moral views evolve, different practices and the power to choose (or move) are important elements of liberty.

The Ringmaster approach also cannot justify judicial review by the "inferior" federal courts and the state courts. (I use this term in its constitutional sense only.) There is one Supreme Court. There are fifty state systems. There are thirteen federal appellate courts, with 168 (authorized) active judges and more than 50 senior judges. There are more than 700 sitting district judges, each an independent agent. Someone filing suit in the federal court in Chicago may find the case assigned to any of 28 active and senior district judges, appointed by presidents from Roosevelt through Reagan, and the appeal will go to 3 randomly selected judges out of 15, appointed by the same nine presidents. Those looking for babble can do no better than to consult the inferior federal judiciary, whose opinions contradict each other on important questions aplenty. And remember that all of these judges purport to be interpreting the decisions of the Supreme Court.

Contrast this helter-skelter decision making with the order that would result if, for example, any decision of the attorney general, supported by an opinion of the Office of Legal Counsel, were to prevail unless set aside by a vote of the Supreme Court (maybe even by a super-majority). The attorney general's is a unitary voice, which can avoid self-contradiction and the splintering of plurality opinions. Much of the existing institution of judicial review simply cannot be justified by the argument that we need uniform declarations on important issues. And if it turns out that the Supreme Court not only sends conflicting signals but also is mathematically certain to keep doing so (and it is), we shall have to throw up our hands in resignation.

The argument that judges have a comparative advantage at preserving the past, the argument Holmes and Hand deployed to justify giving the whip to the judges, does not imply that judges have a comparative advantage at moving us to a better tomorrow. So modern theory is incompatible with the Ringmaster approach. Legislatures have a comparative advantage at innovation, as presidents have a comparative advantage at foreign affairs—and on that account are generally let alone by judges. Judges' insulation ensures that they do not have a comparative advantage at divining the institutions that best suit society. On this score it does not matter whether the maxim is human dignity, wealth, or utiles. Any complex society has a way of surprising those who predict how legal rules will affect human welfare or dignity. One of the great discoveries of modern social science is that people's responses to rules often mean that the rules achieve the opposite of their intended objective, as legislation meant to "protect" women from the rigors of overtime work protected them out of their jobs, for employers turned to men who were allowed to work longer hours.

Detachment has the same effect on the academic lawyers who supply constitutional innovations to judges. These come from a small stratum of society and have tenure. I served on the faculty of the University of Chicago, which is thought very conservative. What that means is that 40 percent of the faculty voted for Reagan in an election in which Reagan got 60 percent. A middle-of-the-road faculty like Yale is one at which 90 percent voted Democratic and 10 percent voted Socialist. A liberal faculty is one in which no capitalist can be considered for appointment—and there are several. This does not suggest to me that the cloisters of the academy or of the bench conduce to keen insight into modern conditions.

The Positivist Argument

Berkeley political scientist Martin Shapiro may be the most blunt of the Positivists. He says: don't trouble me for justifications. Argument is silly. This is government, not argument. Judicial review works. It is what we do. Every government does what it does. In England the queen has all power, except that she can exercise none. The rule of decision in England is that Parliament is dictator. The rule here is that courts make moral judgments, Q.E.D.

The argument can be made more formally. We will scrounge H.L.A. Hart's *The Concept of Law* (1961) for the term "rule of recognition" and opine that our rule of recognition is not the written Constitution but judicial approbation. A law must pass certain forms (approval by the political branches) and secure moral blessing by a court. That is simply the rule. We can put it in many ways. Stanford law professor Thomas Grey says that we have two constitutions, written and unwritten, and that all governmental action must comply with each. Bruce Ackerman, professor of law at Columbia University, says that we have had three revolutions—or conventions of the people—the most recent during the depression, when this convention approved the welfare state. The invisible convention left an unwritten amendment transferring an unspecified amount of authority to Congress. The scope of this new authority will be identified by judges. The locutions are varied, but the result is always that acceptance of judges' words is the authority to demand obedience.

The Positivist approach should sit uncomfortably with exponents of modern constitutional theory. Moral theories contain oughts. The Positivist approach has no oughts. It tells us only what is, what has so far been the practice of governance. The Positivist approach cannot say that President Nixon ought to turn over the tapes when the Court says so, or that President Eisenhower ought to send soldiers to Little Rock to desegregate the schools. If the "right to travel" is a "right" only in the same way the prime minister has a "right" to have the queen read her speech to Parliament, then it is also lawful for the government to change. You cannot derive an *ought* from an *is.* If Congress passes a court-stripping bill, that is OK too. If President Jackson tells Chief Justice Marshall to enforce his own decision, or if President Lincoln ignores a writ of habeas corpus, we cannot pronounce the result other than a success. If President Truman had ignored *Youngstown Sheet & Tube Co. v. Sawyer,* no one could have complained.

You can get around this by explaining why Truman should obey, but the explanation will be driven back to the Ringmaster approach. The only alternative is a utilitarian argument. Heaven forfend that modern theory should appeal to utilitarian arguments! I have avoided them similarly. One cannot mine from the work of Jeremy Bentham a theory of judicial review that will appeal to Professor Dworkin.

The Positivist argument is no argument at all. It is an observation. The observation that a practice "works" does not supply a justification for the continuation of the practice. So far as I can tell, the one-house veto "worked" in curtailing some excessive uses of delegated powers. Nonetheless, in 1981 the Supreme Court held the legislative veto unconstitutional. Only Justice Byron White thought the practical effects of the device mattered. The Court as a whole did not deduce the propriety of the practice from its longevity or its success. A Court that is scrupulous to limit other branches' authority without regard to longevity and success must be equally scrupulous about the justification for its own authority.

People seek to justify judicial review, and the Positivist approach does not. It may explain review with old theories of meaning, but it cannot explain even the function of review with new approaches to constitutional theory. It cannot explain review in this country when other civilized states from England to Sweden do not have the institution. Only Germany among other western democracies has the American style of judicial review. France has three separate systems of courts, each with some power to make constitutional declarations. The French have slogged along for some time, without visible ill effects, with enduring conflicts among these three "highest" courts—each supreme in its domain, and none supreme in some domains. Even Canada's bill of rights, modeled on ours in many respects, has a clause allowing provinces to exempt most statutes from judicial review.

The usual complement of an unwritten constitution is an absence of judicial review. The Law Lords may say on occasion that "the Queen were deceived," but this is just a stalling tactic. If the prime minister insists, she will be obeyed. Constitutional review under an unwritten constitution is, at best, "constitutional common law."

Thoughtful exponents of modern constitutional theory will admit this. One good example is Professor Robert Cover's candid confession, buried in a footnote at the end of "Nomos and Narrative" in the *Harvard Law Review* (1983), that arguments from philosophy make everyone a judge. As he says: "I accord no privileged character to the work of judges. I would have judges act on the basis of a committed constitutionalism in a world in which each of the many communities acts out its own *nomos* and is prepared to resist the work of judges in many instances." If Truman reasons to a conclusion about steel mills in the way judges do, he may act on his own conclusions. The problem is endemic. Dworkin ultimately cannot give a reason why the work of judges is entitled to more respect and authority than Dworkin's own. An argument that gives judges and professors equal standing cannot explain or justify so distinctive an institution as judicial review.

An argument that makes review turn on the supposition that there are "right" answers to questions of moral philosophy ultimately cannot justify judicial review. Most interesting moral questions are no better settled today than they were before Socrates, and it is risible to suggest that the practical men who met in Philadelphia either secretly adopted a view on these contentious questions or silently authorized the unelected branch of government to run the country based on the ethical views that they should come to hold 200 years later. Religious leaders and philosophers through the ages have failed to turn moral philosophy into a system of governance; why should anyone trust former senators, ex–attorneys general, and the others on whom the lot falls to be justices to do better?

Modern constitutional theory does not justify the Positivist approach. The Positivist approach does not justify judicial review. If presidents disobey the court, we are simply embarked on another experiment and will have a new form of government. And since most western democracies have satisfactory government without judicial review, we cannot very well object, because the Positivist argument does not depend in any way on the instrument that separates us from the United Kingdom—our written Constitution.

The Meaning that Supports Judicial Review

Having said all this, let me be clear that I do not think that judicial review is in any trouble. The *Marbury* version is quite hearty—so long as we accept the Constitution as law and confine the theory of meaning to divining rules that fairly bind all branches and do not depend on the will of the interpreter for force. One could even argue that so long as judges regulate only their own conduct, they may take a more expansive version of meaning. They may, for example, proclaim that they will no longer impose punishments once thought acceptable.

The theory of meaning allows more latitude to a branch regulating its own conduct than it does to a branch demanding obedience from the president, Congress, and the states.

Where does this leave us? I think that if we select a form of modern constitutional theory, we end up with no justification for judicial review. We cannot give a reason other than practical politics why the president should pay more attention to a judicial order than to Ronald Dworkin's next article. In all likelihood, Professor Dworkin's article will be better reasoned. When a judge is driven to say: "This document from an earlier day really does not have a meaning, so the living must settle their own affairs," he has given a dispositive reason why he may not demand that everyone else accept his solution. The living speak in appointed ways through legislation rather than through mandarins. To find a justification for review, we must appeal to the quality of the Constitution as law. When we observe that the Constitution is valueless or irrelevant when applied to a modern problem or stands for "human dignity" but not rules, we have destroyed the basis for judicial review. We are left with the fallback, a perfectly acceptable fallback: republican government.

This is not a new observation. Thayer was there long ago. I have not said anything here that would surprise the original Justice Marshall. What I seek to leave you with is that few of today's constitutional scholars, few of the sitting justices, are concerned with producing a theory of meaning that is congruent with a theory of judicial review. The late Alexander Bickel of Yale Law School tried to produce such a theory with partial success. Charles Black, also from Yale, has tried. John Ely, dean of Stanford Law School, has tried. U.S. Court of Appeals Judge Robert Bork has tried. And there are indeed approaches that can supply meaning and review at the same time. These are all rather modest in their claims for the malleability of the Constitution and the power of judges. Black, for example, would let judges roam at the end of a tether, an unbridled power in Congress to withdraw jurisdiction.

The theories that cope well with meaning and the power of review are modest ones. They are theories in which judges are brakes on change rather than the instruments of change. They are theories in which judges answer to a vision of republicanism rather than communalism. They are theories in which people rather than groups hold rights against the political branches. They are theories in which these rights secure the Republic against identified threats rather than established "values" on which new entitlements may be built. They are theories in which the Constitution is law, a set of rules, rather than an empty vessel into which modern theorists pour their own hopes and visions of a better society. They are theories in which the judges are the living voices of the past rather than the sirens of the future. That is, I believe, as it should be.

Technological Change and the Constitution: Preserving the Framers' Balances in a Computer Age

ALAN F. WESTIN

"May I See Your Credit Card, Dr. Franklin?"

Suppose we could use H. G. Wells's (or Captain James T. Kirk's) time machine and transport the fifty-five framers of the Constitution from Philadelphia in 1787 to the bicentennial celebrations of 1987. They would look with wonder at the continental spread of the nation, the size and diversity of its

ALAN F. WESTIN is professor of public law and government at Columbia University, where he has taught since 1959. He has his law degree and his doctorate in political science from Harvard University. Over the past thirty-five years, he has maintained parallel interests in constitutional law and the impacts of technology on individuals, institutions, and society. His books include *Privacy and Freedom, Databanks in a Free Society, Information Technology in a Democracy* (editor), and *The Changing Workplace.* He served as a presidential appointee on the National Wiretapping Commission, helped draft the Federal Privacy Act of 1974, and was senior consultant to the Privacy Protection Study Commission. He has chaired and served on many panels of the U.S. Congress's Office of Technology Assessment and teaches a course at Columbia on "The Impact of Information Technology on American Democracy."

population, the economic wealth that has been accumulated, the urban centers and suburban rings we had created, and many other features of the contemporary United States of America.

But it would probably be the sweeping technological changes our society has produced that would most dazzle the men of Philadelphia. Among the changes they would catalog would be these shifts from their time to ours:

from horse and carriage to auto, train, and jet.

from verbal communication and physically transported writings to telephone, television, and telecommunication networks.

from the citizen's musket over the mantlepiece to nuclear devices, intercontinental missiles, and chemical warfare.

from horsedrawn plows to mechanized agribusiness.

from wood stoves and candles to electricity, oil heat, and nuclear power.

from barrel makers and silversmiths to automated assembly lines and a global marketing economy.

from a medicine of leeches and purges to a wonder drug, high-tech health care system.

and, from an era of police lurking under the eaves or climbing through windows to search to an era of microminiaturized listening devices, videotaping, and computerized file matching.

After they had taken in the enormity of these technological changes, we can imagine the men of Philadelphia asking their contemporary hosts one basic question:

Pray tell us, have these powerful technologies, and especially those that have come on so rapidly in the decades since your World War II, had direct impact on the structure and processes of constitutional government? More specifically, have they worked significant changes in the four central elements of the Constitution (and the Bill of Rights) that we left you as our legacy: separation of powers, federalism, representative government, and individual rights?

How would we answer the framers?

Constitutionally Relevant and Irrelevant Technologies

Technologies involving energy, transportation, production, food, and medicine obviously exert enormous effects on our economic, social, and personal lives. And weapons technology creates the perilous world of nuclear confrontation and portable terrorism we inhabit so nervously today.

Such technologies create major substantive areas for government action, to promote, regulate, and sometimes prohibit. They lead us to create new government agencies and, taken all together, help explain the rise of independent regulatory agencies as a "fourth branch of government."

But, I submit, these kinds of technologies do not affect our constitutional structure and processes per se.

Two other technologies *could* have such effects. These technologies deal with that unique commodity on which government depends for its understanding and decisions, the governors use to administer programs (and also to protect their institutional positions), and the governed rely on to protect themselves and inform their participation. That commodity is *information,* and the two relevant technologies dealing with information are *television* and *computers.*

Television collects information from anywhere in the global village and, through the filter of those directing the "coverage," presents the images of events, people, and transactions directly to the people watching the screen. Most analysts assessing the impact of television over the past twenty-five years would advise the framers that television has helped to weaken political parties (by giving candidates an independent route to the minds and pocketbooks of constituents); has helped some presidents greatly in their relations with Congress and the

public (the "Great Communicator" Reagan) but has harmed
other presidents (Nixon and Watergate or Johnson and Vietnam); and has sometimes helped dramatize serious social injustices, and thereby assisted in their correction by legislation
or judicial decision (as with TV coverage of Southern segrega-
tionists attacking civil rights demonstrators). Television's high
costs have also reinforced the advantages of wealth in American politics, and some believe the "thirty-second political
commercial" with its distortive potential is almost grounds for
removing First Amendment bars to forbidding such practices.

Despite these impacts of television on our political processes, and on the effectiveness or ineffectiveness of political
leaders, I submit that television has still not had a direct effect
on the four central elements of the constitutional blueprint.

This brings us to computers. More precisely, it brings us to
the blend of computer hardware and software, communication
systems, and management science techniques that is increasingly called *information technology.* We would quickly brief the
framers to understand that our's was becoming an information-based society, in which almost all government agencies,
businesses, and nonprofit organizations now own computers
(large, medium, or small) or depend on data processing services. We would sketch for them how large-scale computerized
data bases of information about individuals, groups, events,
and transactions are now relied on to book an airplane ride,
buy an umbrella at a store with a credit card, qualify for government welfare payments, learn whether someone stopped
by the police for speeding is wanted on suspicion of crime
elsewhere, or keep track of exposure of workers or communities to radioactivity. And where once computer systems were
the tools of the already rich and powerful, when systems were
composed of huge mainframes and facilities to house them,
and platoons of high-paid systems experts and programmers
were needed to write their instructions, we had progressed to
an era of cheap, easy-to-use, distributed computing, available
on desktop or even laptop. Today, the American Civil Liberties Union, Jessie Jackson, Jerry Falwell, Ralph Nader's organi-

zations, Cesar Chavez, and the *National Review* all depend on computers to massage their membership, readership, or contributor lists. The fearsome cry "the computer is down" strikes terror into the hearts of black and white, officials or citizens, or liberal, conservative, and middle-of-the-roader alike. Given the ubiquity of information technology, and our heavy dependence on it to carry out the business and affairs of contemporary life, there is a proper sense in which we should regard computers as a *control technology,* and ask whether its potential to change the nature, form, and distribution of information for *public* affairs has—or could—affect basic balances of the constitutional system.

Potential Effects of Information Technology on the Constitutional System

When computer systems began their penetration into organizational affairs in the 1960s, and as their use expanded in the 70s and 80s, social analysts began to warn that the power of this new tool could lead to major power shifts in our constitutional balances. Specifically:

1. Computer power in the hands of executive agencies of federal and state government could enhance the power of those agencies against legislative oversight and control, or diminish the capacities of the judiciary to apply constitutional limitations, thereby upsetting the checks and balances system.
2. Large-scale computerization might expand national power over social programs in ways that would curtail the independence and vitality of state and local government, undercutting healthy federalism.
3. The growth of large databanks and computerized operations could shrink the openness and availability of government information to the public, and to the interest groups and media who facilitate "the people's right to know" what government is doing. Also, advanced computer opera-

tions might lessen the meaning (and incentives) for citizen participation, as policies became more "technocratic" and less "democratic" in execution.

4. Finally, critics warned that computerized data systems in government, collecting and integrating millions of personal records on citizens, could result in massive loss of privacy, denial of due process, and chilling effects on expression and dissent.

These fears make up what might be called the "negative case" or the Orwellian scenario when contemplating the spread of information technology in our era.

There has also been a 180-degree different line of analysis about the potential and the tendencies of information technology for our constitutional system. Some technological enthusiasts have said that computers could be the best thing for constitutional government since the framers did their work in Philadelphia:

1. By providing more information-based and "rational" resources for policy decisions, and developing improved feedback as to program effects, the use of information technology could enhance cooperation between the executive and legislature, and give the judiciary sounder bases for reviewing the actual effects of government programs.

2. By better connecting the contributions and activities of federal and state governments in national social and regulatory programs, information technology could reduce the fractionalizing of policy administration and support the "marble-cake" reality of intergovernmental administration.

3. Proper use of information technology could enhance the public's access to government information, and the development of electronic plebiscites and direct citizen input through telecommunications could expand citizen participation.

4. Finally, because computer systems improve the ability of government to identify individual differences and respond to them, automated information systems can enhance the

diversity of treatment of citizens while protecting those dimensions of rights that call for equality and due process.

In short, we would note to the framers, we have a line of optimistic forecasting that competes vigorously with the pessimistic analysis first reported.

Applying the Framers' Perspectives to Technology Forecasting and Assessment

Once they had learned about the proliferation of information technology, and had been exposed to the pessimistic and optimistic scenarios just summarized, the framers could be expected to offer several general observations derived from their considerable experience with human nature, political processes, and governmental institutions. Drawing on their knowledge about governance from the days of Periclean Athens and the Roman Republic down through Dutch, Swiss, and English constitutional struggles of the sixteenth to eighteenth centuries, they might remark as follows:

"Dear Fellow Republicans, we could not tell a modem from a moped, but we believe we have learned some things about politics and government that would surely be applicable to your age of computers.

"First, it is prudent to assume that new and powerful tools *will* be taken up and used by those in power to advance both the programs they believe in and their capacity to carry those programs out more effectively against opponents inside or outside the government. Therefore, to the extent that new tools *do* confer greater power and cannot be easily matched or overcome, assume that what can be done effectively and what is not flagrantly in violation of public values will probably be sought to be done.

"Second, do not, as a consequence of assuming the worst case, underestimate the forces of custom and inertia, or assign too little strength and vitality to those institutions and processes we gave you for controlling abuses of power. If our checks and balances have not been allowed to fall into disrepair and disuse, do not assume they will be easily thrust aside.

"Finally, when looking at opportunities to improve institutions and processes through new tools, take carefully into account existing interests and beliefs, and consider where the energy and power must come from for such innovations to prevail."

Having reminded ourselves of how the framers would have approached the tasks of technology assessment and forecasting, let us see what we think *has* taken place over the past several decades in terms of information technology impacts on our constitutional system, examining both the pessimistic and the optimistic scenarios.

Information Technology and Separation of Powers

First, despite the proliferation and accomplishments of computer systems in federal and state executive agencies, and the growing dependence of those agencies on computer operations, there have been from early days and *there continue to be* major system design problems and internally destabilizing effects of agency automation. This stems partly from the dynamic and constantly changing arrangements of hardware, software, and telecommunication techniques that make up computer systems. Hardly has an organization settled down to digest what it painfully accomplished with second- or third-generation computer systems when the fourth and fifth generations arrive and wholesale rearrangements and uncertain applications are undertaken.

In addition, after mastering what can be seen as the "easy tasks" of computerization—automating the most objective and routine information-processing functions in government work—most agencies are now attacking far more complex problems. They are seeking to provide more customized services to clients, apply more fine-grained decision-making criteria set by legislators, replace experienced employees with software driven decision systems, improve real-time feedback on operations and trends, and support powerful management information systems for planning and decision making.

Given these realities, accurate observers of agency automation are aware that failures, mishaps, and sheer confusion accompany almost all the experiences of agencies in using information technology. The Social Security Administration, the Internal Revenue Service, the Veterans Administration, and other large computer users, to cite only federal examples, have troubled histories of computer use, and remain caught up in difficult struggles with their present ambitious systems. In short, applications of information technology to the complexities and contradictions of public policy implementation have not been easy, nor have they overcome, even today, serious problems in service delivery and management effectiveness.

This is critical to understand because it helps explain why neither the Congress nor the Supreme Court has lost significant power thus far as a result of executive branch computerization. There was a short period in the mid–1960s, when the so-called McNamara Thrust seemed to mark a pronounced shift of authority away from congressional oversight and toward "expert" executive decisions. This stemmed from the reliance by Defense Secretary Robert McNamara and his cadre of systems analysts on computerized support systems for cost-benefit analysis of defense policies and programs. The language and techniques of program budgeting and systems analysis were touted as a new and scientific approach to policy making, for both foreign and domestic affairs. Congress members and their staffs were sometimes portrayed at that time as traditionalists who lacked both the technical (computer and management science) resources to match the computer printouts of the McNamara team and also the "disciplined mind set" to formulate and support alternative policy positions.

At least as early as 1966–67, that situation had been corrected, from a separation of powers standpoint. Congressional staffs and their support agencies (the General Accounting Office, for example) challenged the cooked computerized statistics of the Defense Department (for the "Safe Village" program in Vietnam, for example), and the mystique of "system analyzing" was exposed by the objective realities and deep policy dissents over the war. On the domestic side, Congress quickly learned how to use its powers of authorization for new agency computer systems, its appropriation controls over spending for machines and personnel, its rules for procurement of ADP equipment, and its oversight powers over program operations and fidelity of agencies to congressional policy directives to keep agency uses of information technology within the bounds that the legislative branch considered wise.

A good example was the total rejection by Congress of the Internal Revenue Service's proposal in 1974 to create a massive automated Tax Administration System. Operating through a panel of its Office of Technology Assessment, Congress examined the IRS proposal for its consideration of issues such as tax equity, privacy, security, and control over large-system complexities, and simply said "no" to the IRS.

The Supreme Court can be seen to have had even less trouble in adapting to the computer age. As long as the justices define what the questions for constitutional decision and interpretation are to be, and as long as they control what elements of the information provided to them by the executive or the legislature the judges will treat as relevant, the Supreme Court retains its customary powers to hold executive actions within the boundaries of what the justices apply as constitutional interpretation. In none of the major Supreme Court decisions of the past twenty-five years involving intergovernmental powers—from the Nixon tapes case to the legislative veto case—has the role or the authority of the judiciary been affected by information technology arrangements. All the computer systems in the federal establishment cannot break through the Court's jurisdictional filter, nor do they change the concepts of rationality and constitutional presumptions that the justices apply.

To sum up, separation of powers and the checks and balances system that reinforces it are alive and well in the computer age. The executive has not blown the other two branches away. Nor has information technology dissolved the interbranch conflicts intended by the framers. Because the framers' concept *requires* president and Congress to compete for authority, policy differences and political considerations inevitably overcome any semblance of "increased rationality" or "empirical data proofs" that executive agency computer systems might offer.

Information Technology and Federalism

By the time that computers entered government administration in the 1960s, federalism had already developed into the post–New Deal cooperative system in which the nationalization of social and economic affairs, the power of federal funding, and the sources of program initiatives had moved decisively to the national government. The question posed by computer use was whether this would propel the federal government even farther into control through centralization of data and its management, or whether state and local governments might use computers to redress or even reverse the "power to Washington" trends of 1934 to 1960.

Again, early developments proved rather misleading. Because of the cost-effectiveness factors in third-generation computing—which were based on giant mainframes holding centralized data bases and accessed by thousands of near or remote terminals—it seemed that either central or at least regional databanks in fields such as welfare, health, or law enforcement would be "inevitable." In such a "technology driven" arrangement, central rules, central databanks, and central oversight would be in Washington and its regional offices, leaving a reduced "local administration" under uniform systems to state and local government.

Both technological changes and political realities thwarted that scenario. Technologically, the development of midsized, micro, and desktop computers, and of cheap telecommunications, made it cost-effective to put both computing power and data bases wherever an organization or a group of cooperating governments chose to locate those resources. As a result, technology no longer dictated highly centralized information systems; depending on what organizations sought to do and how they wanted authority and responsibility to be distributed, they could choose high, medium, or low centralization, and various combinations thereof.

Secondly, political debates over the proper role for "Washington" began in the 1970s and have continued in the 1980s to be far more important in defining the relative power positions of the federal and state governments than the configuration of computer systems. For example, invoking the tradition of state and local predominance in law enforcement and citizen fears about a "national police force," the states, through their representatives in Congress, beat back efforts by the FBI during the 1970s and early 80s to win congressional approval to build a centralized computer system for criminal history records. This was attacked as a threat to state and local law enforcement autonomy, a potential threat to civil liberties, and an unwise increase in police power (by having a police agency control the records also needed by prosecutors, defense counsel, courts, probation, and corrections to carry out their roles in the criminal justice process). The result was that the FBI was allowed to build and improve its National Crime Information Center, which handles wanted person and stolen property records centrally and has local, state, and national police agencies as its users; but the FBI was *not* allowed to build a central National Criminal History Record System. Today, development efforts are proceeding to test a system of central national indexing but retaining storage and control of the actual records by the state agencies. Such a politically crafted system, now entirely supportable by technological capacities, illustrates the primacy of policy over technology in the federalism domain.

It also illustrates that many state and local governments have become adept, experienced, and effective in applying information technology to their own tasks, and offering quite powerful alternative models where there are shared or overlapping governmental functions involving federal and state or federal, state, and local relations.

In short, federalism choices and arrangements remain issues

of social and political policy; they have not been transformed or dictated by technology.

Information Technology and Representative Government

Since campaigns, elections, and the party system were not addressed in the Constitution, the two elements of representative government that need to be examined in terms of information technology impacts are public access to government information and the general level and quality of citizen participation.

The negative scenario warned that shifting information from paper to machine-readable records might diminish the "people's right to know." The assumption was that computerized data bases, accessed through software programs, might be less comprehensible to information seekers, allow the hiding or misdescription of relevant data, increase the cost of getting data, or make less traceable the way in which government decisions were now being made. These concerns, the framers would recognize, are not unfounded, given the long history of efforts at government secrecy, and the tension between executive claims to temporary privacy for responsible decision making and the claims of Congress, the media, and the public to know what government is doing.

Because both freedom of information and privacy became central issues in the late 1960s and early 70s, Congress acted to ensure that no techniques of data handling, automated or manual, would defeat basic rights of access. The Federal Privacy Act of 1974 required federal agencies to publish complete lists of the record systems they maintained (with personal information in them) and guaranteed inspection (and challenge) rights to *record-subjects*. The 1974 amendments to the 1966 Freedom of Information Act (FOIA) strengthened rights of *public* access to information held by the federal government. While neither statute addressed computers per se (unlike European data protection laws, which focused on the technology), the two laws, operating together, have effectively facilitated public access at the federal level. (And, a parallel situation developed in state and local settings.)

In a 1974 field study of how Congress, interest groups, the media, and social critics felt that computerization had affected their existing ability to access government information, I found that (1) computerization as such was not as important as the legal rules and administrative practices in determining the availability of what was sought; and (2) the information seekers reported that, on the whole, and where well-designed systems were present, automation was *improving* the precision, timeliness, and responsiveness of federal agencies to their requests.

When I reexamined this situation in 1984, two conclusions emerged. The facilitating effect of computerization per se continued as before. But the *policies* of the Reagan administration were seen as reducing the timeliness and quality of information sought. Public affairs and freedom of information staffs had been drastically reduced; a policy was followed of requiring lawsuits under FOIA rather than compliance upon request; and whole bodies of information were being sold to the commercial sector for fee-based distribution, where they had once been well disseminated by federal agencies free or at low cost.

Again, information technology was decisively shaped by political and legal debates and their outcomes. And, as the framers would be happy to observe, the tradition of extraordinary openness of American government was well preserved, despite policy issues in the Reagan administration's approach to public access.

On the other hand, efforts to use information technology to *improve* dramatically the public's right to know, or its electoral participation, have not materialized as yet. Despite passionate advocacy by consumer leaders such as Ralph Nader, we do not put public computer terminals in shopping malls or ghetto storefronts and let citizens look up which stores or manufacturers violate safety, health, or other regulatory rules. We *could* do this, but we choose not to spend public dollars that way.

Nor have we designed and funded the "electronic democracy" experiments which would frame key public policy issues and put them to citizen expression or formal vote through terminal, telephone, or two-way television. Two reasons explain this. First, there are serious problems which the framers would quickly recognize in the agenda selection, issue framing, deliberation periods, and binding aspects of such electronic plebiscites. Second, such schemes address the participation of the 60 million "haves" who are already interest group members and active voters, rather than the 40 million "haveless," who are the nonjoiners and nonvoters in our society. Unless a serious political movement to bring nonparticipants into the system were to be the driving force of electronic democracy, the disadvantages of such proposals have been seen as far outweighing their supposed advantages.

Information Technology and Individual Rights

Perhaps the most publicized fear about computerization was that this would lead, inevitably, to the collection of more personal information about people; the consolidation and amalgamation of information from different records; the reliance on such systems to control people's benefits, rights, and opportunities; and the sharing of such files too widely with other government agencies or private organizations. This related not just to privacy rights, but also to due process, freedom of expression (because of "chilling effect"), and equality (because of discriminatory standards in former record systems).

These alarms were raised by social commentators, interest groups, and political leaders when computer use spread in the 1960s. This led, in the United States and other industrial democracies, to a burst of empirical studies and commission investigations to learn (1) just what computers could and could not do; (2) how computers were actually being used, and with what effects on existing individual rights; and (3) whether new laws or organizational rules were needed.

In the U.S., this produced the National Academy of Sciences report, *Databanks in a Free Society* (1972), and the influential report of the HEW Secretary's Committee on Automated Personal Data Systems (1973). These reports concluded that com-

puter use had not yet produced the transformations of data
collection, exchange, and use that critics feared but that the
technology was getting cheaper, more powerful, and more
reliable, and that new laws and rules *were* needed if individual
rights were not to suffer.

Whether we would have enacted national privacy laws had
Watergate not occurred is an interesting question. But with
Watergate as an unequivocal lesson that information could be
abused by an administration, and that records and files now
played a major role in governmental operations, we decided
that new legal safeguards designed to institutionalize "fair
information practices" had to be installed. As a result, there
has been a steady stream of federal and state privacy protection legislation from 1970 to the present, covering government files in general; credit, insurance, and employment reports; bank and financial records; tax information; medical and
health records; educational records; and many other fields.

Interestingly, it has *not* been the Supreme Court that has
pioneered in this updating of the Bill of Rights for the computer age. While the Supreme Court acted in 1967 to reverse
its narrow and inadequate 1928 reading that the Fourth
Amendment was not applicable to government telephone tap-
ping, the Court's new "reasonable expectation of privacy"
standard was *not* extended over the past two decades to cover
citizen interests in government databanks. The Court has left
the definition of such rights to the legislative process. Happily
for the framers' blueprint, federal and state legislatures have
responded. Enactment in the 1980s of federal privacy protections for subscriber data in cable systems and, in 1986, of the
Electronic Communications Privacy Act, covering communications on digital networks, cellular telephones, and other new
media, documents that active protective legislation continues.

The impact of information technology on individual rights
remains perhaps the most volatile of the four areas, in terms
of potential impact on the framers' balances. Today there is
little doubt that our society has more privacy protection laws
and more organizational privacy rules relating to use of personal data than we had before computers arrived. We have

made sure that record systems reflect the post–1960s rules for judging people as to race, religion, sex, life style, and ideology, rather than the 1950s WASP credentialism. In terms of due process, the individual has been "empowered" to see and challenge his or her government records, and we have lively litigation over citizen rights in both public and private data-bank uses. These new rights and procedures are being actively applied by the federal and state courts.

But as government moves in the next decade into federal agency integrated record systems of unprecedented size and complexity; as computer-matching programs pass individual names through dozens of files from various agencies and governmental levels; and as activities such as drug testing and AIDS testing raise the possibilities of national screening-result record systems—a healthy and sustained nervousness may well be called for.

Where Information Technology Impacts Have Been Important

Our inquiry into the effects of information technology, it should be noted, has been framed at the macro or "regime" level, and we have found that neither the negative nor the positive projections have taken place as predicted. However, we hasten to note that information technology is having and will continue to have significant effects on many vital areas of private and public life. For example:

Information technology is reshaping work patterns and employee-employer relationships in both the factory and the office, greatly improving some work and impoverishing other jobs.

Information technology is transforming industry definitions and arrangements, creating a global rather than national production and marketing system, and altering basic public expectations about consumer services.

Information technology is beginning to transform the way that client services are organized and delivered by government agencies, and may well reshape the structures of public agencies in the coming decade.

Information technology continues to cause rearrangements of power and roles within large private and public organizations, in such matters as line-to-management relations, centralized versus distributed operations, and management decision-making processes.

Those changes are deep and important. But they are *not* at the regime level, and they do not, even taken all together, amount to impacts on the great constitutional balances of the Republic.

Summing Up

This account of what information technology has and has not done to the four great mechanisms of the American Constitution tells us, I submit, some very important things about the nature of our constitutional system, the political culture and value system that spawned and sustains it, and the ways that democratic societies have learned to look at and to deal with powerful new technologies.

First, even as powerful a technology as computers and telecommunications flows along the deep, rock-like channels of a society's values, politics, law, and institutions. When we think about how to use computers (or how we will allow government and the private sector to use computers), we follow those channels, and the pathways of action they structure.

Second, the reception and shaping of information technology uses over the past twenty-five to thirty years attests to the strength of our interest group advocacy system, our energetic "guardian" media, our continuing distrust of authority and concern for its control, and our keen readiness to defend constitutional norms of civil liberties, civil rights, and the rule of law. It attests also to the continued vitality of the separation of powers competition and federalism divisions the framers installed to help safeguard against potential abuse of power, whether by new tools or any other mechanisms.

Finally, the men of 1787 would probably react to this review of how technology has affected their handiwork by observing that they would have expected no other outcome. After reminding us of how they had approached regime-level technology assessment (see our earlier section), they might chide us gently:

"We detect in much of your generation's thinking and writing about technology a tendency to seek relief from the struggles over wise policy and its administration through a morbid fascination with new machines. The progress of these United States—if you and your adversaries do not blow up the world, of course—still depends more on the nurturing of a democratic civil culture, the attraction of the best people into government, the vitality of political participation, the pursuit of equality and justice, and the creative use of constitutional balances than on these information machines, for all their amazing properties."

APPENDIX A

The Constitution
of the United States

WE THE PEOPLE OF THE UNITED STATES, in order to form a more perfect Union, establish Justice, insure domestic Tranquility, provide for the common defence, promote the general Welfare, and secure the Blessings of Liberty to ourselves and our Posterity, do ordain and establish this Constitution for the United States of America.

ARTICLE. I.

Section. 1. All legislative Powers herein granted shall be vested in a Congress of the United States, which shall consist of a Senate and House of Representatives.

Section. 2. The House of Representatives shall be composed of Members chosen every second Year by the People of the several States, and the Electors in each State shall have the Qualifications requisite for Electors of the most numerous Branch of the State Legislature.

No Person shall be a Representative who shall not have attained to the Age of twenty five Years, and been seven Years a Citizen of the United States, and who shall not, when elected, be an Inhabitant of that State in which he shall be chosen.

Representatives and direct Taxes shall be apportioned among the several States which may be included within this Union, according to their respective Numbers, which shall be determined by adding to the whole Number of free Persons, including those bound to Service for a Term of Years, and excluding Indians not taxed, three fifths of all other Persons. The actual Enumeration shall be made within three Years after the first Meeting of the Congress of the United States, and within every subsequent Term of ten Years, in such Manner as they shall by Law direct. The Number of Representatives shall not exceed one for every thirty Thousand, but each State shall have at Least one Representative; and until such enumeration shall be made, the State of New Hampshire shall be entitled to chuse three, Massachusetts eight, Rhode-Island and Providence Plantations one, Connecticut five, New-York six, New Jersey four, Pennsylvania eight, Delaware one, Maryland six, Virginia ten, North Carolina five, South Carolina five, and Georgia three.

When vacancies happen in the Representation from any State, the Executive Authority thereof shall issue Writs of Election to fill such Vacancies.

The House of Representatives shall chuse their Speaker and other Officers; and shall have the sole Power of Impeachment.

Section. 3. The Senate of the United States shall be composed of two Senators from each State, chosen by the Legislature thereof, for six Years; and each Senator shall have one Vote.

Immediately after they shall be assembled in Consequence of the first Election, they shall be divided as equally as may be into three Classes. The Seats of the Senators of the first Class shall be vacated at the Expiration of the second Year, of the second Class at the Expiration of the fourth Year, and of the third Class at the Expiration of the sixth Year, so that one third may be chosen every second Year; and if Vacancies happen by Resignation, or otherwise, during the Recess of the Legislature of any State, the Executive thereof may make temporary

Appointments until the next Meeting of the Legislature, which shall then fill such Vacancies.

No Person shall be a Senator who shall not have attained to the Age of thirty Years, and been nine Years a Citizen of the United States, and who shall not, when elected, be an Inhabitant of that State for which he shall be chosen.

The Vice President of the United States shall be President of the Senate, but shall have no Vote, unless they be equally divided.

The Senate shall chuse their other Officers, and also a President pro tempore, in the Absence of the Vice President, or when he shall exercise the Office of President of the United States.

The Senate shall have the sole Power to try all Impeachments. When sitting for that Purpose, they shall be on Oath or Affirmation. When the President of the United States is tried, the Chief Justice shall preside: And no Person shall be convicted without the Concurrence of two thirds of the Members present.

Judgment in Cases of Impeachment shall not extend further than to removal from Office, and disqualification to hold and enjoy any Office of honor, Trust or Profit under the United States: but the Party convicted shall nevertheless be liable and subject to Indictment, Trial, Judgment and Punishment, according to Law.

Section. 4. The Times, Places and Manner of holding Elections for Senators and Representatives, shall be prescribed in each State by the Legislature thereof, but the Congress may at any time by Law make or alter such Regulations, except as to the Places of chusing Senators.

The Congress shall assemble at least once in every Year, and such Meeting shall be on the first Monday in December, unless they shall by Law appoint a different Day.

Section. 5. Each House shall be the Judge of the Elections, Returns and Qualifications of its own Members, and a Majority of each shall constitute a Quorum to do Business; but a smaller Number may adjourn from day to day, and may be authorized to compel the Attendance of absent Members, in such Manner, and under such Penalties as each House may provide.

Each House may determine the Rules of its Proceedings, punish its Members for disorderly Behaviour, and, with the Concurrence of two thirds, expel a Member.

Each House shall keep a Journal of its Proceedings, and from time to time publish the same, excepting such Parts as may in their Judgment require Secrecy; and the Yeas and Nays of the Members of either House on any question shall, at the Desire of one fifth of those Present, be entered on the Journal.

Neither House, during the Session of Congress, shall, without the Consent of the other, adjourn for more than three days, nor to any other Place than that in which the two Houses shall be sitting.

Section. 6. The Senators and Representatives shall receive a Compensation for their Services, to be ascertained by Law, and paid out of the Treasury of the United States. They shall in all Cases, except Treason, Felony and Breach of the Peace, be privileged from Arrest during their Attendance at the Session of their respective Houses, and in going to and returning from the same; and for any Speech or Debate in either House, they shall not be questioned in any other Place.

No Senator or Representative shall, during the Time for which he was elected, be appointed to any civil Office under the Authority of the United States, which shall have been created, or the Emoluments whereof shall have been encreased during such time; and no Person holding any Office under the United States, shall be a Member of either House during his Continuance in Office.

Section. 7. All Bills for raising Revenue shall originate in the House of Representatives; but the Senate may propose or concur with Amendments as on other Bills.

Every Bill which shall have passed the House of Representatives and the Senate shall, before it become a Law, be presented to the President of the United States; If he approve he shall sign it, but if not he shall return it, with his Objections to that House in which it shall have originated, who shall enter the Objections at large on their Journal, and proceed to reconsider it. If after such Reconsideration two thirds of that House shall agree to pass the Bill, it shall be sent, together with the Objections, to the other House, by which it shall likewise be reconsidered, and if approved by two thirds of that House, it shall become a Law. But in all such Cases the Votes of both Houses shall be determined by yeas and Nays, and the Names of the Persons voting for and against the Bill shall be entered on the Journal of each House respectively. If any Bill shall not be returned by the President within ten Days (Sundays excepted) after it shall have been presented to him, the Same shall be a Law, in like Manner as if he had signed it, unless the Congress by their Adjournment prevent its Return, in which Case it shall not be a Law.

Every Order, Resolution, or Vote to which the Concurrence of the Senate and House of Representatives may be necessary (except on a question of Adjournment) shall be presented to the President of the United States; and before the Same shall take Effect, shall be approved by him, or being disapproved by him, shall be repassed by two thirds of the Senate and House of Representatives, according to the Rules and Limitations prescribed in the Case of a Bill.

Section. 8. The Congress shall have Power To lay and collect Taxes, Duties, Imposts and Excises, to pay the Debts and provide for the common Defence and general Welfare of the United States; but all Duties, Imposts and Excises shall be uniform throughout the United States.

To borrow Money on the credit of the United States;

To regulate Commerce with foreign Nations, and among the several States, and with the Indian Tribes;

To establish an uniform Rule of Naturalization, and uniform Laws on the subject of Bankruptcies throughout the United States;

To coin Money, regulate the Value thereof, and of foreign Coin, and fix the Standard of Weights and Measures;

To provide for the Punishment of counterfeiting the Securities and current Coin of the United States;

To establish Post Offices and Post Roads;

To promote the Progress of Science and useful Arts, by securing for limited Times to Authors and Inventors the exclusive Right to their respective Writings and Discoveries;

To constitute Tribunals inferior to the supreme Court;

To define and punish Piracies and Felonies committed on the high Seas, and Offences against the Law of Nations;

To declare War, grant Letters of Marque and Reprisal, and make Rules concerning Captures on Land and Water;

To raise and support Armies, but no Appropriation of Money to that Use shall be for a longer Term than two Years;

To provide and maintain a Navy;

To make Rules for the Government and Regulation of the land and naval Forces;

To provide for calling forth the Militia to execute the Laws of the Union, suppress Insurrections and repel Invasions;

To provide for organizing, arming, and disciplining, the Militia, and for governing such Part of them as may be employed in the Service of the United States, reserving to the States respectively, the Appointment of the Officers, and the Authority of training the Militia according to the discipline prescribed by Congress;

To exercise exclusive Legislation in all Cases whatsoever, over such District (not exceeding ten Miles square) as may, by Cession of particular States, and the Acceptance of Congress, become the Seat of the Government of the United States, and to exercise like Authority over all Places purchased by the Consent of the Legislature of the State in which the Same shall be, for the Erection of Forts, Magazines, Arsenals, dock-Yards, and other needful Buildings;—And

To make all Laws which shall be necessary and proper for carrying into Execution the foregoing Powers, and all other Powers vested by this Constitution in the Government of the United States, or in any Department or Officer thereof.

Section. 9. The Migration or Importation of such Persons as any of the States now existing shall think proper to admit, shall not be prohibited by the Congress prior to the Year one thousand eight hundred and eight, but a Tax or duty may be imposed on such Importation, not exceeding ten dollars for each Person.

The Privilege of the Writ of Habeas Corpus shall not be suspended, unless when in Cases of Rebellion or Invasion the public Safety may require it.

No Bill of Attainder or ex post facto Law shall be passed.

No Capitation, or other direct, Tax shall be laid, unless in Proportion to the Census or Enumeration herein before directed to be taken.

No Tax or Duty shall be laid on Articles exported from any State.

No Preference shall be given by any Regulation of Commerce or Revenue to the Ports of one State over those of another: nor shall Vessels bound to, or from, one State, be obliged to enter, clear, or pay Duties in another.

No Money shall be drawn from the Treasury, but in Consequence of Appropriations made by Law, and a regular Statement and Account of the Receipts and Expenditures of all public Money shall be published from time to time.

No Title of Nobility shall be granted by the United States: And no Person holding any Office of Profit or trust under them, shall, without the Consent of the Congress, accept of any present, Emolument, Office, or Title, of any kind whatever, from any King, Prince, or foreign State.

Section. 10. No State shall enter into any Treaty, Alliance, or Confederation; grant Letters of Marque and Reprisal; coin Money; emit Bills of Credit; make any Thing but gold and silver Coin a Tender in Payment of Debts; pass any Bill of Attainder, ex post facto Law, or Law impairing the Obligation of Contracts, or grant any Title of Nobility.

No State shall, without the Consent of the Congress, lay any Imposts or Duties on Imports or Exports, except what may be absolutely necessary for executing it's inspection Laws: and the net Produce of all Duties and Imposts, laid by any State on Imports or Exports, shall be for the Use of the Treasury of the United States; and all such Laws shall be subject to the Revision and Controul of the Congress.

No State shall, without the Consent of Congress, lay any Duty of Tonnage, keep Troops, or Ships of War in time of Peace, enter into any Agreement or Compact with another State, or with a foreign Power, or engage in War, unless actually invaded, or in such imminent Danger as will not admit of delay.

ARTICLE. II.

Section. 1. The executive Power shall be vested in a President of the United States of America. He shall hold his Office during the term of four Years, and, together with the Vice President, chosen for the same Term, be elected, as follows

Each State shall appoint, in such Manner as the Legislature thereof may direct, a Number of Electors, equal to the whole Number of Senators and Representatives to which the State may be entitled in the Congress: but no Senator or Representative, or Person holding an Office of Trust or Profit under the United States, shall be appointed an Elector.

The Electors shall meet in their respective States, and vote by Ballot for two Persons, of whom one at least shall not be an Inhabitant of the same State with themselves. And they shall make a List of all the Persons voted for, and of the Number of Votes for each; which List they shall sign and certify, and transmit sealed to the Seat of the Government of the United States, directed to the President of the Senate. The President of the Senate shall, in the Presence of the Senate and House of Representatives, open all the Certificates, and the Votes shall then be counted. The Person having the greatest Number of Votes shall be the President, if such Number be a Majority of the whole Number of Electors appointed; and if there be more than one who have such Majority, and have an equal Number of Votes, then the House of Representatives shall immediately chuse by Ballot one of them for President; and if no Person have a Majority, then from the five highest on the List the said House shall in like Manner chuse the President. But in chusing the President, the Votes shall be taken by States, the Representation from each State having one Vote;

A quorum for this Purpose shall consist of a Member or Members from two thirds of the States, and a Majority all the States shall be necessary to a Choice. In every Case, after the Choice of the President, the Person having the greatest Number of Votes of the Electors shall be the Vice President. But if there should remain two or more who have equal Votes, the Senate shall chuse from them by Ballot the Vice President.

The Congress may determine the Time of chusing the Electors, and the Day on which they shall give their Votes; which Day shall be the same throughout the United States.

No Person except a natural born Citizen, or a Citizen of the United States, at the time of the Adoption of this Constitution, shall be eligible to the Office of President, neither shall any Person be eligible to that Office who shall not have attained to the Age of thirty five Years, and been fourteen Years a Resident within the United States.

In Case of the Removal of the President from Office, or of his Death, Resignation, or Inability to discharge the Powers and Duties of the said Office, the Same shall devolve on the Vice President, and the Congress may by Law provide for the Case of Removal, Death, Resignation or Inability, both of the President and Vice President, declaring what Officer shall then act as President, and such Officer shall act accordingly, until the Disability be removed, or a President shall be elected.

The President shall, at stated Times, receive for his Services, a Compensation, which shall neither be encreased or diminished during the Period for which he shall have been elected, and he shall not receive within that Period any other Emolument from the United States, or any of them.

Before he enters on the Execution of his Office, he shall take the following Oath or Affirmation:—"I do solemnly swear (or affirm) that I will faithfully execute the Office of President of the United States, and will to the best of my Ability, preserve, protect and defend the Constitution of the United States."

Section. 2. The President shall be Commander in Chief of the Army and Navy of the United States, and of the Militia of the several States, when called into the actual Service of the

United States; he may require the Opinion, in writing, of the principal Officer in each of the executive Departments, upon any Subject relating to the Duties of their respective Offices, and he shall have Power to grant Reprieves and Pardons for Offences against the United States, except in Cases of Impeachment.

He shall have Power, by and with the Advice and Consent of the Senate, to make Treaties, provided two thirds of the Senators present concur; and he shall nominate, and by and with the Advice and Consent of the Senate, shall appoint Ambassadors, other public Ministers and Consuls, Judges of the supreme Court, and all other Officers of the United States, whose Appointments are not herein otherwise provided for, and which shall be established by Law; but the Congress may by Law vest the Appointment of such inferior Officers, as they think proper, in the President alone, in the Courts of Law, or in the Heads of Departments.

The President shall have Power to fill up all Vacancies that may happen during the Recess of the Senate, by granting Commissions which shall expire at the End of their next Session.

Section. 3. He shall from time to time give to the Congress Information of the State of the Union, and recommend to their Consideration such Measures as he shall judge necessary and expedient; he may, on extraordinary Occasions, convene both Houses, or either of them, and in Case of Disagreement between them, with Respect to the Time of Adjournment, he may adjourn them to such Time as he shall think proper; he shall receive Ambassadors and other public Ministers; he shall take Care that the Laws be faithfully executed, and shall Commission all the Officers of the United States.

Section. 4. The President, Vice President and all civil Officers of the United States, shall be removed from Office on Impeachment for, and Conviction of, Treason, Bribery, or other high Crimes and Misdemeanors.

ARTICLE. III.

Section. 1. The judicial Power of the United States, shall be vested in one supreme Court, and in such inferior Courts as the Congress may from time to time ordain and establish. The Judges, both of the supreme and inferior Courts, shall hold their Offices during good Behaviour, and shall, at stated Times, receive for their Services, a Compensation, which shall not be diminished during their Continuance in Office.

Section. 2. The judicial Power shall extend to all Cases, in Law and Equity, arising under this Constitution, the Laws of the United States, and Treaties made, or which shall be made, under their Authority;—to all Cases affecting Ambassadors, other public Ministers and Consuls;—to all Cases of admiralty and maritime Jurisdiction;—to Controversies to which the United States shall be a Party;—to Controversies between two or more States;—between a State and Citizens of another State;—between Citizens of different States,—between Citizens of the same State claiming Lands under Grants of different States, and between a State, or the Citizens thereof, and foreign States, Citizens or Subjects.

In all cases affecting Ambassadors, other public Ministers and Consuls, and those in which a State shall be Party, the supreme Court shall have original Jurisdiction. In all the other Cases before mentioned, the supreme Court shall have appellate Jurisdiction, both as to Law and Fact, with such Exceptions, and under such Regulations as the Congress shall make.

The Trial of all Crimes, except in Cases of Impeachment, shall be by Jury; and such Trial shall be held in the State where the said Crimes shall have been committed; but when not committed within any State, the Trial shall be at such Place or Places as the Congress may by Law have directed.

Section. 3. Treason against the United States, shall consist only in levying War against them, or in adhering to their Enemies, giving them Aid and Comfort. No Person shall be convicted of

Treason unless on the Testimony of two Witnesses to the same overt Act, or on Confession in open Court.

The Congress shall have Power to declare the Punishment of Treason, but no Attainder of Treason shall work Corruption of Blood, or Forfeiture except during the Life of the Person attained.

ARTICLE. IV.

Section. 1. Full Faith and Credit shall be given in each State to the public Acts, Records, and judicial Proceedings of every other State. And the Congress may by general Laws prescribe the Manner in which such Acts, Records and Proceedings shall be proved, and the Effect thereof.

Section. 2. The Citizens of each State shall be entitled to all Privileges and Immunities of Citizens in the several States.

A Person charged in any State with Treason, Felony, or other Crime, who shall flee from Justice, and be found in another State, shall on Demand of the executive Authority of the State from which he fled, be delivered up, to be removed to the State having Jurisdiction of the Crime.

No Person held to Service or Labour in one State, under the Laws thereof, escaping into another, shall, in Consequence of any Law or Regulation therein, be discharged from such Service or Labour, but shall be delivered up on Claim of the Party to whom such Service or Labour may be due.

Section. 3. New States may be admitted by the Congress into this Union; but no new State shall be formed or erected within the Jurisdiction of any other State; nor any State be formed by the Junction of two or more States, or Parts of States, without the consent of the Legislatures of the States concerned as well as of the Congress.

The Congress shall have Power to dispose of and make all needful Rules and Regulations respecting the Territory or other Property belonging to the United States; and nothing in this Constitution shall be so construed as to Prejudice any Claims of the United States, or of any particular States.

Section. 4. The United States shall guarantee to every State in this Union a Republican Form of Government, and shall protect each of them against Invasion; and on Application of the Legislature, or of the Executive (when the Legislature cannot be convened) against domestic Violence.

ARTICLE. V.

The Congress, whenever two thirds of both Houses shall deem it necessary, shall propose Amendments to this Constitution, or, on the Application of the Legislatures of two thirds of the several States shall call a Convention for proposing Amendments, which, in either Case, shall be valid to all Intents and Purposes, as Part of this Constitution, when ratified by the Legislatures of three fourths of the several States, or by Conventions in three fourths thereof, as the one or the other Mode of Ratification may be proposed by the Congress; Provided that no Amendment which may be made prior to the Year One thousand eight hundred and eight shall in any Manner affect the first and fourth Clauses in the Ninth Section of the first Article; and that no State, without its Consent, shall be deprived of it's equal Suffrage in the Senate.

ARTICLE. VI.

All Debts contracted and Engagements entered into, before the Adoption of this Constitution, shall be as valid against the United States under this Constitution, as under the Confederation.

This Constitution, and the Laws of the United States which shall be made in Pursuance thereof; and all Treaties made, or which shall be made, under the Authority of the United States, shall be the supreme Law of the Land; and the Judges in every State shall be bound thereby, any Thing in the Constitution or Laws of any State to the Contrary notwithstanding.

The Senators and Representatives before mentioned, and the Members of the several State Legislatures, and all executive and judicial Officers, both of the United States and of the several States, shall be bound by Oath or Affirmation, to support this Constitution; but no religious Test shall ever be required as a Qualification to any Office or public Trust under the United States.

ARTICLE. VII.

The Ratification of the Conventions of nine States, shall be sufficient for the Establishment of this Constitution between the States so ratifying the Same. Done in Convention by the Unanimous Consent of the States present the Seventeenth Day of September in the Year of our Lord one thousand seven hundred and Eighty seven and of the Independence of the United States of America the Twelfth. In witness thereof We have hereunto subscribed our Names,

G°: WASHINGTON—Presid[t]
and deputy from Virginia

New Hampshire	John Langdon Nicholas Gilman		Geo: Read Gunning Bedford jun
Massachusetts	Nathaniel Gorham Rufus King	Delaware	John Dickinson Richard Bassett Jaco: Broom
Connecticut	W[m] Sam[l] Johnson Roger Sherman		
New York	Alexander Hamilton	Maryland	James McHenry Dan of S[t] Tho[s] Jenifer Dan[l] Carroll
New Jersey	Wil: Livingston David A. Brearley. W[m]. Paterson. Jona: Dayton	Virginia	John Blair— James Madison Jr.
Pennsylvania	B. Franklin Thomas Mifflin Rob[t] Morris Geo. Clymer Tho[s]. FitzSimons Jared Ingersoll James Wilson Gouv Morris	North Carolina	W[m]. Blount Rich[d] Dobbs Spaight. Hu Williamson
		South Carolina	J. Rutledge Charles Cotesworth Pinckney Charles Pinckney Pierce Butler.
		Georgia	William Few Abr Baldwin

Amendments to the Constitution

ARTICLES IN ADDITION TO, and Amendment of the Constitution of the United States of America, proposed by Congress, and ratified by the Legislatures of the several States, pursuant to the fifth Article of the original Constitution.

ARTICLE I.

Congress shall make no law respecting an establishment of religion, or prohibiting the free exercise thereof; or abridging the freedom of speech, or of the press; or the right of the people peaceably to assemble, and to petition the Government for a redress of grievances.

ARTICLE II.

A well regulated Militia, being necessary to the security of a free State, the right of the people to keep and bear Arms, shall not be infringed.

ARTICLE III.

No Soldier shall, in time of peace be quartered in any house, without the consent of the Owner, nor in time of war, but in a manner to be prescribed by law.

ARTICLE IV.

The right of the people to be secure in their persons, houses, papers, and effects, against unreasonable searches and seizures, shall not be violated, and no Warrants shall issue, but upon probable cause, supported by Oath or affirmation, and particularly describing the place to be searched, and the persons or things to be seized.

ARTICLE V.

No person shall be held to answer for a capital, or otherwise infamous crime, unless on a presentment or indictment of a Grand Jury, except in cases arising in the land or naval forces, or in the Militia, when in actual service in time of War or public danger; nor shall any person be subject for the same offence to be twice put in jeopardy of life or limb; nor shall be compelled in any criminal case to be a witness against himself, nor be deprived of life, liberty, or property, without due process of law; nor shall private property be taken for public use, without just compensation.

ARTICLE VI.

In all criminal prosecutions, the accused shall enjoy the right to a speedy and public trial, by an impartial jury of the State and district wherein the crime shall have been committed, which district shall have been previously ascertained by law, and to be informed of the nature and cause of the accusation; to be confronted with the witnesses against him; to have compulsory process for obtaining witnesses in his favor, and to have the Assistance of Counsel for his defence.

ARTICLE VII.

In Suits at common law, where the value in controversy shall exceed twenty dollars, the right of trial by jury shall be preserved, and no fact tried by a jury, shall be otherwise re-examined in any Court of the United States, than according to the rules of the common law.

ARTICLE VIII.

Excessive bail shall not be required, nor excessive fines imposed, nor cruel and unusual punishments inflicted.

ARTICLE IX.

The enumeration in the Constitution, of certain rights, shall not be construed to deny or disparage others retained by the people.

ARTICLE X.

The powers not delegated to the United States by the Constitution, nor prohibited by it to the States, are reserved to the States respectively, or to the people. [The first ten amendments went into effect December 15, 1791.]

ARTICLE XI.

The Judicial power of the United States shall not be construed to extend to any suit in law or equity, commenced or prosecuted against one of the United States by Citizens of another State, or by Citizens or Subjects of any Foreign State. [January 8, 1798.]

ARTICLE XII.

The Electors shall meet in their respective states, and vote by ballot for President and Vice-President, one of whom, at least, shall not be an inhabitant of the same state with themselves; they shall name in their ballots the person voted for as President, and in distinct ballots the person voted for as Vice-President, and they shall make distinct lists of all persons voted for as President, and of all persons voted for as Vice-President, and of the number of votes for each, which lists they shall sign and certify, and transmit sealed to the seat of the government of the United States, directed to the President of the Senate;— The President of the Senate shall, in the presence of the Senate and House of Representatives, open all the certificates and the votes shall then be counted;—The person having the greatest number of votes for President, shall be the President, if such number be a majority of the whole number of Electors appointed; and if no person have such majority, then from the persons having the highest numbers not exceeding three on the list of those voted for as President, the House of Representatives shall choose immediately, by ballot, the President. But in choosing the President, the votes shall be taken by states, the representation from each state having one vote; a quorum for this purpose shall consist of a member or members from two-thirds of the states, and a majority of all the states shall be necessary to a choice. And if the House of Representatives shall not choose a President whenever the right of choice shall devolve upon them, before the fourth day of March next following, then the Vice-President shall act as President, as in the case of the death or other constitutional disability of the President.—The person having the greatest number of votes as Vice-President, shall be the Vice-President, if such number be a majority of the whole number of Electors appointed, and if no person have a majority, then from the two highest numbers on the list, the Senate shall choose the Vice-President; a quorum for the purpose shall consist of two-thirds of the whole number of Senators, and a majority of the whole number shall be necessary to a choice. But no person constitutionally ineligible to the office of President shall be eligible to that of Vice-President of the United States. [September 25, 1804.]

ARTICLE XIII.

Section 1. Neither slavery nor involuntary servitude, except as a punishment for crime whereof the party shall have been duly convicted, shall exist within the United States, or any place subject to their jurisdiction.

Section 2. Congress shall have power to enforce this article by appropriate legislation. [December 18, 1865.]

ARTICLE XIV.

Section 1. All persons born or naturalized in the United States, and subject to the jurisdiction thereof, are citizens of the United States and of the State wherein they reside. No State shall make or enforce any law which shall abridge the privileges or immunities of citizens of the United States; nor shall any State deprive any person of life, liberty, or property, without due process of law; nor deny to any person within its jurisdiction the equal protection of the laws.

Section 2. Representatives shall be apportioned among the several States according to their respective numbers, counting the whole number of persons in each State, excluding Indians not taxed. But when the right to vote at any election for the choice of electors for President and Vice President of the United States, Representatives in Congress, the Executive and Judicial officers of a State, or the members of the Legislature thereof, is denied to any of the male inhabitants of such State, being twenty-one years of age, and citizens of the United States, or in any way abridged, except for participation in rebellion, or other crime, the basis of representation therein shall be reduced in the proportion which the number of such male citizens shall bear to the whole number of male citizens twenty-one years of age in such State.

Section 3. No person shall be a Senator or Representative in Congress, or elector of President and Vice President, or hold any office, civil or military, under the United States, or under any State, who, having previously taken an oath, as a member of Congress, or as an officer of the United States, or as a member of any State legislature, or as an executive or judicial officer of any State, to support the Constitution of the United States, shall have engaged in insurrection or rebellion against the same, or given aid or comfort to the enemies thereof. But Congress may by a vote of two-thirds of each House, remove such disability.

Section 4. The validity of the public debt of the United States, authorized by law, including debts incurred for payment of pensions and bounties for services in suppressing insurrection or rebellion, shall not be questioned. But neither the United States nor any State shall assume or pay any debt or obligation incurred in aid of insurrection or rebellion against the United States, or any claim for the loss or emancipation of any slave; but all such debts, obligations and claims shall be held illegal and void.

Section 5. The Congress shall have power to enforce, by appropriate legislation, the provisions of this article. [July 28, 1868.]

ARTICLE XV.

Section 1. The right of citizens of the United States to vote shall not be denied or abridged by the United States or by any State on account of race, color, or previous condition of servitude—

Section 2. The Congress shall have power to enforce this article by appropriate legislation.—[March 30, 1870.]

ARTICLE XVI.

The Congress shall have power to lay and collect taxes on incomes, from whatever source derived, without apportionment among the several States, and without regard to any census or enumeration. [February 25, 1913.]

ARTICLE XVII.

The Senate of the United States shall be composed of two senators from each State, elected by the people thereof, for six years; and each Senator shall have one vote. The electors in each State shall have the qualifications requisite for electors of the most numerous branch of the State legislature.

When vacancies happen in the representation of any State in the Senate, the executive authority of such State shall issue writs of election to fill such vacancies: *Provided,* That the legislature of any State may empower the executive thereof to make temporary appointments until the people fill the vacancies by election as the legislature may direct.

This amendment shall not be so construed as to affect the election or term of any senator chosen before it becomes valid as part of the Constitution. [May 31, 1913.]

ARTICLE XVIII.

After one year from the ratification of this article, the manufacture, sale, or transportation of intoxicating liquors within, the importation thereof into, or the exportation thereof from the United States and all territory subject to the jurisdiction thereof for beverage purposes is hereby prohibited.

The Congress and the several States shall have concurrent power to enforce this article by appropriate legislation.

This article shall be inoperative unless it shall have been ratified as an amendment to the Constitution by the legislatures of the several States, as provided in the Constitution, within seven years from the date of the submission thereof to the States by Congress. [January 29, 1919.]

ARTICLE XIX.

The right of citizens of the United States to vote shall not be denied or abridged by the United States or by any State on account of sex.

The Congress shall have power by appropriate legislation to enforce the provisions of this article. [August 26, 1920.]

ARTICLE XX.

Section 1. The terms of the President and Vice-President shall end at noon on the twentieth day of January, and the terms of Senators and Representatives at noon on the third day of January, of the years in which such terms would have ended if this article had not been ratified; and the terms of their successors shall then begin.

Section 2. The Congress shall assemble at least once in every year, and such meeting shall begin at noon on the third day of January, unless they shall by law appoint a different day.

Section 3. If, at the time fixed for the beginning of the term of the President, the President-elect shall have died, the Vice-President-elect shall become President. If a President shall not have been chosen before the time fixed for the beginning of his term, or if the President-elect shall have failed to qualify, then the Vice-President-elect shall act as President until a President shall have qualified; and the Congress may by law provide for the case wherein neither a President-elect nor a Vice-President-elect shall have qualified, declaring who shall then act as President, or the manner in which one who is to act shall be selected, and such person shall act accordingly until a President or Vice-President shall have qualified.

Section 4. The Congress may by law provide for the case of the death of any of the persons from whom the House of Representatives may choose a President whenever the right of choice shall have devolved upon them, and for the case of the death of any of the persons from whom the Senate may choose a Vice-President whenever the right of choice shall have devolved upon them.

Section 5. Sections 1 and 2 shall take effect on the 15th day of October following the ratification of this article.

Section 6. This article shall be inoperative unless it shall have been ratified as an amendment to the Constitution by the legislatures of three-fourths of the several States within seven years from the date of its submission. [February 6, 1933.]

ARTICLE XXI.

Section 1. The eighteenth article of amendment to the Constitution of the United States is hereby repealed.

Section 2. The transportation or importation into any State, Territory or possession of the United States for delivery or use therein of intoxicating liquors, in violation of the laws thereof, is hereby prohibited.

Section 3. This article shall be inoperative unless it shall have been ratified as an amendment to the Constitution by convention in the several States, as provided in the Constitution, within seven years from the date of the submission thereof to the States by the Congress. [December 5, 1933.]

ARTICLE XXII.

Section 1. No person shall be elected to the office of the President more than twice, and no person who has held the office of President, or acted as President, for more than two years of a term to which some other person was elected President shall be elected to the office of the President more than once. But this Article shall not apply to any person holding the office of President when this Article was proposed by the Congress, and shall not prevent any person who may be holding the office of President, or acting as President, during the term within which this Article becomes operative from holding the office of President or acting as President during the remainder of such term.

Section 2. This article shall be inoperative unless it shall have been ratified as an amendment to the Constitution by the legislatures of three-fourths of the several States within seven years from the date of its submission to the States by the Congress. [February 27, 1951.]

ARTICLE XXIII.

Section 1. The District constituting the seat of government of the United States shall appoint in such manner as the Congress may direct:

A number of electors of President and Vice-President equal to the whole number of Senators and Representatives in Congress to which the District would be entitled if it were a State, but in no event more than the least populous State;

they shall be in addition to those appointed by the States, but they shall be considered, for the purposes of the election of President and Vice-President, to be electors appointed by a State; and they shall meet in the District and perform such duties as provided by the twelfth article of amendment.

Section 2. The Congress shall have the power to enforce this article by appropriate legislation. [March 29, 1961.]

ARTICLE XXIV.

Section 1. The right of citizens of the United States to vote in any primary or other election for President or Vice President, for electors for President or Vice President, or for Senator or Representative in Congress, shall not be denied or abridged by the United States or any State by reason of failure to pay any poll tax or other tax.

Section 2. The Congress shall have power to enforce this article by appropriate legislation. [January 23, 1964.]

ARTICLE XXV.

Section 1. In case of the removal of the President from office or of his death or resignation, the Vice President shall become President.

Section 2. Whenever there is a vacancy in the office of Vice President, the President shall nominate a Vice President who shall take office upon confirmation by a majority vote of both Houses of Congress.

Section 3. Whenever the President transmits to the President pro tempore of the Senate and the Speaker of the House of Representatives his written declaration that he is unable to discharge the powers and duties of his office, and until he transmits to them a written declaration to the contrary, such powers and duties shall be discharged by the Vice President as Acting President.

Section 4. Whenever the Vice President and a majority of either the principal officers of the executive departments or of such other body as Congress may by law provide, transmit to the President pro tempore of the Senate and the Speaker of the House of Representatives their written declaration that the President is unable to discharge the powers and duties of his office, the Vice President shall immediately assume the powers and duties of the office as Acting President.

Thereafter, when the President transmits to the President pro tempore of the Senate and the Speaker of the House of Representatives his written declaration that no inability exists, he shall resume the powers and duties of his office unless the Vice President and a majority of either the principal officers of the executive departments or of such other body as Congress may by law provide, transmit within four days to the President pro tempore of the Senate and the Speaker of the House of Representatives their written declaration that the President is unable to discharge the powers and duties of his office. Thereupon Congress shall decide the issue, assembling within forty-eight hours for that purpose if not in session. If the Congress, within twenty-one days after receipt of the latter written declaration, or, if Congress is not in session, within twenty-one days after Congress is required to assemble, determines by two-thirds vote of both Houses that the President is unable to discharge the powers and duties of his office, the Vice President shall continue to discharge the same as Acting President; otherwise, the President shall resume the powers and duties of his office. [February 10, 1967.]

ARTICLE XXVI.

Section 1. The right of citizens of the United States, who are eighteen years of age or older, to vote shall not be denied or abridged by the United States or by any State on account of age.

Section 2. The Congress shall have power to enforce this article by appropriate legislation [June 30, 1971.]

APPENDIX B

Final Report
of the Seventy-third
American Assembly

At the close of their discussions, the participants in the Seventy-third American Assembly, on *The U.S. Constitution Today,* at Arden House, Harriman, New York, April 23–26, 1987, reviewed as a group the following statement. This statement represents general agreement; however, no one was asked to sign it. Furthermore, it should be understood that not everyone agreed with all of it.

Preamble

The purposes of the Constitution ordained and established by the people of the United States were "to form a more perfect Union" which would "establish justice, insure domestic tranquility, provide for the common defence, promote the general welfare, and secure the blessings of liberty to ourselves and our posterity." The participants in the Seventy-third American Assembly convened to discuss the health of the constitutional structure in the bicentennial year of its proposal by the Philadelphia Convention. Their clear overall conclusion, based on their backgrounds primarily in government, law, and scholarship, and on a shared impression of 200 years of constitutional experience, is that the structure has, in general, proved sound, given the Civil War amendments and other adjustments. There is no fundamental reason to believe that it will not work as well for the closing years of this century, and into the next.

In reaching this broad consensus, the participants are, of course, mindful of the fact that the United States faces increasingly complex, indeed seemingly intractable, problems in both domestic and foreign matters. In foreign affairs, for example, the United States has changed from a small nation isolated by oceans to a dominant world leader, while technology has changed qualitatively the factors of the rapidity and the destructiveness of war. Within the United States, vast economic, social, and technological changes have accompanied great historical forces, such as the development of a national economy, diversification of the population, with greatly increased size and mobility, and the introduction of elements of a modern welfare state. These changes have resulted in some erosion of the system of federalism and the role of the states. Further, they have led to the creation of a variety of administrative and regulatory bodies which combine in one place elements of the legislative, executive, and judicial functions. The participants recognize the need for major governmental initiatives in view of all this, but reject, on the whole, the proposition that these fundamental historical changes necessitate corresponding radical changes in the way the United States should be governed.

In reaching this fundamental conclusion, the participants considered a number of proposals for change, both constitutional and nonconstitutional, which would adjust functions and relationships in the constitutional scheme, including changes relating to the political effectiveness of the system, and the important nonconstitutional functions performed from the beginning by the major political parties. They do believe that the failures of government to meet societal problems are political rather than structural in nature, and are not related to, and would not be cured by, the changes in government process proposed. On the whole, to the contrary, the participants are persuaded that no basic constitutional change, such as a fundamental move toward a parliamentary system, is necessary or wise. In general, they are reluctant to open up the amendment process for minor adjustments. In particular, having concluded that constitutional process is not responsible for government failures, they oppose a general constitutional convention under Article V, or an overall revision in the constitutional structure.

The Constitution is not, of course, concerned only with the structure of government. Many of the provisions in the body of its text, including the separation and diffusion of powers, as well as the Bill of Rights and Civil War amendments, are instead directed at the protection of individual liberty and the great principle of equality. The participants recognize that the Constitution guards individual rights and imposes affirmative duty on every branch and level of government, particularly the judicial branch, to protect those rights.

The participants have given considerable attention to judicial review as a power and source of authority claimed by, and in general ceded to, the judicial branch since the beginning. The discussion developed no disagreement among the participants on the proposition that courts have, and should have, the power to declare federal and state laws unconstitutional because they are beyond the power of the legislature to enact, or because prohibited by specific constraints in the Constitution, notably the Bill of Rights or the Civil War amendments. The participants have discussed at length, but have not attempted to resolve, disagreements with respect to particular applications of this power, or methods of constitutional construction used by the courts.

Accordingly, the Assembly concentrated on three areas. The first is whether the political structure established by the Constitution is appropriate for the future. The second is particularly whether it is adequate for the proper conduct of foreign affairs. The third is the vitality of the federal system. The Assembly's specific findings and (in some cases) recommendations on these matters follow.

I. The Structure of the National Government

The participants do have some concerns with respect to the working of the structure of government today, under the Constitution. These concerns, and some recommendations about them, follow.

Findings and Recommendations

1. The Assembly is disturbed that citizen participation in government has greatly declined, and that the importance of wealth in campaigns has greatly increased. It notes as well that political parties have lost much of their power. There are substantial disagreements among the participants over the degree of change with respect to the first two developments and its significance with respect to the third, and over the causal relationships, if any, among these three developments.

2. Congress should have the authority to impose reasonable limits on campaign spending by candidates for federal office, their campaigns, and associated groups.

There is substantial support for this proposition, although some participants strongly believe that it would violate fundamental free speech guarantees. Among the supporters of the proposition, there is a difference of opinion as to the appropriate method for achieving the desired end. Some would support legislation designed to avoid the specific decisions of the Supreme Court invalidating aspects of previous congressional action on the subject, and thus invite the Court to limit or reconsider those decisions. Others would, if necessary, proceed by constitutional amendment. The supporters also urge Congress to authorize public financing of congressional campaigns.

In addition, the participants have considerable unease about the length of campaigns, and the amount of energy spent on campaign fundraising, but do not think it feasible or wise to impose express limits on the time devoted to those activities.

3. A number of additional proposals have been considered and

rejected or tabled. After considerable debate, the participants rejected the proposal that the terms for members of the House of Representatives should be changed from two to four years. The Assembly is also unwilling (a) to authorize legislators to be cabinet members, or to separate an elected head of state from a chief executive chosen by the legislature; (b) to recommend a unicameral legislature; (c) to bring the initiative and referendum to the national government; and (d) to lengthen Senate terms from six to eight years. While it would not have approved in the first instance the Twenty-second Amendment, limiting presidents to two terms, it does not support a new amendment repealing the twenty-second. It did not act on a proposal to require including legislators in the nominating conventions of the parties.

4. The constitutional doctrine of separation of powers, and a tripartite system of government, cannot easily be reconciled with the existence of independent regulatory agencies that combine in one entity legislative, executive, and judicial power.

Nevertheless, the Assembly rejects a series of proposals to limit the power of the agencies, to give the president the power to remove members of the agencies, to restore the one-house legislative veto, and to reduce the deference given by reviewing courts to the legal (as distinguished from factual) determinations of administrative agencies. The result is that the Assembly is left with a sense of unease about lack of accountability, but makes no recommendation for structural change.

II. Foreign Affairs, Military Power, and Intelligence Activities

Consistent with the Constitution's basic notion of separate but overlapping powers, the president and Congress each have major roles to play in all forms of international affairs, including making foreign policy, involving the nation in military operations, and pursuing foreign intelligence gathering and operations.

Actual practice under the Constitution has evolved from a premise that the newly independent nation, largely isolated from the rest of the world by physical barriers, could be and should be reluctant to involve itself in entangling alliances and in the affairs of foreign nations. In addition, successive presidents, from Washington through Reagan, have assumed and exercised the prerogatives to initiate military and intelligence operations without express congressional approval.

The nation's emergence as a world power raises fundamental constitutional questions about these kinds of activities. Some presidents assert virtually complete autonomy because of the president's roles as "sole organ of foreign affairs" and as commander-in-chief of the armed forces. Congress asserts, but infrequently exercises, power and responsibility because of its constitutional charge to regulate foreign commerce; to control imports and exports; to raise, support, and regulate the armed forces; and to declare war. The Senate's role in advising and consenting to treaties and to appointment of American diplomats, cabinet officers, and military commanders provides it with a specialized claim to involvement in foreign and military affairs. As with most other functions of government, the Constitution provides no clear boundaries on these issues, and instead assumes a process of consultation, coordination, and accommodation.

The constitutional provision giving the Senate alone, but not the biennially elected members of the House, a formal role in approving treaties raises an important question today about whether institutional arrangements that have the significance and formality of treaties should require bicameral consensus. At the same time, the current insistence that the nation may only commit itself to international treaties if two-thirds of the senators concur may impede the government's ability to enter into important, but controversial, commitments. To the extent that the requirement of a super-majority may reflect a presumption against entering into international relationships in the absence of overwhelming consensus, that requirement may no longer coincide with the modern reality of an interdependent world and America's leadership role in it.

Finally, the Constitution does not expressly address the question whether the conduct of foreign policy, military operations, and intelligence activities is subject to congressional or judicial restrictions, or whether these issues are remitted solely to political discretion and expediency. Especially in times of international stress and tension, which may well now be the norm rather than the exception, executive branch officials have suggested that the president has plenary powers constitutionally entrusted to him alone. Yet, the Constitution expressly recognizes the existence and force of international law. And it authorizes Congress, both generally under the necessary and proper clause and specifically with reference to international commerce and governance of the armed forces, to adopt appropriate legislation.

Findings and Recommendations

After considering these issues of constitutional law and policy, we reach the following findings and recommendations.

Foreign Affairs

1. The conduct of relations with other nations requires the projection of national policy in foreign arenas in a reliable and unified fashion. This goal requires greater consultation and cooperation between the executive and legislative branches aimed at achieving a bipartisan approach and consensus.
2. The Assembly recognizes that the Constitution permits some and perhaps all agreements with other countries to be accomplished by use of congressionally approved executive agreements (i.e., agreements ratified by joint resolutions passed by ordinary majorities of both houses). It rejects the proposal that the treaty-ratification process should be altered to permit three-fifths of the Senate, rather than the two-thirds presently required, to approve treaties.

Military Operations and Foreign Intelligence Activities

1. The Assembly notes a long tradition under which presidents have initiated military operations without formal congressional approval.

2. The Assembly endorses the principles and aims of the War Powers Resolution. Although the participants are divided on the issue, the majority believes that greater congressional involvement is appropriate in decisions about the use of military force than the resolution requires.

3. In conducting military and intelligence activities, the executive must act in accordance with limitations imposed by the Constitution and constitutionally authorized acts of Congress.

4. Only those means should be used to implement those policies—even where legitimately carried out in secret—that would be considered defensible if publicly aired. In no event should it be assumed that public approval of policy goals justifies whatever means the executive might choose to carry it out.

5. No structural changes need be made in the constitutional arrangements governing foreign military and intelligence operations. Respect for constitutional restraints, vigorous congressional oversight, and the political process are adequate to restrain unwarranted executive action.

III. Federalism

The original allocation of powers and responsibilities in the Constitution between sovereign national and state governments was a wise accommodation. The purpose underlying the federal structure was to give the national government the power to address, on a unified national basis, matters of genuine national scope. At the same time, the structure reserves local matters to state government and thus provides for a significant measure of self-determination, preserves local values, protects local initiative, and encourages diversity.

Findings and Recommendations

1. Although the balance of power and responsibility between state and federal government has changed over time, the basic concept of federalism retains its power.

2. As the nation's economy has changed from an aggregate of

intrastate and regional markets to markets national and international in scope, the role of the national government in economic regulation has necessarily expanded.

3. The commerce clause broadly empowers the national government to address matters having national economic impact and has been one vehicle for the expansion of national domestic economic regulation. The taxing and spending powers have provided an alternative constitutional basis for this expansion.

4. Federalism provides the opportunity for continuing experimentation in governance at the state and local levels. This "laboratory" aspect of federalism involves "we the people" more directly in our self-governance, and these experiments often provide models for solutions to problems which we face as a nation in a changing, complex society. State and local governments should be encouraged to experiment with the caveat that such experimentation should be sensitive to the implications of such action on the people of other states.

5. The national government has a responsibility to act where national action is appropriate or necessary, but Congress should take into account the constitutional values of federalism in deciding when and how to act.

6. It is essential to guarantee the same basic individual rights and liberties to all people; consequently, the application of the Bill of Rights to the states through the mechanism of the Fourteenth Amendment, and the application of the principle of equality to the federal government, has been an important alteration in our federalist doctrine.

7. Attention by state courts to their state constitutions is another important source of diversity. State court decisions interpreting state constitutions accordingly may appropriately extend protection for individual rights and liberties beyond that afforded by the federal Constitution.

Conclusion

The Assembly's conclusion that the U.S. Constitution, as amended, remains essentially sound is not an expression of complacency.

The Assembly recognizes our many problems as a nation. It does not see the need for—or has been unable to agree on—structural constitutional change, but is disturbed by failures and distortions in how our institutions work. Individual rights are beyond the scope of our deliberations, but the participants are keenly aware of the need for eternal vigilance to assure that they are respected and protected for all individuals in respect of all activities of government. Our continued success as a nation will depend on our ability to make our inherited institutions fulfill the purposes and promises for which the people ordained and established the Constitution two centuries ago.

Participants
The Seventy-third American Assembly

SHIRLEY S. ABRAHAMSON
Justice
State of Wisconsin
Supreme Court
Madison, Wisconsin

RENATA ADLER
The New Yorker
New York, New York

CHARLOTTE E. BALDWIN
Vice President
First Kentucky Trust Company
Louisville, Kentucky

RICHARD BLUMENTHAL
State Representative
Connecticut General Assembly
Stamford, Connecticut

**Rapporteur

EARL V. BROWN, JR.
Associate General Counsel
United Mine Workers of
America
Washington, D.C.

**SARAH E. BURNS
Legal Director
NOW Legal Defense &
Education Fund
New York, New York

LINCOLN CAPLAN
Washington, D.C.

STEPHEN L. CARTER
Yale Law School
Yale University
New Haven, Connecticut

JAMES W. CEASER
Woodrow Wilson Department
of Government & Foreign
Affairs
University of Virginia
Charlottesville, Virginia

ROBERT L. CLAYTON
Tulane Law School
Tulane University
New Orleans, Louisiana

‡CHARLES J. COOPER
Assistant Attorney General
Office of Legal Counsel
U.S. Department of Justice
Washington, D.C.

†LLOYD N. CUTLER
Wilmer, Cutler & Pickering
Washington, D.C.

‡J. DAVID ELLWANGER
Member
Commission on Public
Understanding About the Law
American Bar Association
San Francisco, California

JOHN HENRY FAULK
Austin, Texas

MICHAEL FRANCK
Executive Director
State Bar of Michigan
Lansing, Michigan

PAUL GARVER
Contract Director
Service Employees
International Union
Pittsburgh, Pennsylvania

‡Panel Member
†Delivered Formal Address
*Discussion Leader

ROBERT GEARY
Consultant
North Carolina Commission on
the Bicentennial of the U.S.
Constitution
Raleigh, North Carolina

JOSEPH GOLDSTEIN
Yale Law School
Yale University
New Haven, Connecticut

CHRISTOPHER L. GRIFFIN
Secretary
Young Lawyers Division
American Bar Association
Tampa, Florida

NORMAN GROSS
Division for Public Education
American Bar Association
Chicago, Illinois

*MARK HARRISON
Chairman
Commission on Public
Understanding About the Law
American Bar Association
Phoenix, Arizona

LOUIS HENKIN
Columbia University
New York, New York

PAUL HOLTZMAN
Harriman Scholar
Yale Law School
Yale University
New Haven, Connecticut

PAUL L. JOFFE
Counsel
House Subcommittee on
Commerce, Consumer
Protection & Competitiveness
Washington, D.C.

NICHOLAS DE B.
KATZENBACH
Riker, Danzig, Scherer, Hyland
& Perretti
Morristown, New Jersey

THOMAS M. KERR
Graduate School of Industrial
Administration
Carnegie-Mellon University
Pittsburgh, Pennsylvania

JOHN W. KIERMAIER
President
Foreign Policy Association
New York, New York

RICHARD P. KLEEMAN
Consultant
Association of American
Publishers
Washington, D.C.

ALAN S. KOPIT
Chairperson
Young Lawyers Division
American Bar Association
Cleveland, Ohio

JUDITH F. KRUG
Director
Office for Intellectual Freedom
American Library Association
Chicago, Illinois

*PHILIP A. LACOVARA
Hughes Hubbard & Reed
Washington, D.C.

CINDY LEBOW
General Counsel
Senate Committee on the
Judiciary
Washington, D.C.

BURKE MARSHALL
Yale Law School
Yale University
New Haven, Connecticut

JUDY PERRY MARTINEZ
Simon, Peragine, Smith &
Redfearn
New Orleans, Louisiana

MICHAEL McGOUGH
Editorial Page Editor
Pittsburgh Post-Gazette
Pittsburgh, Pennsylvania

LOUISE MELLING
Harriman Scholar
Yale Law School
Yale University
New Haven, Connecticut

WILLIAM H. NEUKOM
Vice President
Law & Corporate Affairs
Microsoft Corporation
Redmond, Washington

*JON O. NEWMAN
Circuit Judge
United States Court of Appeals
for the Second Circuit
Hartford, Connecticut

CHERYL NIRO
Illinois Commission on the
Bicentennial of the U.S.
Constitution
Chicago, Illinois

*Discussion Leader

ELI M. NOAM
Graduate School of Business
Columbia University
New York, New York

**ROBERT PECK
Director
Commission on Public
Understanding About the Law
American Bar Association
Chicago, Illinois

JOHN PODESTA
Chief Counsel
Senate Committee on
Agriculture
Washington, D.C.

‡H. JEFFERSON POWELL
Yale Law School
Yale University
New Haven, Connecticut

LLEWELYN G. PRITCHARD
Karr, Tuttle, Koch, Campbell,
Mawer, Morrow & Sax
Seattle, Washington

CHARLES STEPHEN
RALSTON
First Assistant Counsel
NAACP Legal Defense &
Educational Fund
New York, New York

*FREDERICK A.O.
SCHWARZ, JR.
Cravath, Swaine & Moore
New York, New York

NADINE STROSSEN
School of Law
New York University
New York, New York

**Rapporteur
‡Panel Member
†Delivered Formal Address
*Discussion Leader

MARK V. TUSHNET
Georgetown University Law
Center
Washington, D.C.

**BARBARA D.
UNDERWOOD
Chief of Appeals
Counsel to the District
Attorney
District Attorney of Kings
County
Brooklyn, New York

ROBERT WEDGEWORTH
Dean
School of Library Service
Columbia University
New York, New York

JOSEPH F. WEIS, JR.
Circuit Judge
United States Court of Appeals
for the Third Circuit
Pittsburgh, Pennsylvania

CATHERINE WEISS
Harriman Scholar
Yale Law School
Yale University
New Haven, Connecticut

JOEL WELLS
Law Clerk
State of Wisconsin
Supreme Court
Madison, Wisconsin

†ALAN F. WESTIN
Department of Political Science
Columbia University
New York, New York

LEROY W. WILDER
Portland, Oregon

Index